Approaches to Acting

Approaches to Acting

Past and Present

ഇൽ രൂ

Daniel Meyer-Dinkgräfe

CONTINUUM
London and New York

Continuum
The Tower Building, 11 York Road, London SE1 7NX
370 Lexington Avenue, New York, NY 10017-6550

First published 2001
© Daniel Meyer-Dinkgräfe 2001

British Library Cataloguing-in-Publication Data
A catalogue record for this book is available from the British Library.

ISBN 0-8264-4900-X (hardback)
0-8264-4901-8 (paperback)

Library of Congress Cataloging-in-Publication Data
Meyer-Dinkgräfe, Daniel, 1958–
    Approaches to acting: past and present/Daniel Meyer-Dinkgräfe.
        p. cm.
    Includes bibliographical references and index.
    ISBN 0-8264-4900-X—ISBN 0-8264-4901-8 (pbk.)
    1. Acting. 2. Acting—History. I. Title.

PN2061.M397 2001
792′028—dc21   00-043136

Typeset by BookEns Limited, Royston, Herts.
Printed and bound in Great Britain by
Biddles Limited, Guildford and King's Lynn

Contents

ℰℐℂℬ

Acknowledgements

I would like to thank the A-level Drama students at Phoenix College, Morden, Surrey, and the undergraduate students at the University of Wales, Aberystwyth, for their comments during the writing of this book.

To my mother

Introduction

Whenever we go to see a 'show' at a traditional theatre or any other performance venue, what we see in the first place are actors or performers on some shape of stage. Numerous other people are involved in the production: the playwright, perhaps a dramaturg, a director, designers, administrators, front-of-house staff and many more. However, the audience does not see them directly. What we see, and hear, are the actors. And yet, were we to believe some recent twentieth-century books written about the theatre, we might think that acting and actors occupy a relatively marginal position in the theatre, compared with dramatists and especially directors. In several publications, the captions underneath production photos carry credits for the photographer, the dramatist and the play, often the director and designer(s), but hardly ever the names of the actors we see on it. Newspaper reviews may devote much space to describing the play's plot, the director's concept and aspects of stage design, only to mention that the actors on the whole did a good job, too. If actors are mentioned by name, comments about them tend, on the whole, to be vague and general: 'X was very well able to immerse herself into the role.'

Many members of the public, whether they go to the theatre or not, appear to have some knowledge of what it means to be an actor, because they may have had some amateur experience at school. As a result, they assume competence to judge an actor's work at a level that, say, a physicist would never expect from anyone not educated in this field.

In this book I want to demonstrate the obvious importance of the actor for the theatre by describing and analysing approaches to acting, both in the West (Europe and the USA) and in India, Japan, China and Islamic countries as examples of non-Western theatre and performance traditions. Following some observations on the worldwide origins of acting, I initially focus on the Western tradition, providing succinct surveys of approaches to acting in Greece and Rome, the Middle Ages, the Renaissance and the period from 1550 to 1900. The twentieth century takes up most space, with a close look at Stanislavsky and his legacy in the development of realistic acting. The wide range of developments in anti-realism and their implication for approaches to acting is demonstrated in sections on German Expressionism, Bauhaus, Futurism, Dada and Surrealism, Brecht, Artaud and Grotowski.

As I suggested above, at least in the twentieth century, the director has tended to dominate the theatre. Therefore, a chapter is dedicated to the role of the director in relation to the actor. Over the last thirty years of the twentieth century, traditional theatre has been compared more and more often to innovative forms of what is no longer theatre, but performance, and as such the subject not of theatre studies, but performance studies. This development has been linked with the rise of postmodernism as a general trend in our time. I examine those issues in an attempt to differentiate between acting for the theatre and performance.

Any survey of approaches to acting over the centuries in the West should be complemented by an introduction to the approaches adopted in the non-West. I take India, Japan, China and the Islamic countries as examples. I go into most depth in my discussion of India, relating the position of the actor in Indian theatre aesthetics to Indian philosophy. Although a similar depth would be possible for Japan, China and the Islamic countries, too, I decided against it, as delving into four different philosophies and corresponding mind-sets would be too complicated for such an introductory survey.

Once the basic information on approaches to acting in non-Western cultures is available, it is possible to address a development in the late twentieth century in the West: intercultural theatre. Typically, a Western theatre director takes elements of plot, philosophy or acting techniques from a non-Western culture and uses them in some way in his or her own production, often with a Western, sometimes with a multicultural, cast of actors. Such a directorial approach has implications for acting, which I discuss in a separate chapter.

Actors do not 'just do their work'. They undergo a thorough training in preparation for it. Approaches to actor training have varied considerably over the centuries, and among different cultures. In Chapter 8 I provide a survey of those approaches, comparing Western and non-Western, and past with present. Theatre everywhere, West and non-West, is subject to criticism, most often in the form of newspaper reviews that appear a day or more after a production's press night. In addressing theatre criticism, I rely on my own experience of it in the past, and expectations from it in the future.

The future of acting is at the centre of the final chapter. Taking up some of the issues raised in the course of the book, I outline my own, personal ideas about the potential of acting, and with it the theatre, for the twenty-first century and beyond.

References to quotations from books and journal articles have been collected in the endnotes. In the text, numbers in superscript refer to those endnotes. All references in the endnotes are listed in an alphabetical bibliography. I had originally considered to provide an annex with names and addresses of drama schools which offer actor training programmes. In the end, I have decided against this: the number of such schools is very high indeed, and some seem relatively short-lived. Selection would have been necessary to remain within the limits of this book, and selection criteria are always problematic. In addition, I have found that a number of simple searches on the Internet reveals that the vast majority of relevant schools are represented through their own highly informative websites. Alternatively, the web leads you to print publications which may list those institutions who have decided not to go on-line yet.

80C3

1

Worldwide Origins of Acting

⚯⚮

Any discussion of approaches to acting has to begin with the issue of how theatre is thought to have developed in the first place. The conditions under which it arose and its context in ancient society have a direct impact on, for example, the way actors were regarded by their peers: were they highly esteemed, for instance, as custodians of a tradition closely related to religious ritual? Or were they regarded as people who imitated real life, thus providing second-hand accounts of reality more or less undesirable in comparison with the real thing? Western theatre scholars approach the issue of the origins of theatre from a scientifically influenced perspective, through the discipline of history. In contrast, many non-Western theatre forms, especially in India and Japan, have their own myths that explain the creation of theatre. It is interesting to look at both in sequence.

Data on which historians of the theatre could base their ideas about how (and why!) theatre developed are very few indeed. Many theories have been put forward, based on intelligent guesswork rather than facts, and none of the theories can be verified. Several prominent candidates for the source of theatre have emerged, possibly interrelated, and all concerned with fundamental characteristics of human nature: myth and ritual, storytelling, imitation and a gift for fantasy. Whichever source one favours, from each of them the actor emerges along similar lines of progression: an activity which was originally an integral part of the source, and which can be described as theatrical, is further elaborated and developed, and ultimately becomes independent of the source both regarding the format of the source and its function for the individual and society.

Take storytelling, for example. It has been regarded as fundamental to human nature, and can be observed in children as early as two or three years old. An account of an event, real or imagined, is initially presented by a narrator, who may use change of voice and pantomime to demonstrate the differences of various characters in the story. Theatre develops when a story's individual characters are impersonated by different actors.

Ritual can have various functions in a society. It is an expression of how the members of the society understand their world. It may serve to teach children and adolescents about that understanding and its implications for their lives. In many societies, rituals are carried out to influence, possibly to control, events, such as the appropriate amount of rainfall. Ritual is often used to glorify (supernatural powers, gods, a hero, etc.), and, finally, ritual may entertain and give pleasure. Brockett argues that most of those functions are shared with those of theatre. In addition, ritual may employ some of the same basic ingredients characteristic of theatre, such as music, dance, speech, masks, costumes, audience, stage and performers.[1] Some rituals involve all, or most, members of a community, whereas in others the majority of people observe (and through observation participate in) the ritual activity carried out by a few individuals. These performers have to be highly skilled and trained, especially if minute details are to be followed precisely. Such skilled individuals may be regarded as precursors to actors in theatre events.[2]

In the course of time, societies abandon their original rituals, but the stories and myths that have accumulated around them remain, and they are taken up in dramatic, theatrical form for their own aesthetic sake, no longer serving the original religious function. Theatre may thus have developed from ritual, and some contemporary theatre artists attempt to lead secular theatre practice, now devoid of religious or, in more general terms, spiritual purpose, and dominated by commercialism, back to its ritual origins. In this endeavour, they are often inspired by non-Western theatre traditions whose philosophical texts on theatre provide a deeply spiritual purpose. The *Natyashastra*, the oldest Indian treatise on drama and theatre, is one example. It was written down between the second century BC and the eighth century AD, but is most likely much older, transmitted in an oral tradition. Towards the beginning of the text we find a passage describing how theatre was created: the golden age, in which all human beings enjoyed a state of enlightenment, complete health and fulfilment, had come to an end. The silver age had begun, and humans were afflicted by the first symptoms of suffering. The gods, with Indra as their leader, were concerned and approached Brahma, the creator, asking him to devise a means that would allow humans to regain their enlightenment, to restore the golden age. Indra specified that this should take the form of a fifth Vedic text, an addition to the four main texts of Indian (Vedic) philosophy (*Rig-Veda, Sama-Veda, Yajur-Veda and Atharva-Veda*). The fifth Veda must be both pleasing/entertaining and instructive, and should be accessible to the *shudras*, the lowest caste, because they were not allowed to read or listen to recitations of the other Vedas. Brahma considered Indra's request, immersed himself in meditation and came up with *natya* (drama), which he asked Indra and the gods to implement. Indra assured Brahma that the gods would be no good at this task, and so Brahma passed on his knowledge about *natya* to the human sage Bharata, who in turn taught it to his hundred sons, who were thus the first actors. The knowledge imparted to Bharata by Brahma is contained in the text of the *Natyashastra* (*shastra* is a holy text).

Theatre in this context thus has the direct and explicit function of restoring the golden age for humankind, implying restoration of the state of perfection, liberation (*moksha*) and enlightenment for all people on earth. The text then sets out in stunning detail highly specific means of acting (movement and gesture, voice, costume and make-up, and emotional characterization), all aimed at achieving specific aesthetic effects in the audience, and which function as means of raising the level of consciousness of all involved in the theatre, in both its production and reception. There is a tendency in Western theatre scholarship to water down (or preferably annihilate) the implications of this claim for the function of theatre by arguing that its inclusion in the text of the *Natyashastra* is merely a trick used by the author to justify the book to his readers. Another argument might be that the claim must not be taken at face value, because theatre in line with the *Natyashastra*, at least so far, has not achieved restoration of the golden age (we are currently in the darkest of the four ages according to Indian philosophy). Theatre artists, however, appear to take the claim at least a bit more seriously when they acknowledge inspiration from the *Natyashastra* and contemporary forms of Indian dance/drama (which are said to have their roots in the aesthetics of the *Natyashastra*) in their attempts to lead theatre back to its ritual origins.

In Japanese theatre, the first recorded professional actor is Umihiko. He was a divine fisherman, and older brother to Yamahiko, divine hunter. One day, the brothers decided to exchange their tools so that they could experience each other's work. Neither of them was very happy with this exchange, and Umihiko returned arrow and bow to his brother. Yamahiko, however, had meanwhile lost his brother's angling hook. Umihiko was very angry and would not accept any replacement, insisting that Yamahiko return it. In despair, Yamahiko went to the ocean shore and wailed, whereupon he was invited to the palace of the sea-god, who ordered the fish of his kingdom to find the hook. Yamahiko returned the hook to his brother, married the sea-king's daughter and lived in his palace for three years. When he wanted to return home, to his own palace, he received two jewels from the sea-king, which could influence the tide. Umihiko was still angry at his brother, and would taunt and abuse him. Yamahiko, in turn, used the jewels to influence the tide in such a way that Umihiko's fishing would be disrupted. Umihiko gave in, and said: 'From now on I will be your subject, performing plays.' And he smeared his face and hands with red earth and presented the mime of someone drowning. Records describe how he stops short in surprise at the rising water, lifts his legs when the water reaches knee level, runs around in a circle when it reaches his hips, expresses his inner anguish when the water reaches his shoulders, and cries for help with raised arms when the water is up to his chin.[3]

Another mythical story about the origins of theatre from the Japanese context revolves around the Sun-goddess, Amaterasu. She had been offended by her brother, and retreated into a cave. As a result, the world was left in darkness. The gods perfom a ceremony, at the climax of which the goddess Ama no Uzume goes into a trance and performs a religious striptease. The assembled gods all start laughing at once, rousing Amaterasu's curiosity. She opens the door to the cave and asks the reason for the gods' laughter. Ama no Uzume answers: 'We are happy and jolly because there is a god who is even more wonderful than your Highness.' She is shown an iron mirror, and on seeing her own image for the first time, her curiosity grows even more, and she comes out of the cave. One of the gods now grabs her and drags her out of the cave altogether. Thus, the sun has been restored to the world.[4] Interpretations of this mythical story vary. The gods' laughter could be a ceremonial response to Ama no Uzume's dance. It could be the natural response to a comical, 'obscene' disrobing, or it could be the joy at the restoration of the sun expressed in advance of the event. The exposure of the genitals has also been interpreted as the mythical moment of the birth of a theatrical event: the moment when the actual function of the organs of reproduction is set aside, and their 'theatrical' use for sole entertainment is discovered and celebrated.[5]

Theatre history is the business of locating data and interpreting them to arrive at a story, a narrative. Myth provides the story in the first place. As indicated, few data exist that could help us say anything conclusive about the origins of the theatre. From among the ideas that have been offered by theatre historians, and from the story of how theatre was created in the *Natyashastra* and in the two unrelated Japanese myths, we can derive the following preliminary information about the actors:

- immensely skilled, suggesting a demanding training;
- likely to be highly esteemed by peers, both for providing a rewarding experience and for their skills.

෨෭෬

2

The Foundations of Western Approaches to Acting: Greece and Rome

ࡘ)Ƈ

As with views on the origins of theatre, anything we can say about the actor in ancient Greece is based on few, and evidently contradictory, data. Drama is closely associated with the festivals in honour of Dionysus, the god of fertility and wine, son of Zeus and Semele (daughter of Theban king Kadmos). Semele died while giving birth, and Dionysus was raised by satyrs (half-human, half-beast creatures). Legend has it that he was killed, dismembered and resurrected, symbolic of the cycle of the seasons in nature. His worshippers sought to reach a state of union with his inspiring creativity, and to maintain the fertility of their land. Worship of Dionysus is said to have started in the Near East, and when it reached Greece it initially met with suspicion, because it was associated with ·intoxication and sexual orgies. In the course of several centuries, however, those excesses disappeared. By the sixth century BC, in Athens, four annual festivals were held in honour of Dionysus. At one of those, the City Dionysia (held towards the end of March), the assumed precursor of drama proper, the dithyramb was first presented. The dithyramb was a hymn sung and danced in honour of the god. It is thought that a chorus of some fifty men sang a refrain to a story based on mythology, improvised by a chorus leader.[1] The dramatist Thespis modified the dithyramb by emerging from the chorus and playing one of the characters of the story, thus developing into the first actor in Western theatre history. It is important to note that the chorus leader maintained his limited function, and is not related to the first actor. The Greek term for actor was *hypocrites*, 'answerer'. The new form of drama, involving chorus, chorus leader and initially one actor, became known as *tragedy*, with dithyrambs continuing to exist independently. By 533, contests for the best plays were part of the City Dionysia; apart from Thespis, we know the names of three further dramatists of the sixth century BC – Pratinas, Choerilus and Phrynichus – but none of their plays has survived.

More is known about dramatists, plays and performance conventions in the context of the City Dionysia contests of the fifth century BC. Performances were held over a five-day period. On each one of three days devoted to plays, a different dramatist would present three tragedies and a satyr play (a burlesque treatment of mythology[2]). After 487, five dramatists also had to present one comedy each, independent of the tragedy contests. Up to 449, prizes were awarded for plays; after that year also for individual actors.

The members of the chorus were performers in their own right. With Aeschylus, the chorus consisted of twelve men; Sophocles increased their number to fifteen. The men were not professionals, but were not inexperienced either: choral dancing and singing were popular, with around a thousand participants in dithyrambic contests at the City Dionysia alone. Historical sources show that the members of the chorus were allocated to a competing dramatist eleven months before the competition, during which time they would complete their training. Initially, the dramatist himself trained and choreographed the chorus, but in due course, professional trainers took over, probably working closely with the dramatist. Training is said to have been intense, long and arduous, involving special diet, exercise and disciplined practice. In return, members of the chorus were often pampered and given special treatment, remarkable in view of the rather spartan treatment of soldiers.

Initially the dramatists were actors as well, performing in their own plays. Aeschylus introduced the second actor, and with the introduction of the third actor by Sophocles, the dramatist no longer acted himself. All speaking parts of a play were shared among the actors available, and on many occasions one actor had to play several parts. Mute parts were taken by any number of supernumeraries. Initially, the dramatist selected his own cast; later (after 449), the leading actor was allocated to the dramatist by lot, and the two remaining actors were selected by joint decision of the dramatist and leading actor. A contest for tragic actors was introduced in 449, and only leading actors could compete. All actors were paid by the state. The close relation of dramatist and actor implies that the actor took direction directly from the dramatist. The written text did not have stage directions, and it is likely that actors were illiterate and learned their lines through listening to the dramatist reciting them. Both dramatist and actors were held in high esteem in the country.

More details about the acting process can be gathered from three main sources: scholia (that is, commentaries on editions of the plays which may contain references to productions); vase paintings showing actors in performance; and evidence from the related field of oratory.[3]

As before, data obtained from these sources are at times contradictory and have to be scrutinized carefully: the dates of useful comments in the scholia are often uncertain, and with them the validity of the evidence. Vase paintings are not realistic camera shots, but artistic impressions, which may be accurate, but may also express the artistic freedom of the artist. Much of the evidence adduced from oratory comes from the writings of Roman orators, who based their work on Greek origins dating from several centuries earlier.

In general, it appears that the style of acting in ancient Greece was rather unrealistic: one actor would play more than one part, only men would appear on stage, also playing women, and there was a rich mixture of song, recitative, choral passages, dance and the use of masks. The size of the theatre had an important impact on acting: the buildings seated more than 10,000 spectators, with the front row positioned about 60 feet (18 m) away from the stage, and the back rows some 300 feet (91 m). This compares, for example, with a distance of 48 feet (14 m) between the stage and the middle of the dress circle at the Theatre Royal, Drury Lane, London.[4] Gestures had to be broad to be intelligible, and indeed we find that simple gestures were employed to express fundamental emotions: to express grief, the actor may have covered his head with his cloak, or simply looked down. Mourning may be expressed by 'tearing the hair, cheeks, and garments'.[5] In supplication the 'petitioner kneels at his interlocutor's feet, throws one arm around his knees and with the other hand grasps his chin or beard'.[6] Prayer to a deity in heaven was expressed by stretching the arms forward, palms turned up; whereas a deity in the underworld was roused by striking the ground with the foot. Dance often expressed joy, and characters joined hands to swear an oath. Suitably wild gestures, appearing uncontrolled, accompanied pain, sickness and madness. All such gestures are clearly visible even at a great distance, and immediately convey the respective emotion to the audience. In the case of hiding one's face to show grief, the gesture carries a deep psychological meaning: life and light are associated in Greek belief, and the gesture of excluding light is thus 'a powerful visual expression of the death-wish'.[7]

Given the size of the theatre, any minute details of facial expression would have been futile. This may be one of the reasons for the use of masks in Greek theatre. They were made from linen, cork or light wood, which means that today we have to rely on marble or terracotta copies made at the time, and vase paintings. Masks covered most of the head, and had hair attached. It is possible to trace 'deep psychological and even metaphysical'[8] implications of the mask in the fields of psychology, culture, ritual, metaphysics and religion: a mask allows the actor to identify fully with the character it represents. Spectators can project any emotion expressed by the actor's words on to the mask: it seems to laugh or weep depending on the circumstances in the play. According to

Rehm, first and foremost, masks in Greek theatre were a theatrical convention: all actors wore them, endowing them with dramatic power. Together with costumes, they provided the spectator with an immediate insight into a character's type, 'gender, age, social status and economic class'.[9] On a practical level, wearing masks meant that one actor could play several parts in the same play, while the large open mouth of the mask allowed the actor's voice to project powerfully. This was important not only within the large theatre space but also in view of the fact that life in ancient Greek society was 'dominated by rhetoric and oral exchange'.[10]

In Rome, theatre was as closely linked to religious festivals (in honour of gods such as Jupiter, Apollo and Ceres) as it had been in Greece. In addition, performances were put on for special public occasions, such as victories at war, the dedication of new buildings or the funerals of important public figures. The number of days per year devoted to theatre rose from between four and eleven in 202 BC to more than a hundred in AD 354. As the political system of Rome changed from the Republic to the Empire, more and more other forms of entertainment competed with theatre, such as races, gladiatorial contests, wild animal fights and sea battles.

At festivals, magistrates received a specific sum of money from the state to arrange theatre performances. They contracted the managers of acting troupes, who were in charge of the staging. The size of a troupe is not known from the sources of the time. However, it is possible to work out that most plays could have been performed with five or six actors, occasionally doubling up parts. Many of the actors in Rome were originally slaves. When considered talented by their masters, they were given for training to established actors, and subsequently hired out to managers. The profit was shared between master and teacher. All actors received a basic fee, often also personal gifts from favourable audiences. Thus, slave-actors could possibly, depending on their success, buy their freedom from their salaries. Free-born actors appear only late in Roman history, because being an actor would have contravened the code of honour of free-born citizens. Actors were expected to speak, dance and sing, and their training placed special emphasis on the angle of the head, the placement of feet, the use of hands and vocal intonation to convey their characters' emotions. Movements, for which there were strict codes, were exaggerated. The great actors, such as Roscius and Aesopus, listened to the renowned orators of their time to improve their vocal delivery and gestures.

Roman actors wore masks modelled on their Greek precursors. They were made from linen, with wigs attached. However, there was a striking difference between Greece and Rome regarding the cultural and religious implications of masks in general. Wiles suggests that the Greek 'who put on a mask created a new form of life'. The Roman, however, 'who put on a mask resurrected a dead being'.[11] Whereas Greek culture is dominated by the life cult related to Dionysus, Roman culture is dominated by the death cult, which finds most prominent expression in the *imago*, the death mask, as Wiles describes:

> When a man of noble family died, a death mask was made using a wax mould. A person who had the same physique as the dead man, and had been trained in life to imitate him, sometimes a professional actor, would participate in the funeral as the living incarnation of the dead man. Others would wear the robes of office and masks of the dead man's ancestors, and would take their places on ivory chairs mounted on rostra, so that the entire family line was, as it were, brought back to life on stage. ... To be a noble in Roman society was to have the right of receiving a death mask.[12]

In this context it was important for theatre to avoid any possibility of mistaking the masks used in it for death masks. As a result, masks were 'imbued with ignobility'.

ঙ৩ ৫৪

3

Renewing the Sources: Approaches to Acting in the Middle Ages and the Renaissance

ಬಿಂಬ

After the Roman empire disintegrated, theatre entered a long period of near non-existence during the early Middle Ages (900–1050). Brockett, however, identifies three remnants. First, there were travelling troupes of mimes, which included all kinds of 'performers' such as storytellers, jesters, tumblers, jugglers, rope dancers and exhibitors of tamed animals.[1] Second, there were Teutonic minstrels, who sang and told stories of their traditional heroes and thus preserved history. Originally held in high esteem in their community, following conversion to Christianity, they became infamous, little better in social status than travelling mimes. Third, theatre survived at local festivals, which attracted travelling entertainers. Most of these festivals were originally derived from pagan rites.

The Church also had its ceremonies, which some critics have associated with drama. Mass was rather set in its structure, offering little scope for dramatic elements. The Hours, however, were more flexible. Since they involved ceremonies at regular intervals throughout the day, they were not suitable for working people, and were thus restricted to the monasteries. Here, acting out some of the episodes of the Bible was considered beneficial for the monks' understanding of their religion. The only one early exception to the restriction of any dramatic element in Church liturgy are the plays written by the German nun Hrosvitha of Gandersheim (935–73?); it is not certain, however, whether these plays were actually performed.

In the middle period of the Middle Ages (1050–1300), the Church rose in power and importance, demonstrated by the building of vast cathedrals, and the schools and, later, universities associated with them.

They became open to laypeople, who were subjected to the dramatic elements of liturgy and the similar didactic intention that had characterized their use in the monasteries. The 'actors' were members of the clergy or choirboys. They were probably not expected to provide naturalistic representations: especially in the portrayal of God or Christ, presenting a real human being would have come across as blasphemous. Rather, an iconographical representation must have been expected, focusing on restraint and decorum.[2] Performers of evil characters, however, were given more freedom to engage in appropriate physical activity. In the records of different productions, Herod, for example, has been described as greeting the Magi with a kiss, inviting them to sit on thrones beside his own, angrily throwing the book of prophecies to the ground and brandishing his sword.[3] More emphasis was placed on the depiction of action rather than on conveying emotions directly, most likely because the actors were amateurs, who were not professionally trained in any modern sense of the word.

In the late Middle Ages (1300–1500), vernacular religious drama developed. On the Continent, it was taken up by the religious guilds, in Britain by the trade guilds. Long cycles of plays based on the birth, life, death and resurrection of Christ were divided up among various guilds, so that each one only needed a few actors. Those actors remained amateurs, although the demands made on them by the plays could become considerable: they might have to double up parts (evidenced, for example, by one event in which 300 actors played 494 roles), and were expected to learn their lines by heart (there is evidence of a woman memorizing 2,300 lines as St Catherine in 1468).

Acting in the Middle Ages, Elliott argues, was 'regarded as an art requiring both talent and training; its principal aim was to move the emotions of an audience'.[4] The actors were chosen by audition and various other formalized means of selection. One source states that the selection criteria were 'cunning, voice and person', which Tydeman equates with 'acting ability, vocal range and delivery, and physical presence'.[5] They were then given some two weeks to accept the part, after which they had to swear an oath, in some cases in front of a notary, to attend rehearsals and performances diligently as instructed, or face a range of fines for breaking the contract. Considering the length of the performances themselves, which could extend over four full days, there were relatively few rehearsals.

When plays were not performed by guilds, anyone could participate, although apparently the major parts were quickly taken by the most influential and rich people of the area. Actors were given free food and drink during rehearsals and on performance days, and in some cases there are records of the guilds or town councils working with them on the production of plays, paying actors for income lost because of their commitment to the play. Most actors were men, but there were exceptions: in particular, the Virgin Mary was at times played by a woman, and records indicate that the woman playing St Catherine had such an impressive stage presence that she later married a rich nobleman who had fallen in love with her during the performance.

The late fourteenth and fifteenth centuries have been cited as the period when acting became more professionalized, in the sense that actors increasingly made a living from their work, ceasing to be amateurs who only performed for a small part of the year as an additional activity to their main profession or job. These troupes of actors were usually associated with noble households, carrying letters of recommendation to prevent them from being 'whipped as rogues and vagabonds'.[6]

The end of the Middle Ages overlaps with the tendencies and currents of the Renaissance. Historians date the Renaissance approximately as the period from 1300 to 1550. Its major characteristics include a humanist tendency to regard life on earth as worth living in its own right, and not merely as preparation for eternity. Although such a shift represented a process of secularization, life remained related to God. A further feature of the Renaissance is the rediscovery of ancient Greece and Rome: long-lost manuscripts were found, studied and often translated, and influenced philosophy and creative writing in literature and theatre.

For several reasons, Italy was dominant in the development of the Renaissance. Geographically, it was placed at the centre of Europe. Financially, it enjoyed a period of affluence. The Catholic Church, which had its seat in Italy, was undergoing a crisis, with internal struggles for power and, between 1305 and 1377, two rival popes. The vacuum left by the dissolving authority of the Church was filled by the rulers of the small Italian states. They sought to demonstrate their power through the number and status of the scholars, writers and artists whom they attracted to their courts.

Within this rich cultural atmosphere, three forms of theatre developed in Renaissance Italy: plays paying homage to important people present at the performance; new productions of Roman plays; and performances of newly written plays of Italian origin. Characters in the plays of homage were taken from mythology. In a play written and performed on the occasion of an important wedding in Milan, Jason and the Argonauts, accompanied by music, appear, carrying the golden fleece, which they leave on a large table on the stage as a wedding present after having presented a dance in homage of the couple. Mercury, followed by three quadrilles of dancers, offers a calf as a present to the couple. Diana as huntress appears, accompanied by nymphs. To the sounds of forest instruments, they carry onto the stage a gorgeous stag on a golden stretcher, covered with leaves. Orpheus bemoans the early death of his Eurydice, and other characters of this three-part play are Atalanta and Theseus, Iris and Hebe (goddess of youth). A scene in which Marital Fidelity elaborated on her principles in the presence of numerous gods of love, Hymen and the Graces is interrupted by Helena, Medea and Cleopatra. They in turn praise the excesses of passion and seduction, but are stopped by the deeply offended Marital Fidelity, who has them removed by the love gods. A number of mythical women now appear who carry crowns of chastity in their hands, which they present to the bride.

Plays of homage were later developed into *Trionfo*, processions, sometimes lasting up to four hours, with several wagons or ships on water on which similarly elaborate scenes were created. Such performances are also found in Germany and France (in the latter called *Entrées Solennelles*), where they were usually held in honour of the King. The design was equally elaborate, with records of imitations of ancient Troy, or a village in Brazil.

In Italy, Roman plays by Seneca, Plautus and Terence had been known only through reading in the Middle Ages; during the Renaissance, interest turned to performing them on stage. The emphasis was on comedies, pastorals and intermediaries, and the actors were rarely professionals, but mainly amateurs, occasionally students and schoolboys. In Holland, Roman plays were staged at the universities, in their original Latin. Inspired by the success of such productions for educational and aesthetic purposes, professors wrote their own plays in the style of Roman, and also Greek, models. In due course, religious topics entered the canon. The rediscovery for performance of Terence and Plautus in Latin at schools is also characteristic of late fifteenth- and early sixteenth-century Germany. Plots based on the Bible emphasized the open stance of the Protestant movement, attracting competition from Catholic schools. Here, credit must go especially to Jesuit attempts to create a synthesis of the Catholic belief system and Renaissance secular trends.

To the Jesuit teachers, there was no question 'but that acting was a theatrical extension of the art of rhetoric'.[7] This understanding is reflected in a major manual, written in neo-Latin and published in 1620, by Jesuit teacher Louis Crésol: *Autumn Vacations, or the Complete Action and Pronunciation for the Orator*. According to Crésol, the process of appropriate and moving delivery is twofold: in the majority of cases, the actor/orator would create an image in his mind, and a split second later translate it into facial expression, followed by bodily attitude and gesture. Speech comes last:

> usually only being allowed to emerge after the body was set into an attitude predicting the meaning of the words to be spoken. These congruent postures and movements were usually held until the completion of the statement which they amplified; only then was a new attitude taken, as the speaker again produced an image in his mind to induce subsequent physical and vocal activity.[8]

Crésol was very specific as to the use of individual parts of the body. The right hand, for example, was to be used for making universal or noble statements, such as giving a blessing. The left hand was used to express commonplace or private thoughts, such as 'striking the breast in pretended faithfulness', or 'striking the thigh in anger'.[9] When stronger emotions were required, the actor/orator turned to the device of *personificatio*: 'In this procedure the orator emphatically identified with the character he wished to impersonate. In this way the emotion generated by the association provided a strong motivating force for the action rather than a string of images.'[10]

At the schools, emphasis was on the recitation of the Latin words; instructions on movement, gesture and facial expression, regarded as the final interpretation of the words, were added only if time permitted. In due course, school plays used the vernacular rather than Latin; they became so popular that adults joined the playing, and the demand for public performances led to the establishment of theatre buildings. Strasbourg had an open-air theatre seating 2,000; the Jesuit productions of *Konstantin* (1575) had 1,000 participants, and *Esther* (1577) 1,700.

Popular theatre was frequently found in craft guilds. The special development in Germany within the general trends characterizing the Renaissance is probably associated with Hans Sachs (1494–1576), who wrote and performed stylized comedy and tragedy, and more realistic carnival plays with the mastersingers. There are indications of a clear awareness of appropriate casting. Stage directions are precise for the movement, gesture and diction required to portray madness, for example. The range of possibilities is strictly limited, though, in order to make things easier for the amateur performers, all of them craftsmen. In Holland, too, popular theatre was organized in relation to the crafts, with special acting associations, *Rederijker*; by 1700, Holland boasted 200 of these. They enjoyed aristocratic patronage, and at times the patrons participated actively in the activities. These took the form of competitions; we have records of sixty-five such events having taken place between 1431 and 1620, which were attended by between ten and nineteen associations each. The competition lasted for six days. On the first, a grand procession of all the visiting associations marched into the host town's playing area. On the second day, slots for the individual presentations were allocated by lot. On the third day, all competitors attended church together, followed by a welcoming presentation by the host company. On the fourth day, all the companies' fools were guided by the host's fool to a drinking competition. On the fifth day, all competitors enjoyed a festive meal. Finally, on the sixth day, the performances took place: each company presented a play on a given subject, a prologue and a farce, concluding with a song. The host company closed the proceedings with a farewell presentation. The set subjects on which plays had to focus, such as 'what rouses human beings most for the arts?', implied the choice of symbolic characters. The texts for the plays were not printed.

The Renaissance in Europe is thus characterized by plays of homage performed with great pomp by amateur performers, and school performances of Roman plays and new plays in a Roman style on religious topics; initially presented for pedagogical reasons in Latin by students at schools and universities, they were increasingly performed in the local languages by students and adult amateurs. In addition to such forms of theatre, each country developed its own modes of new drama, performed by professional actors, defined as people who earned their living through work in the theatre. In Italy, *commedia erudita* developed as a mirror of contemporary times, especially between 1520 and 1570, with Ariosto as a major representative. Besides this, pastoral plays and fishermen plays were written, as was tragedy based on Roman models, with an increase in the depiction of horror and violence. Performances by professional actors were commissioned by academies or literary and academic societies. Compared with the large spaces and outdoor settings of theatre in the Middle Ages, Renaissance professional theatre took place in smaller spaces indoors, which should have led to an increased emphasis on detailed and less exaggerated movement and more differentiated depiction of age, social status, sex, character and nuances of the dialogue.

In France, the professionalization of acting developed more slowly than in Italy, because of censorship introduced in 1515. There was also religious opposition, leading to a ban on productions of the mysteries, and allowing only secular plays from 1548. The first appearance of professional acting in France arrived via travelling Italian troupes, who are first recorded in 1530, initially at court, later beyond. These troupes consisted mainly of members of the same family, who only later added hired actors. Both men and women performed. Theatre historians indicate that professional actors appear to have been rather poor, and from all walks of life, including adventurers, romantics and failed students.

With the flourishing of theatre in its various forms during the Renaissance, it is not surprising that theatre itself became the subject of discussion and analysis. The first known writings on the art of acting date from the late Renaissance. One of them, by Leone di Somi (1527–92), is entitled *Third Dialogue about the Art of the Theatre*. The director, Somi tells us, writes out the parts, selects and assembles the cast and distributes parts, and requests all actors to read the whole play. There are clear criteria for selecting actors. They should be appropriate for the part physically: a lover must be good-looking, a soldier should be of strong build, a parasite should be fat and a servant nimble. The tonality of the voice, too, must be suited to the role. The actors should avoid the use of masks or false beards, because they hinder the free expression of the voice. All effects must instead be achieved through make-up. As far as speaking is concerned, actors have to be audible at the back of the auditorium. Somi places emphasis on the ability to speak with a powerful voice without screaming. He thus criticizes over-hasty delivery, suggesting instead appropriately slow delivery, without lowering the voice at the end of syllables. Movements should be appropriate to the use of the voice and the mood of the situation, not merely the part's character. For example, it is not enough if the actor who plays a spendthrift only has his hand in his pocket, as if he were constantly afraid of losing the key to his treasure. He has to play the madman when he learns that his own son has turned into a thief. If he plays a servant, he must know how to start a lively dance when he hears good news, wipe away tears with his handkerchief in moments of sadness and push back the cap on his head when he is at a loss. If he plays the fool, he has to make sure that while speaking the dialogue written by the author, he also acts the fool: for example, catching flies or looking for fleas. On exiting, a chamber maid should, for example, make her skirt move in a vulgar manner and suck her thumb – actions which the author cannot prescribe in the manuscript. In acting, the most important element is the person(ality) of the actor. He has to be full of life and active in his performance. Movement must appear natural, and dialogue improvised, like a conversation among family. It is striking that some of these key characteristics resurface throughout Europe across the centuries. In seventeenth-century France, for example, the list of what is desirable in an actor includes vivid facial expression, impressive bearing, unconstrained movement, absence of extravagant posturing or provincial accent, and good memory.

ഇൗ൫

4

Nature or Form: Approaches to Acting from 1550 to 1900

❧❧❧

Up to this point it has been relatively unproblematic to describe approaches to acting within quite clear boundaries of geography (Greece, Rome) and time (Middle Ages). As we have seen when looking at the theatre of the Renaissance, a common denominator can be established, but there are marked differences between the countries. Therefore, rather than proceeding by listing developments century by century and, within those centuries, country by country, I want to isolate two characteristics of approaches to acting that have emerged from the discussion so far – the internal organization of theatre as far as it concerns the actor and the acting style adopted at any given time – and show how they have developed up to the end of the nineteenth century.

Professional theatre across Europe developed initially in troupes travelling throughout their countries of origin, and beyond. These troupes were often made up of members of the same family, who in due course hired additional performers. English acting troupes were the first to travel abroad; they merged with local actors, and gradually, several countries developed their own independent troupes, inspired by the English example. In Denmark, English troupes are recorded as early as 1586, followed by German and Dutch troupes after 1663 and the appearance of French companies after 1669. With increasing interest in the theatre, more sophisticated troupes, from their own country or from abroad, became established. The first permanent troupe in Sweden (1699) came from France. Some companies could attract royal patronage. In England, for example, we know of the existence of the Queen's Men (1583–93), a company whose life was curtailed by the closure of the theatres during the great plague, and which, after the theatres reopened, became the Lord Admiral's Men. They were in competition with the Lord Chamberlain's Men, run by the Burbage family, whose name changed to the King's Men when James I succeeded to the throne in 1603. Queen Elizabeth I saw an average of five productions per year, James I seventeen and Charles I (who reigned from 1625 to 1649) twenty-five. Royal patronage was one of the factors contributing to a rise in the status of actors in England between 1580 and 1642. Ben Jonson was the first to publish his plays in an elaborate folio edition, rather than the pamphlet editions in which plays has been published until then. He was also the first to mention the actors who had performed in his plays by name. Thomas Heywood published a detailed *Apology for Actors* in 1612, followed by a similar piece by Nathan Field in 1616. The good name of actors also benefitted from Edward Alleyn's 1619 deed of foundation of his College of God's Gift in Dulwich.

In Italy, the troupes developed a special form of theatre, *commedia dell'arte*, a form of improvised theatre in which actors played to detailed scenarios. Its tradition was kept alive mainly in families, with fathers teaching sons, or mothers their daughters. Among the players were many of high education: one, for example, was reported to have been fluent in Italian, French, Latin, Greek and Turkish, in addition to playing many instruments, acting and writing poetry.

Seventeenth-century Spain was shaken by its increasing loss of power throughout the world. Theatre took on a surrogate function, providing an appeal to the divine in the struggle with a tough fate. Faith and honour developed as dominant motifs in both worldly and religious forms of drama. Theatre became tremendously popular, and numerous troupes travelled through the country. In a text from 1602, entitled *Viaje entretenido* (*Entertaining Journey*), Augustino de Rojas provides what amounts to a typology of troupes. Altogether, eight categories can be differentiated:

- *Bululu*: the solo entertainer, who travels from village to village, presenting comedies in which he plays all parts himself.
- *Ñàque*: two men who use blankets as costumes and beards from fur. They perform *entremeses*, *autos*, and recite *Loas* accompanied by Tambourine.
- *Gangarilla*: three to four actors, one of whom is expert at playing the fool, and another of whom is young and plays the female parts. They have beards and wigs, and like to borrow (and not return) women's clothes from among their audience. Their payment is higher than that of the *Ñàque*.
- *Cambaleo*: consists of an actress, who appears mainly as a singer, and five men who accompany her in play and song (Rojas characterizes their singing as howling, though). They stage a comedy, two *autos*, or three to four *entremeses*. They have a basic stock of costumes. On their travels, the woman is at times carried in a sedan chair. They stay four to six days in one place and rent a bed for the woman, while the men sleep on straw in the kitchen, covered by a blanket.

- *Garnàcha*: consists of an actress who plays the leading ladies, a boy who plays other female parts and five to six men. Their costume stock, carried in a box, consists of two skirts, a wide cloak, three furs, beards and wigs, and a lady's dress. The repertory consists of four comedies, three *autos* and three interludes. The costume box is carried by a donkey, and behind the donkey there is some space for the actress, whose suffering is wittily conjured by Rojas.
- *Boxigranga*: consists of two actresses, a boy actor and six or seven male actors. They have a repertory of six comedies, three or four *autos* and five interludes. Their stock material is kept in two suitcases. When travelling they use four mules, one for the suitcases, one each for the actresses and one for the rest of the company, with fifteen-minute shifts. In general, their performances take place in the evenings. Company members often change, and Rojas mentions that dubious characters are found among them.
- *Farándula*: consists of three actresses and up to eighteen actors. They have two suitcases, travel on mules or carts and perform only in major places.
- *Compañias*: they represent the highest level of sophistication among travelling companies. Their members come from a good family background and boast a good education. They have a repertory of some fifty comedies, and their stock of 4,000 kg is transported in coaches. The company comprises sixteen actors and actresses, with staff and family members increasing this number to about thirty. The large repertory was necessary to please their audiences; as a result, they had to rehearse almost continuously.[1]

From Spain, we also have records of the average daily life of professional actors. They would rise early and study their role from 5 to 9 a.m., followed by rehearsals from 9 a.m. to noon. After lunch they would perform in the theatre until about 7 p.m. In the evening they might be summoned to private performances by officials or nobles. They were always paid straight after the performance.

In Germany in the early eighteenth century, the actor Konrad Ekhof (1720–78) describes his impressions of a travelling troupe he saw perform when he was young:

> Troupes of travelling players, who speed through the whole of Germany from one fair to another, amuse the mob with common farces. ... One comedy, performed everywhere with the greatest frequency was called *Adam and Eve or the Fall of the First Beings*. It has not yet been completely banned, and I recall seeing it performed in Strasbourg. Eve was a fat woman whose body was covered in canvas painted in unconvincing flesh-colours and who had a little belt of fig-leaves stuck to her skin. Poor Adam looked just as ridiculous, but God the Father wore an old dressing gown and had a huge wig and a long white beard. The devils were played by clowns. ... Otherwise everything was hideous: a poor wooden booth

served as a theatre; the decorations were pathetic, the actors, clothed in rags and second-hand wigs looked like coachmen disguised as heroes; in a word, the comedy was a success only with the rabble.[2]

Although performances may appear to have been rather basic, there was nevertheless a strong hierarchical structure in the troupes, as this recollection by Iffland (1759–1814) of the middle of the eighteenth century shows:

> The second hero had to greet the leading tragic hero first whereas the latter only returned the greeting. Those who played the confidant took their hats off the moment the first hero or the one who played the tyrant turned up. In public places the leading actors kept to themselves, the others withdrew on their own accord and were only allowed to approach when condescendingly invited to do so. . . . Any comment on the acting of senior members was regarded as a sign of madness.[3]

As indicated, aristocratic patronage was common throughout Europe. In some cases, such as Denmark and Sweden, however, the court developed a preference for opera and ballet, respectively, at the expense of acting in plays. In Russia, theatre thrived under Tsar Peter the Great (1689–1725), adopting the style predominant in Western Europe. Following his reign, however, the theatre deteriorated for some years, because his successors, Katharina I (1725–7) and Peter II (1727–30), were not interested in the theatre. Matters improved again under Anna Ivannovna (1730–40), but well into the period of Elisabeth Petrovna's reign (1741–61), court theatre was almost exclusively in the hands of German or French troupes. Russian companies initially imitated the style of their visitors. However, Russia was also the scene for a special 'form' of the relationship between aristocracy and actors, in which numerous nobles kept theatre companies made up of 'christened property', i.e. serfs. Clearly well trained, when they performed in plays together with professional actors, spectators were reportedly unable to tell the difference.

In other countries, theatre was preferred throughout. In Germany, many of the numerous small states run by aristocrats gave considerable support to the arts, including theatre. With the decline of the aristocracy and the rise of municipal bureaucracies, patronage, or at least financial support, either shifted or ceased altogether. The commercial element, on the back burner during the comfortable years of support by the local or national court, returned to the forefront, and on a larger scale than had been the case for the independent travelling troupes at the onset of professional theatre. With developments towards the creation of unified nation-states (rather than a loose conglomerate of independent small units), attempts were made to create National Theatres, with France's Comédie Française (1680) being the first.

Organizationally, the first sophisticated professional companies worked on the sharing principle. A number of actors were shareholders in the company. To become a shareholder, the actor had to put down a sizeable sum of money, and on his departure he (and in case of his death someone named by him for that purpose) would get the share back. Admission to the rank of shareholder became more complex as time went by: in eighteenth-century France, for example, admission to the troupe was decided by a panel of actors: those approved were tested in three public performances, and if successful, became salaried actors, until a sharing position became available. The risk and profit of the company were divided among the shareholders. In addition to the shareholders, the theatre companies employed hired men to play smaller parts and work as prompters, wardrobe keepers, stage keepers, janitors and musicians. On the whole, leading actors were shareholders, and besides acting, they may have served as dramatists or been involved in managing the company financially.

In most companies up until the end of the nineteenth century, actors were expected to follow a line of business. In Restoration and eighteenth-century England, the hierarchy was as follows: player of leading roles, player of secondary roles, player of third-line parts and general utility performer. In Germany the categories of male and female stock characters became more differentiated: first hero, youthful hero, heroic father, young character actor, young comic and bon vivant; and first heroine, first sentimental, heroic mother, comic old lady, innocent naive and soubrette. Actors were expected, and sometimes had the contractual right, to play all parts within their line of business.

There were several problems with this approach to casting: stock roles led to repetitive mannerisms and stereotyped characterization. When applying for a new position, an actor would draw up a list of parts in his repertory, and could be expected to play any role on that list at very short notice. Nobody would check whether the list presented upon application was accurate or exaggerated. One can imagine the kind of acting that resulted from an actor playing a part he had never played before without rehearsal and at such short notice. Another problem was one of credibility: if an actress was able to present a tender voice and a soulful glance, her line of business became the first sentimental. Only when she was clearly too old to play the parts in her line, such as Gretchen in Goethe's *Faust* or Ophelia or Desdemona in *Hamlet* and *Othello* respectively, was she promoted to first heroine. She would then play a part such as Lady Milford in Schiller's *Kabale und Liebe* to a Ferdinand young enough to be her son.

The system of lines of business also led to the development, especially in the nineteenth century, of a strong star system. Star actors would travel all over the country, appearing in the provinces in plays of their choice, in which they played the leading part to great public acclaim. Frequently, they did not bother to rehearse with the local actors, and often even had their own tailor-made scripts that contained new lines, cues and stage business that the local actors had to adapt at very short notice. No wonder that in many such cases the quality of the star actor appeared even greater in contrast with the inevitably poor performance of the locals. Reviews for the locals were bad, and in future local audiences would attend only if they had the assurance of a star actor. In several cases, this vicious circle nearly led to the bankruptcy of many local theatres, which could not afford to pay the expensive stars without receiving sufficient income from the box office.

The line of business approach implied that relatively little time was spent on rehearsals: the actor was expected to know his business. There were a few attempts to remedy this situation. In Germany, Goethe introduced three read-throughs in his house, followed by time given to the actors to learn their parts. On the stage, exits and entrances were blocked, followed by two full rehearsals on stage, one of them in full dress. Altogether, some twenty hours were spent on rehearsals. Just how generous this was in the context of nineteenth-century practice becomes clear when we note that in 1867, a leading German court theatre had a total of eighty staff, including the opera chorus. In a season of six months, sixteen new productions were mounted in addition to six revivals. This left literally no time for rehearsals beyond arranging basic entrances and exits.

The Duke of Saxe Meiningen (1826–1914) carried through fully Goethe's attempts at abandoning the lines of business, the related star system and the dire lack of rehearsals. He developed a cohesive company, in which actors played both leading parts and members of the crowd. Actors hired as guest artists were not regarded or used as stars, but as honorary members of the company, with the same duties, including that of playing small parts. Leading actors were often successfully employed to serve as a focus for a number of super-numeraries in crowd scenes. Thus, each member of a crowd knew precisely what to do at any given point in time, and they had their psychological motivation for such action. The crowd scenes were one of the strongest points of the Saxe Meiningen troupe, despite claims that such exciting spectacles diverted attention away from the main characters, and that interjections from the crowd broke the flow of the play's poetry. The following description of Caesar's death scene in Shakespeare's *Julius Caesar* highlights the impact of such crowd scenes:

> When Casca strikes the blow to Caesar, a single, heart-shattering cry runs through the mass of people gathered around the Curia. There follows a deadly silence; the murderers, the senators, the folk, stand a moment as if bewitched and frozen before the body of the mighty Caesar; then a storm breaks out, the movement of which one has to see, the roaring of which one has to hear, to realize how powerful, how high and how deep, the effect of dramatic art can go.[4]

To cast a play, the text was read on stage. Reading rehearsals were then held to discuss and analyse the play. Rehearsals on stage began once lines had been learned, always in full set and costume. The Duke's wife gave individual lessons to actors in delivery. Sometimes, the Duke interrupted the actors to make suggestions, and often he made notes that formed the basis of discussions following the presentation of a scene. Here is a selection of his notes for a production of Shakespeare's *Winter's Tale*:

> Get Floritzel better hat – fountain terrible – clean jewellery – Görner keeps saying, 'aaah aaah!' – scene change to 'Time' and to Bohemia far too long – Richard not understandable – better chair for Leontes – the three court ladies should not have identical headdresses – the headdresses of everyone must fit the costumes better – streaks on the backdrop paint – the bear kicks over the set pieces every time he goes off.[5]

Visiting actors were surprised by the Duke's attention to detail during rehearsals. Two actors from Berlin were hired for parts in *Julius Caesar*, which they had played often at home. They expected two scene rehearsals and were initially shocked and bored at having to work through four full general rehearsals of this three-year-old production. They later commented:

> The duke sat in the auditorium and made his remarks in a loud, energetic voice. ... Each of his directions astonished us and earned our admiration. We had never even heard of any such well-thought-out instructions given to the actor on any stage.[6]

Over the centuries, the acting profession had undergone a remarkable development from the humble beginnings of the travelling players described by Ekhof to the level of sophistication characteristic of the Saxe Meiningen troupe at the end of the nineteenth century. During this time, the role of the director, at first virtually unknown, grew in importance, and was set to dominate the stage for much of the twentieth century.

Having briefly surveyed the organization of the theatre as it affected the actor, it is now appropriate to look in more detail at the style of acting in the theatre of Europe from the Renaissance to the end of the nineteenth century. It is characterized by regularly shifting from formal to realistic, and back. George Taylor discovered a paradox in the development:

> why, in the last couple of centuries, each actor has been greeted as more 'natural' as the one before, and how the naturalism of one generation becomes the 'ham' action of the next. It cannot be entirely due to changing techniques of speech and gesture, but to the underlying creative method. Once such a method has been recognised by an audience, it no longer convinces them. They may still be moved, excited, and impressed by a performance, but they call it art rather than nature.[7]

The issue was whether the actors should concentrate on the artifice of the theatre, or whether they should attempt to portray 'real' people. It is important to understand that acting styles deserving the description of 'natural' in earlier centuries differ greatly from what we today traditionally associate with the concepts of 'realistic' and 'naturalistic', with the movements of realism and naturalism in the theatre, which flourished in the last part of the nineteenth century in the works of Ibsen, Chekhov and Strindberg. Compared with the level of realism achieved in those plays and their productions on stage, what critics and contemporaries labelled 'natural' in earlier times would register as quite unrealistic for us. This observation has, of course, implications today for our understanding of the styles called *formal* and *natural*.

In some cases, the distinction between formal and realistic can be made quite easily; in others, the issue has generated controversial discussion. In Shakespeare's England, for example, female roles were played by boys, and the scripts suggest a non-realistic style, because the stage background was conventional and there was a large repertory. All these factors appear to support the position of a formal style of acting. Critics supporting this view also cite the relation of acting to the art of oratory, pointing to the use of the voice in a declamatory manner, in which phrasing, figures and literary qualities are observed. Hand gestures are used to emphasize words. The actors intend to arouse the spectators' emotions rather than express the characters' emotions. Other scholars support the view that acting in Shakespeare's time tended towards the realistic. They draw their support from Hamlet's advice to the players, from documents implying actor Burbage's convincing performances, the truthfulness of human psychology in the plays and the physical closeness of the actors to the audience in performance. Burbage is said to have been fully immersed in his role right from the beginning of the performance to the end, and even when he came off-stage.[8]

Cervantes' comedy *Pedro de Urdemáles* contains a comment by the main character, Pedro, which suggests that full emotional involvement is required of the good actor:

> Above all, an actor must have a good memory, then a lively tongue, and thirdly his outward appearance must be pleasing. He cannot do without a beautiful figure if he wants to act. His bearing must not be mannered, his recitation not exaggerated. He has to act unforced, but with care; as an old man, he has to be serious, as a young one lively, as a lover passionate, and as a jealous man he has to be angry. He has to act in such a way and with such art that he transforms himself completely into the person he plays. With apt tongue he has to do justice to the verse, and bring the dead plot to life; he has to conjure tears from his smiling face, and be able to change back to laughter immediately. The highest test he faces is whether the expression he takes on himself will show on the spectators' faces. If that is the case, the actor can be called brilliant.[9]

Apart from the common requirements of actors regarding memory, physical appearance and verse-speaking, Cervantes implies that the actor should *become* the character, surely an indication of the natural approach to acting. Yet other documents of the time suggest otherwise: as Schack and Rennert have pointed out, abrupt changes from one passion to another were frequent, as were exaggerations of everyday life.

Italian *commedia dell'arte* represents an intriguing mix of formal and natural acting. Although the plays were improvised in performance, this did not mean a free-for-all; rather, detailed scenarios had been worked out and agreed in advance. Emphasis was placed on both individual skills and ensemble acting. The plays employed stock characters. The actors playing comic roles wore half or partial leather masks, covering forehead, eyes, nose and cheeks. The serious roles were unmasked, thus allowing greater kinship to the spectators.[10]

One of the most important actors of the English Restoration was Thomas Betterton (1635–1710), who convinced through his deeply felt emotions, accompanied by decorum of movement. His successors, Booth (1681–1722) and Wilks (1665–1732), adopted a more externalized style, and shifted towards a declamatory delivery. Macklin (1699–1797) and Garrick (1717–79) urged the adoption of a style based on direct observation of life. Again, the result was not late nineteenth-century realism but a less declamatory delivery, which still idealized life. The natural style of acting characteristic of much of European theatre in the middle of the eighteenth century is perhaps epitomized by Garrick. In his acting, observers noted 'sudden and noticeable shifts from one passion to another'.[11] These were due to the understanding of the nature of passions at the time, which, as Taylor describes, was 'a mental state, not necessarily an emotional motive; it is a state recognized and controlled by the mind, not, as a modern psychologist would maintain, a subconscious response controlled by unconscious memories and physiological reactions'.[12] Garrick, in particular, was aware of the importance of the use of artifice in creating the impression of naturalism.[13] Actors such as Garrick exercised their intellect and brought an almost scientific observation 'to those outward symptoms of a passion, the gestures and the tones of voice'.[14]

Among the issues discussed in theories of the theatre, the extent of the actor's involvement in the emotions of the character he is playing has gained a prominent position. The Spanish theorist Alonso Lopez Pinciano (1597–1627) argued that although the actor 'must transform himself into the character he is imitating so that it appears to everyone else as no imitation, ... it seems more likely that the best actor would concentrate on technique and move to tears without weeping himself'.[15] Jusepe Antonio Gonzalez de Salas, on the other hand, held that the actor 'must truly experience the passions of the play as interior feeling rather than guileful appearance'.[16] Pinciano, then, champions technique; Salas emotional involvement. This dichotomy of technique versus emotional involvement is taken up by the subsequent major theorists of the theatre: Luigi Riconboni (involvement); Antonio Riconboni (technique); St Albine (involvement).[17]

The best known of the earlier theorists to tackle the question of the actor's emotional involvement in acting is Denis Diderot (1713–84). Diderot differentiates between two types of actors. The one plays from the heart, from 'sensibility', immersing himself, while acting, in the feelings of the character he plays. According to Diderot, this way of acting yields poor results: 'their playing is alternately strong and feeble, fury and cold, dull and sublime.'[18] Moreover, the actor loses his self-control and the acting varies from performance to performance, because it depends on the actor's daily ups and downs. The actor is unable to pull together his 'individual actions into a coherent whole'.[19] Such acting will have much less effect on the spectators than acting based on the actor's self-control.

Rather than playing from the heart and experiencing the emotions of the character, the actor 'must have in himself an unmoved and disinterested onlooker. He must have, consequently, penetration and no sensibility'.[20] Such an actor, Diderot's ideal, is guided by the intellect. He will have a highly developed ability to observe nature, to imitate it and accurately repeat a pattern of acting that has developed during the rehearsal period. He is thus able to create a coherent and unified role. He does not feel while acting, but makes his impression on the audience by 'rendering so exactly the outward signs of feeling'.[21] Diderot cites the English actor David Garrick as an example of such acting:

> Garrick will put his head between two folding doors, and in the course of five or six seconds his expression will change successively from wild delight to temperate pleasure, from this to tranquillity, from tranquillity to surprise, from surprise to bland astonishment, from that to sorrow, from sorrow to the air of one overwhelmed, from that to fright, from fright to horror, from horror to despair, and thence he will go up again to the point from which he started. Can the soul have experienced all these feelings and played this kind of scale in concert with his face?[22]

The paradox is that emotions in the spectators are stimulated by their unemotional imitation by the actor.

Diderot's paradox is rooted in the history of theatre, science and philosophy of his time. According to Grear, seventeenth-century France saw a 'revival of interest in *pronunciatio*', the 'theory of oratorial delivery'.[23] Diderot's central concern, 'the extent to which an actor should identify ... with the emotions of the character he portrays',[24] is also the major issue discussed in the *pronunciatio* of classical rhetorics. Grear refers to Cicero and Quintilian: Cicero advised the orator to use the rules of the art to portray those emotions he wanted to create in the spectators. Quintilian also emphasized the rules of the art, but added to the 'rationally prepared pathos ... an element of imaginative identification'.[25] The mechanism was this:

> The same devices of style and delivery worked out by the orator to move his audience would, during the performance itself, work upon the orator himself, enabling him to imagine the scene and further assist his ability to portray passions realistically.[26]

Grear shows that French seventeenth-century theatre theory initially followed Quintilian's advice. However, from 1670 onwards, this 'formalist' position was challenged, as part of 'a larger movement against hypocrisy and insincerity'.[27] The emphasis shifted from rational principles of acting to an emotional approach.[28] It is against the latter that Diderot's *Paradox* argues.

To evaluate the implications of Diderot's theory, its central term, 'sensibility', has to be understood within the context of the theories of psychology and physiology that influenced Diderot. Roach takes up this key term, pointing out that in Diderot's time the word 'sensibility' 'resonated through complex layers of meaning in science, literature, and moral philosophy, ascending from the most rudimentary responsiveness of nervous fibres to the highest expressions of humane sympathy and imagination'.[29] In his discussion of the physiological background of the *Paradox*, Roach refers to Diderot's own work in the fields of psychology and physiology.[30] Here, Diderot's views on the relationship between mind and body become relevant.

Despite the variety of approaches in philosophy and psychology to the relationship of mind and body, each with its own terminology, some major strands can be isolated from Diderot's time. Mind and body can be regarded as fully distinct entities. This view is termed 'dualism'. Within this approach, it is possible to distinguish at least two lines of argument. One is usually associated with Descartes (1596–1650). It has been termed 'concrete dualistic interactionism',[31] and holds that both mind and body can mutually influence each other. The other line of argument, termed 'concrete dualistic parallelism',[32] is associated with Leibnitz (1646–1716). It asserts that mind and body unfold in a parallel but causally unrelated manner.

Opposed to dualism and its varieties is monism. Subjective monism 'argues that the physical world does not have an existence independent of either an individual or universal consciousness and thus absorbs physical reality into a consciousness-based monism'.[33] This variety of monism is also called 'mentalism', and is associated with Berkeley (1685–1753). Later developments in physiology led to objective monism, which argues that consciousness is based on, and an expression of, the neurophysiological activities of the brain. This theory is known as the reductionist or mechanistic model.

Diderot was also influenced by the empiricist philosophers Locke (1632–1704) and Hume (1711–76) in putting forward 'a theory of mind which based everything on discrete sensations provided by the senses'.[34] In this context, Diderot regards the body as a 'virtually soulless machine' which has 'biological drives but not will'.[35] The functioning of the human machine depends on the control of the mind over the nerves. When the mind is in control of the nerve activities, the machine functions properly. When the nerves dominate, the functioning of the machine is disturbed: 'Rationality and self-possession inevitably yield before the inexorable pressure of strong feelings.'[36] The feelings, in turn, have specific corresponding involuntary effects on the physiology. For example, the feeling of fury 'inflames the eyes, clenches the fists and the teeth, furrows the brows'.[37] Diderot believed most feelings to be directly related to what he regarded as the physical centre – the diaphragm. Just as the brain 'propels the mechanism of thought',[38] the diaphragm propels the mechanism of feeling. Negative emotions lead to a contraction of the diaphragm; positive, such as happiness, to an expansion. As any feeling has an involuntary effect on the body in general, the specific reaction of the diaphragm is also involuntary and cannot be intentionally suppressed. Once the diaphragm starts reacting – that is, once feelings dominate – the mental faculties such as reason and judgement are rendered ineffective.

In this context, the term 'imagination' is to be separated from the term 'sensibility' as discussed above. In the rehearsal process, not during the actual performance, imagination has an important function for the actor. In creating the pattern for a role that is to be repeated performance after performance without emotional involvement, the actor draws on two important functions: memory and imagination. 'Memory retains the image, imagination revives it, vivifies it, and combines it with other images to form the living mosaic of the inner model.'[39] Roach explains that again this theory is grounded in Diderot's understanding of physiology: if patterns enlivened in the memory of the actor are increased in their intensity by the actor's imagination, the revived sensations 'can duplicate actual experiences'.[40] Thus, during the rehearsal period the actor can feel and physically experience the emotions of the character he is playing, observe them, and thus develop the pattern of the automatized performance. This process is intellectually controlled and leads to a performance equally controlled by the intellect. By contrast, acting from the heart, dominated by emotions and by the diaphragm, is never controlled, because the cause–effect chains of feeling and physiological reaction are involuntary.

Diderot's basic assumption about the relationship of mind and body, their functioning as one entity in the process of combining memory and imagination, leads to an apparent contradiction: 'If the actor's mind and body constitute a single entity, then how can his mind coldly direct his body through sequences of passions without mentally experiencing the same emotions?'[41] According to Roach, Diderot followed the notion common in his time that mind/body can simultaneously be engaged in two separate activities because 'its components resemble those of a stringed instrument'.[42] The more the actor's discriminating qualities of the mind are developed, the more will he be able consciously to detach himself from the emotions of the character, so bringing him closer to Diderot's ideal. According to Diderot, such a level of acting presupposes a nature-given talent and a long process of learning and experience.[43]

Diderot argued in favour of mind and body as an entity, at least as far as the process of combining memory and imagination is concerned. His view is therefore more closely related to monism than to dualism. However, clearly associating Diderot with either subjective or objective monism is difficult. Although his understanding of mental processes is closely related to his understanding of physiology, he does not argue for a dominance of the physiology. Rather, intentional control of the interplay between feeling and physiological reaction is possible through the activity of the intellect.

This, then, is the theoretical background against which approaches to acting developed throughout Europe. The shifts from deeply felt emotions to the externalization of emotion (Betterton and Booth), and forward again to acting based on the observation of life (Garrick), are mirrored elsewhere in Europe. In Holland, early eighteenth-century acting strove to be natural. In tragedy and demanding comedy (as opposed to bloody spectacle and popular comedy), gesture was moderate and in accordance with the emotions represented. Differences in holding a glass or a spoon, expressing goodwill, giving flowers or standing gracefully or at ease were indicative of the characters' social status. All are meticulously captured in a book of the time, also translated into German, French and English.[44] The subsequent development towards a grand rhetorical manner, representing the peak of the neo-classical style, was characteristic of the actor Jan Punt (1711–79). Marten Corver (1727–94) was in favour of a more natural style of acting, closer to Garrick in England and Lekain in France. Corver's students, Ward Bingley (1757–1818) and Johanna Cornelia Wattier (1762–1827), further developed 'psychological insight instead of fixed passions; sensitiveness instead of rhetoric; muted instead of vehement climaxes; and harmonious unity of all the actor's physical means instead of salient vocal effects'.[45]

Naturalism, as an attempt at reproducing naked reality on the stage, found many supporters in the late eighteenth and early nineteenth centuries. In Germany, the question 'what is natural' was at the centre of one of the weekly committee meetings called by Dalberg (1750–1806), the managing director of the theatre in Mannheim. The discussion brought up several suggestions from the actors:

- It is an exact re-creation of reality, based on the actor's experience.
- To achieve naturalness, the actor has to develop a specific technique.
- Theatre brings a painting to life.
- The training of technique is the prerequisite for inspiration, which may lead to the emergence of anything 'natural'.

Dalberg summarized the discussion as follows:

> The most natural actor is therefore the actor who, after thorough exploration of every detail of both his own role and that of the play itself, and after the precise correction of each passage in rehearsal, surrenders himself in the actual performance to his own feelings and to the mood and inspiration of the moment.[46]

In this kind of naturalism, the actor's business was 'to imitate Nature through Art, to come so near to Nature that appearance must be taken for reality and that things which have already occurred are represented as though they were now occurring for the first time'.[47]

Counter-movements against the natural style followed. In Germany, this was epitomized by Goethe (1749–1832) and Schiller (1759–1805); in England by John Philip Kemble (1757–1823) and Sarah Siddons (1755–1831). Goethe developed ninety-one rules for actors, emphasizing that 'First and foremost, the actor must consider that he should not only imitate nature but should also present it in an idealised form, that in his performance he should unite the true with the beautiful'.[48] For the actors of the time, the demand of combining natural acting with the idealized form, usually understood as declamatory pathos,[49] appears to have been taken too far, leading to an over-emphasis on empty declamation. Kemble and Siddons in England tended to look for the *ruling passion* in a part, thus showing emotions leading naturally from one to another. They emphasized stateliness, dignity and grace, aiming at a classical style similar to Goethe and Schiller's in Weimar. In France, François-Joseph Talma (1763–1826) also combined fire and passion with an appropriate level of beauty and measure.[50]

After Schiller's death in 1805, Goethe lost most of his interest in practical theatre work, and naturalism regained its dominance, especially in the work of Iffland, who had been praised by Goethe:

> Laudable features are his vivid imagination, by means of which he knows how to discover whatever his part calls for, then his talent for imitation by means of which he knows how to represent what he has found and as it were created, and finally the humour with which he carries out the whole thing in a lively manner from beginning to end.[51]

It is difficult, however, to assess his acting in view of Schiller's opinion of the same actor:

> I cannot begin to understand how an actor, even a very incapable one,

can so much forget the aims of his art as to go through such pains in front of the audience to create such a cold, empty and unnatural grimace. In addition to all that, Iffland has never been able in all his life to either feel or portray on stage any kind of enthusiasm or exalted mood, and was always dreadful when playing a lover.[52]

During the Romantic period in Germany, leading theorist Tieck (1773–1853) argued against external emotions (taken to be character-istic of the Weimar school). Instead, the 'ideal actor would embody a role with total conviction, allowing the emotional expression to flow from within'.[53] However, Tieck's ideals failed in practice, because the actors in general, apart from a few stars, were not yet ready for the shift, especially given the lack of proper professional training. The most extraordinary actor of the Romantic period in Germany was Ludwig Devrient (1784–1832). His strength was playing wild passions, at the expense of any kind of measure or reason in everyday-life situations.

Isidoro Mayquez (1768–1820), who studied with Talma in Paris for three years, spearheaded Romantic acting in Spain with his portrayal of Othello (1802): approached from within, not outside, and revealing all the confusion of mind characteristic of Romantic thinking. Talma's equal in Russia was Michail Scepkin (1788–1863). He had begun his career in the neo-classical, declamatory style, and shifted to the Romantic approach after he had seen the strikingly passionate performance of an amateur actor. He studied his parts in depth, and strove to ignore his own personality while portraying a character on stage. In Holland, the Romantic period was still influenced by the previous generation of *natural* actors, such as Wattier and Bingley, thus leading to some restraint on the expression of passions. Andries Snoek (1766–1829) said that he could only play or speak a part if he had the imagined awareness of actually being the character.[54] In England, the Romantic style took over from Kemble and Siddons, with Frederick Cooke (1756–1812), then Edmund Kean (1787–1833), as major representatives. As Booth describes, Kean was paradigmatic for the actor who played

his part from situation to situation, playing each significant dramatic moment for what it was and extracting the maximum passion and effect from it, plotting his course through the play from emotional climax to emotional climax, saving himself in between and making a 'point', if appropriate, at each climax.[55]

In England, Romantic individualism placed a strong emphasis on the character: 'The poet created the agonised Romantic hero; the critic wrote about him; the actor played him.'[56] The Romantic ideal declined, however, into melodrama. The increasing popularity of the theatre necessitated larger theatre buildings: Covent Garden seated 3,000, Drury Lane 3,600, and new theatres were built. In 1843, there were twenty-one companies in London, compared with only six in 1800. Only Covent Garden, Drury Lane and the Haymarket were licensed to produce regular plays. Other theatres put on minor drama, with performances lasting up to five or six hours. The popularity of such fare led the three licensed theatres to imitate the popular trends. The large size of the theatres had an impact on the acting style: the spectators were further removed from the stage, and more emphasis on the visual aspects of the production led to the development of spectacle at the expense of subtlety of acting. In this spectacular kind of melodrama, 'moments of intense physical or emotional action' were 'momentarily frozen in a powerful attitude or tableau'.[57] A contemporary critic of 1834 satirizes the acting style employed in melodrama:

> I was curious enough, even on the first night of attending a theatre, to ask myself why Mr Almar made such incessant use of his arms. Now they were antithetically extended, the one skyward, the other earthward, like the sails of a windmill; now they were folded sternly across the bosom; now raised in denunciation; now clasped in entreaty, and considerately maintained in their positions long enough to impress the entire audience at leisure with the effect intended.[58]

The first stage of psychological realism characteristic of Tieck is mirrored to some extent in the attempts of Macready (1793–1873) to combine Kemble's 'dignity and studiousness with Kean's fire'.[59] According to Booth, Macready viewed the character as dramatically unified and attempted to show this unity, the governing 'idea' of the character, on stage.[60] The Duke of Saxe Meiningen in Germany, along with Charles Kean (1811–68) in England, developed and perfected pictorial realism. Psychological realism became the major new development in dramatic writing, and acting followed suit. Henry Irving's (1838–1905) Hamlet of 1874, Booth argues:

> was a Victorian benchmark for psychological analysis on the actor's part and the meticulous construction of a psychologically complex but credible character within the bounds of the doctrine, which Irving did not question, that the meaning of the play could be found in the meaning of the central character.[61]

Indeed, Irving maintained that individual characters should be examined with care for more than their theatrical opportunities. Irving valued originality and individuality, devalued declamation and encouraged gesture and stage business, all with the aim of creating the illusion of a consistent character.[62]

In France, Elise Rachel (1821–58) excelled in giving a realistic touch to classical parts, whereas others specialized in the realistic portrayal of social criticism in contemporary French plays by Scribe (1791–1861), Sardou (1831–1908) and Labiche (1815–88). In 1857, French writer Théophile Gautier (1811–1872) complained that theatre of his time lacked idealism and poetry. 'All is only prose, leaving no space for imagination. Actors perform in the same clothes they wear in private life, and display the same manners, too.'[63] In Italy, the major actors representing the shift towards realism included Adelaide Ristori (1822–1906), Tommaso Salvini (1829–1915) and Ernesto Rossi (1829–96). Michail Scepkin in Russia, who had started in the neo-classical declamatory style, developed via the Romantic dominance of the passions towards a vital realism which emphasized the character types rather than the individual. Prov Sadovsky (1818–72) was able to 'project both internal and external realism' and thus 'created more fully rounded characterization than any previously seen'.[64]

Psychological realism was favoured vehemently in Germany by Otto Brahm (1856–1912). Actors should act with their whole body, not just the voice and gesture. They should be unconscious of the audience's presence, avoid posturing, playing for effect or making points, and should never pause for applause. They were expected to be in character all the time when on stage. Brahm aimed at photographic naturalism, with an emphasis on the sordid side, usually with rather drab decor.[65]

While realism and naturalism were in full swing, the counter-movements of anti-realism had already developed. They emphasized that in human life, science and objectivity cannot reveal all. Rather, much is left unknown and relative. To show the unknowable is the main aim of anti-realist theatre in its manifold versions, beginning, perhaps, with symbolism in France at the end of the nineteenth century. One of its proponents, Stephane Mallarmé (1842–98), saw drama 'as an evocation of the mystery of existence through poetic and allusive language, performed with only the most essential and atmospherically appropriate technical aids, for the purpose of creating a mystical experience'.[66] The two dominant symbolist dramatists were Maurice Maeterlinck (1862–1949) and Paul Claudel (1868–1955). In the theatre, Paul Fort (1872–1960) was the first to establish an independent symbolist theatre (1890), followed soon after its demise in 1892 by Aurélien-Marie Lugné-Poë (1869–1940) at the Théâtre de l'Oeuvre (until 1899). For his symbolist productions, Lugné-Poë developed a strikingly unrealistic acting style, characterized by vocal delivery in the form of chant, and 'angular, stylised gestures'. An 1894 critic wrote:

> The most simple and sensible things take on a different appearance in passing through the mouth and gestures of the l'Oeuvre actors under the direction of Lugné-Poë. They have a continual ecstatic air of perpetually being visionaries. As if hallucinatory, they stare before them far, very far, vaguely, very vaguely. Their voices are cavernous, their diction choppy.[67]

The contrast between realism and anti-realism at the end of the nineteenth century is characteristic of much of twentieth-century theatre.

The development of scenic realism into psychological realism at the end of the nineteenth century runs parallel with the growing importance of the role of the director for theatre production. The tendency is said to have begun with the Duke of Saxe Meiningen, and is prominent in the theory of the total work of art, *Gesamtkunstwerk*, developed by Richard Wagner (1813–83). The idea of combining several art forms in the theatrical event is not new. Lessing speculated on a synthesis which would respect the limitations of the separate arts while using them to supplement each other. Herder argued that there is no reason to doubt the exalted effect which an intelligent alliance of music, poetry and dance, these arts which so naturally belong together, would produce. Schelling saw the universe itself as a perfect work of art, and demanded a combination of all the arts that can possibly be brought onto the stage.

Wagner initially held that the language of music is eternal, infinite, ideal. It expresses nothing specific, not, say, the passion of an individual, but love and other feelings themselves, in the abstract, and in most universal terms. Influenced by the Romantic period, and eighteenth-century doctrine of the limitations of the arts, he moved on to argue, in *The Art-Work of the Future*, that a more comprehensive massing together of the effects of art will produce a more sublime artistic effect. At this stage of Wagner's theory, the spoken word was given priority over other means of expression. In *Opera and Drama*, he shifts the emphasis towards music. *Gesamtkunstwerk* can only communicate to the senses and through them exclusively to the emotions. Reason, the conceptual and the intellectual are to play no part. Music serves to intensify the direct sensory appeal of the verse to overcome the conceptual level of poetry (alliteration, condensation, free rhythm). In *Beethoven*, finally, Wagner is influenced by Schopenhauer's view that music is a direct objectification of the real essence of the universe (will). Ideal drama becomes dramatic music, in organic connection with dramatic action, in which the metaphysical will is transmitted to our consciousness. The sole determining agent for the music in the ideal drama is the dramatic action. All forms of art coming together in the *Gesamtkunstwerk* should be, ideally, under the command of a single master artist.

In such a context, the function of the performer can become a rather subordinated one; the legacy of the development of directors' theatre can still be felt today, when much review space is devoted to at times detailed analyses of the production, compared with far less discussion of the performers. Equally, photos from productions in many books on contemporary theatre drama credit the author, the director, the designer, even the photographer, but hardly ever the actors.

ಬಿೆೇಙಿ

5

Approaches to Acting in the Twentieth Century

ଚଠଉଔ

Stanislavsky and His Legacy: Realism and Naturalism from Psychotechnique to Physical Actions

Psychotechnique and Method of Physical Actions

The movements of the pendulum between natural and artistic/ heightened styles of acting became even more pronounced throughout the twentieth century, with an explosion of -isms in which realism and anti-realism represent opposite poles. At the end of the eighteenth century, Goethe and Schiller had brought new impulses to theatre through their texts. Despite their efforts, however, they were unable to forge a style that allowed actors to do justice to their plays. Melodramatic acting prevailed, leading to the realistic/naturalistic counter-movement, initially in scenic realism (elaborate, historically accurate sets and costumes), later in dramatic realism (epitomized by the plays of Ibsen), which led on to naturalism (Strindberg, Chekhov). A more realistic style of acting followed, which Stanislavsky system-atized from 1906 onwards, first in practice, and subsequently in writing. In developing his own ideas, Stanislavsky in turn shifted from an emphasis on the psychology of the actor (mainly associated with Stanislavsky today), towards an emphasis on the actor's body (which appears to have been marginalized by Stanislavsky scholarship).

Stanislavsky's system of actor training and acting has had a major influence in Western theatre history of the late nineteenth and twentieth centuries. If it is not directly practised, the differences most frequently represent conscious developments of Stanislavsky's theories (for example, Strasberg and his 'Method'), or outspoken opposition to them (for example, the early Brecht). Stanislavsky takes up the serious issue as to whether or not the actor should be involved with the emotions supposedly felt by the character.

On the issue of the actor's emotional involvement while acting, Stanislavsky appears to take the opposite view from Diderot: 'an actor is under the obligation to live his part inwardly, and then to give to his experience an external embodiment.'[1] This obligation of the actor is in line with Stanislavsky's view of the fundamental aim of the art of acting: 'the creation of this inner life of a human spirit, and its expression in an artistic form'.[2] The inner life has to be created and lived in every performance, not just in rehearsal as Diderot argued. The important force that has to be tapped to allow such 'inspired' acting is the subconscious. Thus, the more the actor can use his subconscious forces, the more he will be able to 'fit his own human qualities to the life of this other person, and pour into it all of his own soul'.[3] Stanislavsky describes the ideal of acting in the following terms:

> The very best that can happen is to have the actor completely carried away by the play. Then regardless of his own will he lives the part, not noticing how he feels, not thinking about what he does, and it all moves of its own accord, subconsciously and intuitively.[4]

This ideal appears to imply that the actor has lost self-control, a state that Diderot had warned against.[5] Stanislavsky recognized that the subconscious, and whatever arises from that realm, is not only inaccessible to consciousness[6] but also lies beyond the control of the will. For that reason he sought to develop procedures that allow the actor to use the subconscious forces through conscious techniques.

In preparing for a part, the actor begins by dividing the play into units 'which, like signals, mark his channel and keep him [the actor] in the right line'.[7] Understanding the structure of the play constitutes the outward purpose of the division into units. This outward purpose is complemented by an inner purpose which, according to Stanislavsky, is far more important. The inner purpose is the 'creative objective' which lies 'at the heart of every unit'.[8] Stanislavsky provides a detailed definition of right objectives. To be able to 'live his part inwardly',[9] the actor's objectives must be 'directed toward the other actors, and not toward the spectators'.[10] This orientation towards fellow-actors means that the actor concentrates on the fictional reality of the play. This fictional world, through the actor's objectives, is to be 'real, live, and human, not dead, conventional, or theatrical'.[11] The objectives must be precise and clear-cut, and should attract and move the actor; they should be personal to the actor, but still analogous to those of the character the actor is portraying.

Establishing the units and objectives of play and character allows the actor to arrive at a comprehensive understanding – both intellectual-outward (units) and emotional-inward (objectives) – of the play and the character he has to portray. The emotional, intuitive grasp of the role is not completed, however, with the association of the objectives resulting from the units of the play. Stanislavsky recognized that 'direct, powerful and vivid emotions do not ... last over long periods or even for a single act. They flash out in short episodes, individual moments.'[12] Moreover, Stanislavsky asserts that we cannot control such 'spontaneous eruptions of feeling'[13]: 'They control us. Therefore we have no choice but to leave it to nature ... we will only hope that they will work with the part and not at cross purpose to it.'[14] No matter how irresistible and moving a force those direct, powerful and vivid emotions may be, they are not sufficient for the actor's daily task of performance.

Stanislavsky does not argue, then, in favour of a loss of self-control, of leaving it to nature and hoping for the best. He recognizes the creative potential of a spontaneous eruption of emotions, but at the same time realizes the inherent dangers of an eruption that is beyond the actor's control. It is in this context that Stanislavsky explicitly warns the actor: 'Never lose yourself on the stage. Always act in your own person, as an artist.'[15]

Once the actor has established the emotion-dominated objectives of his part, he can use the technique of emotion-memory to gain controlled and repeatable access to his unconscious. Stanislavsky explains that

> just as your visual memory can reconstruct an inner image of some forgotten thing, place, or person, your emotion-memory can bring back feelings you have already experienced. They may seem to be beyond recall, when suddenly suggestion, a thought, a familiar object will bring them back in full force. Sometimes the emotions are as strong as ever, sometimes weaker, sometimes the same strong feelings will come back but in a somewhat different guise.[16]

Thus, the actor uses his own past emotions as creative material, assisted by 'feelings that we have had in sympathising with the emotions of others'.[17] Stanislavsky all along emphasized that the emotions should be spontaneous: 'The work of the actor is not to create feelings but only to produce the given circumstances in which true feelings will spontaneously be engendered.'[18]

While the emotion-memory is a technique, allowing the actor to suffuse his acting with genuine emotions of his own which are analogous to the emotions the character is supposed to experience, several techniques in turn are used by the actor to stimulate the emotion-memory: initially, the actor has to believe in the validity of the objectives for the play and the character. Such belief, a sense of truth, is spontaneously followed by desire, in turn leading to action. The action takes the form of physical motor adjustments which are in line with the emotions felt. A further technique to stimulate the emotion-memory is an awareness of tempo-rhythm, both of movement and regarding speech. Stanislavsky explains how both our actions and our speech

> proceed in terms of time. In the process of action we must fill in the passing time with a great variety of movements, alternating with pauses of inactivity, and in the process of speech the passing time is filled with

moments of pronunciation of sounds of varying lengths with pauses between them.[19]

Indeed, there is 'some kind of tempo-rhythm inherent in every minute of our inward and outward existence'.[20]

Each actor will have to find his own tempo-rhythm for both movement and speech, in line with the requirements of the part. Tempo-rhythm is closely interrelated with feelings, the 'inward existence': as Stanislavsky points out, 'every human passion, every state of being, every experience has its tempo-rhythms'.[21] The actor can intuitively apply the tempo-rhythm appropriate to a character and a situation on the stage. If the actor, however, lacks such intuition, he can work 'from the outside in',[22] beating out the rhythm. By intentionally adopting a tempo-rhythm appropriate to specific emotions, those emotions can be triggered, stimulated in the form of emotion-memory. Through an awareness of tempo-rhythm the actor can 'be put into a state of genuine excitement and get from it an emotional impact'.[23]

The emotions certainly have an important function in acting, but they are not isolated. Feeling unites with mind and will to form a 'triumvirate' of motive forces.[24] They can be stimulated independently and in their interaction. Again, Stanislavsky argues that the motive forces sometimes function spontaneously, subconsciously. However, if they do not, the actor can turn to any of the three components of the 'triumvirate'. If he turns to the mind, the mechanism will be as follows: 'The actor takes the thoughts in the lines of his part and arrives at a conception of their meaning. In turn, this conception will lead to an opinion about them, which will correspondingly affect his feeling and will.'[25] Using the interaction between the three inner motive forces is at the basis of Stanislavsky's psychotechnique. It encompasses emotion-memory to stimulate feelings (and, in turn, tempo-rhythm of movement and speech to stimulate emotion-memory). The mind is directly affected by thought. However, Stanislavsky argues that 'there is no direct stimulus by which you can influence the will'.[26] There appears to be a contradiction at this point: when arguing for will as the third inner motive force, Stanislavsky points out that units and objectives are techniques of 'arousing inner living desires and aspirations'.[27] He clarifies the point by proposing that will and feeling are inseparable, and that some objectives 'influence the will more than the feeling and others enhance the emotions at the expense of the desire'.[28]

All elements of the psychotechnique assist the actor's energies to converge towards a holistic and organic expression of a character on the stage. Stanislavsky regards the holistic value of acting on two levels: on the level of action, he coined the phrase 'through line of action'.[29] On the level of speech, the equivalent to 'through line of action' is called the 'subtext'.[30] Stanislavsky defines the subtext as a web of innumerable, varied inner patterns inside a play and a part, woven from 'magic ifs,' given circumstances, all sorts of figments of the imagination, inner movements, objects of attention, smaller and greater truths and a belief in them, adaptations, adjustments and other similar elements.[31]

All the elements that compose the subtext lead to the ultimate super-objective of the play, which gives the play and the characters their holistic and organic shape.

The actor approaches a part both intellectually and intuitively, stirring his motive forces – feelings, mind and will – to reach into the unconscious, the subtext of the play, in order to develop a grasp of both play and character that leads to genuinely felt and experienced performances. The technique of emotion-memory appears to be crucial, because it most efficiently enables the actor to gain access to the subconscious: 'the subconscious creative objective is the best, because it takes possession of an actor's feelings, and carries him intuitively along to the basic goal of the play',[32] the super-objective. Such unconscious objectives are consciously 'engendered by the emotion and will of the actors themselves'.[33] The unconscious is set to work by a conscious stimulus. The unconscious objectives 'come into being intuitively'.[34] If the actor left the unconscious objectives to themselves once they have been consciously stimulated, he might well lose his self-control. Stanislavsky, however, points out clearly that once the unconscious objectives have come into being, 'they are then weighed and determined consciously'.[35]

Diderot saw an actor who fully involves himself in the emotions of the character he has to portray as being in danger of losing his self-control. He therefore advised actors to act without emotional involvement, instead perfecting the art of imitating real-life emotions. Stanislavsky was also well aware of the risk of an actor's loss of self-control. On the other hand, he maintained that acting in which the emotions are not genuinely felt, but merely mechanical, does not do justice to the demands of the art of acting. He thus provided the actor with techniques intended to stimulate as much unconscious, intuitive, emotional material as possible, while at the same time ensuring that such techniques did not lead to an undesirable state of lost self-control. Stanislavsky quotes the actor Salvini: 'An actor lives, weeps and laughs on the stage, and all the while he is watching his own tears and smiles. It is this double function, this balance between life and acting that makes his art.'[36] Stanislavsky's reference to this double function – the witnessing of the process of acting by the actor himself – resembles Diderot's call for the 'unmoved and disinterested onlooker'.[37]

Thus, the paradox takes a decisive shift from Diderot to Stanislavsky. Diderot's paradox is the emotional stimulation of the audience through an emotionally uninvolved actor. In the case of Stanislavsky, the paradox exists not in the interaction between actor and spectator, but within the actor: his capacity to be both deeply emotionally involved – down to the level of the unconscious – and yet still in conscious control of the acting through this ability to watch.

The discussion of Diderot's theory of acting has revealed the important influence physiology and psychology studies had on the development of the theory. Placing his theory of acting into a wider framework of philosophical arguments about the relationship of mind and body has also proved useful. The same is true for an assessment of Stanislavsky's concepts.

The importance that Stanislavsky placed on the subconscious for inspired acting reflects the increasing interest in the psyche, pioneered by Freud. The foundation of Stanislavsky's system, gaining access to the subconscious through conscious procedures, has led scholars to draw parallels between Stanislavsky and the basic principles of Freudian psychoanalysis. Kesting proposes further parallels between Stanislavsky's theory of acting and Freud's seminal discoveries in psychology: one of Freud's techniques of assessment was the *free association procedure*, in which the patients reported on whatever 'thoughts and memories occurred to them'.[38] Likewise, Stanislavsky sought to use the emotion-memory of the subconscious as a vehicle to free the actor's inspiration.[39] Stanislavsky's concept of 'subtext' – those elements implied in the play and the part but not directly expressed – mirror, according to Kesting, Freud's construct of the id, while the super-objective of the play, in turn, resembles his concept of the super-ego.[40] Such parallelisms are in danger of being mechanical, however: the subtext, though invisible in itself, can be made visible through the actor; whereas by definition the unconscious cannot be made visible. The super-objective is defined as giving the play and the characters their holistic shape; whereas the super-ego is defined as 'the individual's internalization of societal moral values ... preventing the individual from expressing primitive urges publicly, and ... encouraging the individual to set goals that would establish him or her in a career as a productive citizen'.[41]

It is perhaps more appropriate to draw parallels between Stanislavsky's system and Freud's first topography, where he differentiates the unconscious, the preconscious and the conscious. The area of the mind Stanislavsky wishes to access, which he calls the subconscious, could resemble the preconscious in Freud's first topography of the mind: whereas unconscious contents are in principle not accessible to consciousness, preconscious contents are not yet available to consciousness but can be made available.[42] In any case, Freudian psychoanalysis only provides parallels, points of contact, with Stanislavsky's theory of acting, and not historical sources of influence.

Roach regards the unconscious, to which Stanislavsky attributed 'major powers of artistic creativity', as 'a subconscious repository in a pre-Freudian physiological sense'.[43] The physiological sense of the subconscious is further explained by taking up Strasberg's statement about the concept of emotion-memory central to the American Method: 'The emotional thing is not Freud, as people commonly think. Theoretically and actually, it is Pavlov.'[44] Roach convincingly argues the influence of Pavlov's theories of reflex on Stanislavsky's system. For example, Pavlov saw the relationship between the inner and outer world as a continuous process, a chain of interdependent learned or conditioned reflexes: learned mental reflexes are substitutes for innate physical ones. In parallel, Stanislavsky's system

> defines individual units and objectives as 'bits' in what will eventually, after sufficient rehearsal, become the 'unbroken line of action' or 'the score of the role.' This line is a chain of mutually interdependent reflex desires and reflex actions.[45]

Regarding the affective memory, it has been shown that Stanislavsky directly derived this concept from Theodule Ribot's *The Psychology of the Emotions*, translated into Russian in the 1890s, and one of the books in Stanislavsky's library.[46]

A comparison of Diderot and Stanislavsky leads to the conclusion that apart from the shift of emphasis in the paradox from the actor–spectator relationship in Diderot to the actor–actor dimension in Stanislavsky, there are, as Roach points out, many parallels between the evolution of Diderot's and Stanislavsky's theories:

a) Emotion is beyond the direct reach of the will.
b) Major powers of artistic creativity are attributed to the unconscious mind.
c) The unconscious mind is interpreted as a subconscious repository in a pre-Freudian physiological sense.
d) The actor's creativity is regarded highly, but an inner model of character brought forth collectively with the playwright is conceived of.
e) Belief in long rehearsal periods to prepare a role meticulously.
f) Emphasis on the need for absorption in the stage task.
g) The role is regarded as a score or inner model of physical actions overseen by the dispassionate half of a divided consciousness.[47]

Not only do the scientific theories influencing Diderot and Stanislavsky have to be considered but also the individual ways in which the authors arrived at their theories of acting. Originally a follower of the emotional approach to acting, Diderot arrived at his views as documented in *The Paradox* after his acquaintance with the sensibility debate in science and after having seen Garrick perform. He was further influenced by his contacts with actors, and by frequently attending performances. Thus, Diderot was well informed, but still an outsider. Stanislavsky, on the other hand, arrived at his system through direct experience in acting and directing. His own experiences led him to abandon the mechanical, uninspired and ultimately frustrating way of acting he had been accustomed to, and to develop his own system. This inside approach and its unique experiences made Stanislavsky take the same concern that had guided Diderot – the risk of the actor losing self-control through (over-)indulging in an involvement with the emotions of the character – to a different end. Stanislavsky was primarily concerned with providing practical assistance to actors and directors, leading to an emphasis on practical techniques that can be applied in the day-to-day routine of rehearsal and performance. As a result of this emphasis on practical matters, Stanislavsky refers to the paradoxical nature of the conscious control over simultaneously occurring phenomena of emotional involvement only in passing.

The majority of Stanislavsky's writing was occupied with the psychotechnique (its legacy will be discussed in the next chapter). However, less well documented is his shift of emphasis towards the body and its role in acting. Stanislavsky developed the *method of physical actions* late in his life, and the best record of it appears in the writing of the actor Vasily Osipovich Toporkov, especially about his work on Molière's *Tartuffe*. At the beginning of the work, Stanislavsky informed his cast that their rehearsals were not intended to create a new production, but that he would like to explore with them the method of physical actions. Compared to his work on the psychotechnique, the method of physical actions was not a completely new development; rather, it strove to achieve the same aim, to provide a technique

> for mastering the laws of the creative nature of man. With the understanding of these laws comes the ability to influence this nature, control it, to discover at every performance one's own creative possibilities, one's own intuition.[48]

The method of physical actions, however, took a different point of departure. Psychotechnique and method of physical actions were never ends in themselves, but sought to enable the actor to achieve *the fullest embodiment of the stage character*. Thus, the 'choice of the physical actions is always dictated by the given circumstances and the final intention'.[49]

In rehearsal for *Tartuffe*, Stanislavsky would often ask: 'Well, now, what is the physical line here?'[50] By taking physical actions as a starting point, Stanislavsky intended to emphasize those elements involved in creating a role which are clearest, most accessible and can be easily established. Once truth of physical actions has been established, feelings will arise naturally from that basis in the actor. Thoroughly established physical actions have the added advantage of very clearly transmitting to the audience the 'spiritual condition' of the character.[51]

The cast were allocated rehearsal space on two floors, and, in character, they had to assign rooms to the characters as if the rehearsal space was Orgon's house in *Tartuffe*; later, they played scenes, again in character, which are not in the play, such as the implications of the mistress of the house being ill: how does it change all the activities of the other people in the house? Slowly, they proceeded to scenes from the play, but without being allowed to use Molière's words. The initial result was deplorable: the actors were unable to be truthful, their bodies did not transmit the appropriate inner state. In one particular scene, the actors were expected to present inner tension, but failed to achieve this. Challenged to show them, Stanislavsky obliged. Toporkov's description merits full quotation:

> And there, seated on the sofa, he was transformed instantly. Before us an extremely perturbed person was sitting as if on hot coals. He took out his watch and, hardly glancing at it, thrust it back again; he then became completely still, at any moment ready to spring. Without stopping, he made use of a series of very quick movements. Each of these movements was inwardly justified, completely convincing.[52]

The physical actions will have a logical sequence which develops in the course of the play, and just as with the psychotechnique there is a through-line of action. The actor has to determine the logical sequence, and to make that his own. On the basis of hard work on the physical actions, mainly in the form of improvisations, the cast proceeded to work with Molière's text, which in turn led to a refinement of the physical actions as more insights into the characters' motivations developed. Initially, only the broad outlines of individual scenes were established and translated into physical actions. With the addition of the author's text, rehearsal of the details took over. In this emphasis on detail, physical actions merge with elements of the psychotechnique to give rise to a unity of psychophysical action.

As one aspect of this amalgam of mind and body, Stanislavsky placed special importance on the need for the actor to be in constant communion with his partner(s) on stage. The problem with such communion is that the traditional actor will come on stage as set down during the blocking rehearsals, will go wherever he has been told to go, and then he 'immediately enters into conversation with others, not troubling to find out whether they're disposed to listen to him or not'.[53] Communion, Stanislavsky suggests, consists of seven distinct aspects:

1. Orientation,
2. searching for the object,
3. getting the attention of your partner,
4. making contact with your partner,
5. creating images and making your partner see them as with your eyes,
6. thinking only in the images, never of the intonation of the words, and
7. considering how best to transfer these images and events to your partner.[54]

Ultimately, for the older Stanislavsky, mind (psychotechnique) and body (method of physical actions) work together as a unified whole. However, his followers focused on one or the other, either preferring to work with the mind or with the body. It is only late in the twentieth century that the notion of *bodymind* began to take hold in approaches to acting, mainly influenced by non-Western acting paradigms.[55]

Stanislavsky's Legacy 1: Psychotechnique and the American Method

Stanislavsky's system was further developed, modified and made popular in America as the Method, a term mainly associated with Lee Strasberg (1901–82). First of all, it is important to place this development in the context of the history of approaches to acting in the USA. Here, developments closely mirrored those in Europe. In the mid-eighteenth century, the first actors from the UK are recorded in America. They were from the beginning stigmatized and even subject to legislation against the theatre. Especially in the Puritan-dominated North, the authorities were opposed to the theatre, while the South was more open. The style of acting, according to records, was initially declamatory. Following the revolution and subsequent independence, theatre in the USA did not produce the movement towards natural acting epitomized in Europe by Garrick. George Frederick Cooper (1756–1812), born in Ireland, was influenced by Kemble and added only a little more passion to his dignified, statue-like acting. Edwin Forrest (1806–72) became the first American-born star, one of a number of touring stars who emerged during the period from 1810 to 1865. Unlike the English models of Kemble and Macready, Forrest developed a physical, heroic style.

After a split between elite and popular entertainment from about 1865, the style of acting became more realistic, with Edwin Thomas Booth (1833–95) expressing rudimentary realism in unassuming, intellectual and refined performances, a trend that was developed further by William Gillette (1853–1937). Stars from abroad, such as Jenny Lind, Mlle Rachel, Adelaide Ristori, Sarah Bernhardt, Eleonora Duse and Salvini, continued to influence the US theatre, but by the turn of the century, the star system was being abandoned in favour of ensembles. It was one of these later ensembles, the Group Theatre, founded in 1931 by Harold Clurman, Lee Strasberg and Cheryl Crawford, that Stanislavsky's system was developed into what is now commonly known as the Method, mainly associated with the name of Strasberg.

The major point of departure for Strasberg was Stanislavsky and his 'magic if'. For Strasberg, this concept meant a series of questions which the actor has to ask himself: 'Given the particular circumstances of the play, how would you behave, what would you do, how would you feel, how would you react?'[56] Strasberg agrees that this understanding of the 'magic if' helps the actor in plays that are 'close to the contemporary and psychological experience of the actor',[57] but fails in works that do not fulfil that requirement, for example, classical plays. In recognizing the principal value of the 'magic if', and in an attempt to escape its drawback, Strasberg developed the principles of motivation and substitution. Regarding motivation, he credited Stanislavsky student Vakhtangov with the initial reformulation of Stanislavsky's proposition: 'The circumstances of the scene indicate that the character must behave in a particular way; what would motivate you, the actor, to behave in that particular way?'[58] The actor should not try to imagine that he is the character and derive his emotions from such an imagination. Instead, the actor should use the substitution technique. Strasberg comments as follows:

> The actor is not limited to the way in which he would behave within the particular circumstances set for the character; rather, he seeks a substitute reality different from that set forth in the play that will help him to behave truthfully according to the demands of the role. It is not necessarily the way he himself would behave under the same circumstances, and thus does not limit him to his own natural behavior.[59]

To achieve this substitute emotion, the actor uses several techniques, with an emphasis on the emotion-memory. An example should illustrate the principle. The actor has to portray extreme existential fear. The situation in the play in which that fear is called for is unlike anything the actor has ever experienced in her own life. The actor, therefore, is in trouble if required to imagine how she would react if she were in that situation (as Stanislavsky would have demanded). So, following Strasberg's Method, for each performance she recalls the emotions of terror experienced as a teenager when she was swimming in the ocean off the coast of Florida and suddenly saw herself pursued by a shark, and had to swim for her life back to the shore.

Other representatives of the American Method do not place as much emphasis on psychology as Strasberg, but took up different aspects of Stanislavsky's (and Vakhtangov's) ideas. Stella Adler (1901–92) 'suggested that the actor's inspiration should come from the world of the play itself'.[60] Within that world, the primary emphasis should be on the actions, and only the secondary one on the words. Uta Hagen (1919–) differentiates what she calls *formalism* and *realism*. In formalism, the artist 'objectively *predetermines* the character's actions, deliberately watching the form as he executes it'. In realism, on the other hand, the actor strives to identify with the character to the fullest extent possible. The given circumstances provided by the dramatist in the play serve as guideposts. Any action carried out by the actor in line with those given circumstances will 'involve a moment-to-moment *subjective* experience'.[61]

To achieve involvement and identification, the actor uses his own psyche, because the basic components of any character an actor may be asked to play lie somewhere within the actor's psyche. Hagen points out that we 'change our sense of self a hundred times a day as [we] are influenced by circumstances, [our] relationship to others, the nature of the event, and [our] clothing'.[62] We may begin the day as a sleepy student, or father, or mother or child; once we are on the bus or train to work or school, we perform different roles, and are different again when we reach our workplace or school. In the theatre, the actor makes use of this natural ability, transferring elements from his own experience to those of the play until these become synonymous with the experiences of the role. Such identification relates both to the character's assumed past (prior to the dramatized material that is actually seen on the stage) and to stage events. With reference to the character of Blanche in Tennessee Williams's *A Streetcar Named Desire*, Hagen explains the principle of transference:

> Blanche has coped with the agonizing death of her relatives, nursing them as they clung to her in their pain. Hopefully, you have never experienced anything exactly like it, but you will have sat by the bedside of a loved one while his teeth chattered from chills and fever, or held the hand of a sibling or friend with the flu or bronchitis. ... Anything similar is sufficient to transfer to the illness of Blanche's cousin Margaret, for example.[63]

Establishing the character's past in this way is the actor's homework, preceding rehearsals. During rehearsals, the emphasis will be on the dramatized events, and here, transference is assisted by particularization:

> the making of each event, each person, and each place down to the smallest physical object as particular as possible, exploring these things in detail to discover in which way they are relevant to the character, in which way they are perceived, in which way they further or hinder the character's needs.[64]

Transference and particularization together will allow the actor to express emotional experiences in physical behaviour that is precise and efficient in communicating the experience to the audience. Hagen explains that the actor should, in preparing for the part, determine from the given circumstances provided in the play what the condition is, and what causes the condition. What are the effects of the condition on the particular, most suggestible part of the body? Let us assume that the condition is stifling heat, caused by the climate and the lack of air conditioning. The part of the body affected is the armpits, where the actor 'feels' perspiration. The physical adjustment needed to alleviate or overcome this is, in this case, to raise his arm a little while pulling the sleeve away.

For Hagen, however, the actor's use of his own psyche by way of transference does not mean a psychoanalytical probing of the subconscious, as Strasberg's approach may suggest. Indeed, she warns against probing into 'any past experience that may have traumatized you to the point of your still being unable to deal with it'. Those are experiences from which we do not have any objective distance: we may never have spoken, or wanted to speak, about them to anyone. If we were to probe into such experiences, we would be on dangerous ground: 'You will risk becoming hysterical. And hysteria is a state to be avoided by the actor at all costs.'[65]

A question arises about the degree of truthfulness in acting to which such transference or substitution leads. If the actor follows Stanislavsky's line, he will, with all the training of body, voice and mind at his disposal, attempt to 'inwardly live the character'. To the extent that his training and his gift allow, he will become the character, and the degree to which he is able to affect the audience emotionally will be directly dependent on his ability to live the character. The Stanislavsky actor is thus guided in his attempts to internalize the character's emotions by the causal conditions set forth in the play as leading to the emotions of the character. The actor following Strasberg, or other Method representatives, it appears, initially understands the emotions that the character is believed to be feeling. Instead of trying to live the character inwardly, he substitutes the causal conditions leading to the character's emotions, as set forth in the play, by causal conditions of his own making, which are then supposed to lead to the same emotions as if the causal conditions were taken from the play. The spectator is confronted with an emotion that outwardly might fit the situation of a specific scene in the play. However, what the spectator is not aware of is that the emotions do not originate in the sequence of causal conditions in the play, but from potentially 'arbitrary', unsequenced, unrelated, individual substitutes: substitute A for emotion A, substitute B for emotion C, with C following causally from emotion A, whereas substitute B is not necessarily related to substitute A.

Two questions result: will the spectators feel the difference between genuine and substitute emotions, and does the use of substitutes make acting easier for the actor, does it require less technique, less skill, less art, than a 'through-line' of emotion?

Stanislavsky's Legacy 2: An Emphasis on the Body

We have seen that in the course of his career, Stanislavsky shifted his emphasis from the actor's psyche to the method of physical action. It is striking to note that three contemporaries in Russian theatre, Evgeny Vakhtangov (1883–1923), Aleksandr Tairov (1885–1950) and Vsevolod Meyerhold (1874–1940), developed their own ideas of theatre in general, and acting in particular, which increasingly emphasized the actor's body, thus paving the way for many late twentieth-century developments.

Vakhtangov started off as a devoted student and follower of Stanislavsky. In his own early work, he insisted on 'temperament from the essence'.[66] In due course, he shifted his emphasis to acting that was both inwardly inspired by the use of Stanislavsky's 'magic if' and outwardly precise and fixed. The actor was 'answerable for every gesture, for the slightest movement, for each intonation'.[67]

Tairov was opposed to naturalism, which he saw as the main cause for the deterioration of the theatre. He wanted to raise this art form to the level of its sister arts such as ballet, painting and music. Like Copeau (1879–1949) in France, he sought to resurrect the archetypal forms of pantomime and harlequinade as found in *commedia dell'arte*, and to derive new theatre forms from ancient Greek and Eastern myths. The Kamerny Theatre, which he founded in Moscow in 1914, aimed for a theatre of pure aesthetics, based on the 'master actor', someone 'armed with rhythmical and musical sensibility and capable of handling all the dramatic genres from tragedy to operetta and pantomime'.[68] Tairov felt that Meyerhold had insufficient regard for the actor. He held that actors must be taught how to care for the material of their art, their own natures and their own bodies. Mastery of their own instrument (inner and outer) would be achieved through mastery of inner and outer technique. Like the violinist mastering his violin, the actor must 'embody in clear-cut forms the delicate vibrations of his own creativity'.[69]

The emphasis on the body is most strongly developed in Meyerhold's ideas. We have seen that Diderot changed his views on acting from an endorsement of the actor's emotional involvement to the position documented in *The Paradox*. From an initial adherence to mechanical acting and dictatorial directing, Stanislavsky graduated to the psychotechnique, followed by the method of physical actions. He supported the experiments of Vsevolod Meyerhold, who maintained that the 'truth of human relationships and behavior was best expressed not by words, but by gestures, steps, attitudes and poses'.[70] Consequently, Meyerhold placed much emphasis on the actor's physical training and discipline: he wanted an actor so 'thoroughly trained that he could respond immediately, as if by reflex action, to the needs dictated by his part or by the director'.[71] To achieve this aim, Meyerhold developed a set of simple and complex exercises which he called *biomechanics*. Theatre researchers have had difficulty assessing this concept for two reasons: first, because 'it was a means to an end, not an end in itself'; and second, because 'it was never fully explained or codified by Meyerhold'.[72] Biomechanics incorporated many elements of acrobatics and gymnastics. Simple exercises included 'deep knee bends, with spine erect, stretching and contracting in various planes and at various tempi',[73] walking and running exercises, and various falls, backwards and forwards. The *dactyl* was a preparatory exercise carried out before more complex *études*:

> In this, the actor stands relaxed, arms down, on the balls of his feet which are place one in front to the other as in a boxer's stance, with the toes pointing slightly inwards. Leading with the hands, which describe a wide semi-circle as they move upwards through 180°, clapping twice sharply as they go, the whole body is brought to a position stretching upwards, with the heels raised off the ground and the head thrown back. Then the hands describe a downwards semi-circle, clapping twice, ending flung backwards behind the actor; the arms again lead the movement – when they are parallel with the ground, the knees begin to bend and the head is flung backward. The knee of the rear foot is no more than an inch off the ground, the back is bowed, the head beside the forward knee. By swinging the arms forward, enough momentum is created to return the actor to the initial standing position.[74]

Especially in the *études*, the sequence of movements was based on a principle of three consecutive phases: preparation for the action, the action itself and its corresponding reaction. A marked pause separates these three elements. For example, 'Throwing the Stone': 'The actor runs, halts, crouches and leans back to pick up the imaginary stone, rises and leans forward to aim, takes the stone around in a wide arc backwards, poises, throws, leaps forward to land two-footed with a cry.'[75]

In addition to exercises for individual actors, Meyerhold developed others for pairs. Again the aim was for the actor to develop perfect control of the body, together with an awareness, at every moment, of the body and what it looked like from outside. Once the actor had mastered biomechanics, 'he could go beyond the needs of psychological character depiction and "grip" his audience emotionally through physiological process'.[76] According to Meyerhold, the actors were not to identify emotionally with the characters they had to portray, as in Stanislavsky's approach to acting, 'but to consciously comment on the character by remaining clearly distinct from it'.[77] This concept foreshadows Brecht's views. Meyerhold's insistence on non-involvement also mirrors Diderot, and is in contrast to Stanislavsky. The paradox in Meyerhold's argument, however, differs from Diderot's: Meyerhold asserted that the 'correct postures and moves', which the actor achieves through mastery of biomechanics, will 'lead naturally to an emotional state in the actor and, by extension, affect the audience'.[78] The paradox lies in the assumption that physical movements are not the result of emotion but their stimuli. I used Diderot's theory of acting as one example to demonstrate the relation of approaches to acting to the general tendencies of the time, in particular in science. It helps to engage in another, similar exercise of theatre history to better understand Meyerhold's approach.

In developing his theory of acting, Meyerhold was influenced by his materialistic world view. The general *Zeitgeist* of the nineteenth century, with the industrial revolution, colonialist international politics and hunger for money, had suggested materialism. It was consciously theorized by left Hegelians and some scientists.[79] In pre- and post-revolutionary Russia, Marxism, and its particular variety of Leninism, had exerted strong influences on Meyerhold, claiming that all phenomena of reality are of a material nature, and all cognition like a copy or photocopy of that material reality.[80]

The machine was regarded as 'the representative symbol of modern life',[81] and biomechanics was devised as an acting system 'as technically precise as the miracles of technology'.[82] This influence was further supported by Meyerhold's interest in Pavlov's studies of conditioned response behaviour, the origin of behaviourism. The paradox of emotions as stimulated by and resulting from physical movement, rather than themselves initially causing physical reactions, was founded on William James's and C. G. Lange's originally independent, later co-authored studies in the psychology of the emotions. They viewed emotions as 'perceptions of physiological disturbances': for example, 'we do not cry because we feel sad, but we feel sad because we cry'.[83] The physiological reaction is central to emotion, but in a reversed order: in the above example, ' "feeling sad" is not the cause of this reaction, but instead our experience of that reaction'.[84] Critics of the James–Lange theory have pointed out that the authors 'leave largely unspecified how events and objects in our environment come to produce these physiological disturbances'.[85] The most severe criticism is that the physiological changes are so unspecific that it becomes difficult to distinguish between many different emotions and their nuances merely on the basis of unspecific physiological reactions.[86] In recent years, however, experiments with voluntary facial action have shown emotion-specific changes in the autonomous nervous system. Ekman studied the emotions of anger, disgust, fear, happiness, sadness and surprise. In the experiment, he provided subjects with muscle-by-muscle instructions and coaching to produce facial configurations for those emotions. During the experiment, some of the subjects' functions, such as heart rate, skin conductance, finger temperature and somatic activity were monitored. These are functions of the autonomic nervous system, beyond the influence of the will. Ekman found that

> voluntary facial activity produced significant levels of subjective experience of the associated emotion, and that autonomic distinctions among emotions: (a) were found both between negative and positive emotions and among negative emotions, (b) were consistent between group and individual subjects data, (c) were found in both male and female subjects, (d) were found in both specialised (actors, scientists) and nonspecialised populations, (e) were stronger when the voluntary facial

configurations most closely resembled actual emotional expressions, and (f) were stronger when experience of the associated emotion was reported.[87]

In addition, stimulation of emotional states in the actor and spectator by specific movements of the actor's body is also characteristic, at least in part, of the Indian theories of acting as stated in the *Natyashastra*. Thus, Meyerhold's view that the actor's postures and movements could arouse an emotional state in the actor, which then affects the audience, cannot be regarded as scientifically falsified and therefore should not automatically be discarded in further discussions of acting.

Developments in Anti-Realism

Vakhtangov called his theatre imaginative realism, and Tairov aimed at a purely aesthetic theatre of balletic beauty. Meyerhold's theatre, too, is everything but naturalistic. Whereas it was reasonable to discuss those three theatre artists in the context of Stanislavsky's legacy, this chapter is devoted entirely to anti- or non-realistic, developments in the theatre in general, and approaches to acting in particular.

German Expressionism

While German theatre at the beginning of the twentieth century also showed signs of the counter-movement against naturalism, it also built upon the foundations of that very movement. By 1905, naturalism as advocated by Brahm was already in decline, but it was nevertheless influential for the future development of theatre in Germany. It had been based on the assumptions that truth is more important than beauty, that theatre must be concerned with contemporary society and that individuals must be examined in relation to their environment. Naturalist theatre had rejected totally the declamatory style of acting dominant in most of earlier nineteenth-century theatre, had shown the importance of gesture and movement for underlining the text, and had abandoned the conceit of the star performer.

German theatre in the wake of naturalism was seminally influenced by actor-turned-director Max Reinhardt (1873–1943). He regarded theatre in general as a community ritual. Faithful to the dramatist's intentions, he developed no style of his own, because he explored every possible style, according to the plays he chose to direct. The actor was the focus of his attention, and rather than hand out prescriptive instructions, his intention was to 'give the actor and his work the atmosphere in which they can breathe more freely and more deeply'.[88] Overall, the acting style observed in his productions has been described as 'a little larger than life, more theatrical than the flatter tones of the realists would have allowed, but avoiding the heavy style of the German 19th century theatre'.[89] Reinhardt's form of realism has been called impressionistic or stylized realism. One aspect of his productions was the use of stage machinery. In naturalism it would have been used to 'create remarkable imitations of real events'. Reinhardt maintained that approach, but added a further dimension: for example, he created a very realistic woodland scene for *A Midsummer Night's Dream*. However, he placed the wood on a revolve, thus making it clear to audiences right from the start that they were in the theatre. As Patterson puts it, Reinhardt facilitated 'the aesthetic enjoyment of it as an autonomous artefact'.[90]

The reaction against naturalism was evident also in the set designs, supported by theoretical writing, of Adolphe Appia (1862–1928) and Edward Gordon Craig (1872–1966). They created abstract sets inspired by the plays, and worked much with atmospheric lighting. Craig, in particular, was very critical of the art of the actor as he saw it: 'That ... which the actor gives us is not a work of art; it is a series of accidental confessions.' Actors have to develop a new form of acting, Craig argued: 'today they *impersonate* and interpret; tomorrow they must *represent* and interpret; and the third day they must create.'[91] The ideal actor for Craig is not a human being, but an *Übermarionette*, which does not compete with (real) life, but goes beyond it: the ideal 'will not be the flesh and blood but rather the body in trance – it will aim to clothe itself with a death-like beauty while exhaling a living spirit'.[92]

These developments in early twentieth-century German theatre, as well as several others to be discussed later, gave rise to Expressionist playwrighting and theatre production, including acting style. The term *Expressionism* was coined in France in 1901, initially in painting, to distinguish Van Gogh (1853–90) and Gauguin (1848–1903) from the Impressionists. Whereas the Impressionists captured the appearance of objects in a certain light and a particular moment, Expressionist painters emphasized strong inner feelings about the objects of their perception; portraying life as they saw it, they did not aim to depict objective truth, but to express the external, objective world as filtered through the artist's inner, subjective world to express an inner reality (rather than an outside one perceived through the senses). The major assumption of Expressionism is that the inner reality is the psychological reality behind appearances.[93]

The rise of Expressionism across the arts is closely linked to the philosophical developments of the time. German philosopher Immanuel Kant (1724–1804) argued that beyond all of the observable world is a transcendent field, *Ding an sich*, which gives rise to all manifestations, but which is not knowable on its own. The mind imposes its own order on the observable world. As a result of this view, much of nineteenth-century philosophy had excluded the transcendent, emphasizing instead aspects of the observable world. Compte's positivism and the dialectic materialism of Marx and Engels are examples of this development, which was influential in shaping realism and naturalism at the end of the nineteenth century and Piscator and Brecht in the twentieth century. Schopenhauer (1788–1860) conceptualized the transcendent, underlying field as *will*, maintaining that when will is obscured by the intellect and civilization (together conceptualized as *idea*), unhappiness results. 'Through art, especially music, we can penetrate the false structures of the idea to arrive at a direct experience of the will.'[94] Expressionism took up the possibility of using art to break the boundaries artificially created by human reason. Instead, Expressionist artists sought access to the essence of human beings (Kant's *Ding an sich*, Schopenhauer's *will*) through non-rational means. Such a non-realistic approach, reflected both in playwrighting and acting styles, was further supported by the philosophy of Friedrich Nietzsche (1844–1900). He argued that we need to abandon an ethics, based on the Christian religion, which denies life and advocates 'humble conformity and repression of the human spirit'.[95] Instead, we should return to high values such as good, noble, mighty, beautiful, happy, beloved by the gods. To achieve this high aim, most means are justified. Expressionists took this argument to justify the often immoral and destructive behaviour of the plays' protagonists.

Expressionism, then, exists in a multifaceted context of naturalism, Impressionism, the philosophy of Kant, Schopenhauer and Nietzsche, and positivist materialism. Naturalism emphasizes positivism, the phenomenal, the scientific, determinism, the objective, the representational and the reproduction of superficial detail, and assumes that the environment conditions the individual. Expressionism, on the other hand, sets idealism, the noumenal, the supra-rational, the assertion of moral freedom, the subjective and the visionary against those concepts, and maintains that the environment is an extension of the individual.[96] In this context:

> The Expressionist does not see, he beholds. He does not describe, he experiences. He does not reproduce, he creates. He does not accept, he seeks. There is no longer the chain of facts: factories, houses, disease, whores, screams, hunger. Now there is the *vision* of these things. Facts have importance only because the artist reaches through them to what is beyond. He recognizes what is divine in factories, what is human in whores. He incorporates the accident of individuality into the totality that constitutes the world.[97]

What do Expressionists see? They see a world that has lost much of its traditional meaning. According to Nietzsche, language has lost its power of consoling; there was not much to be hoped for in the world that had just seen the First World War, and the crushed illusions of a new beginning that followed it. According to an early twentieth-century cultural critic, Wilhelm Worringer, when a civilization feels at ease with the world it is living in, it will produce realistic art. However, if a civilization feels ill at ease with the times – as was clearly the case during the period when Expressionism flourished – it produces art that follows an impulse to abstraction.

In terms of the plays, abstractionism means a decidedly episodic structure, in contrast to the causally stringent development of events characteristic of realistic plays. The form of *Stationendrama*, as it came to be called, was inspired by the structure of Büchner's *Woyzeck* and especially Strindberg's *To Damascus*, which traces the spiritual progress of an anonymous stranger through a series of stations where he encounters unnamed characters. Characterization employs little reference to the characters' past, and the dialogue is employed to express the dramatist's argument rather than add to the information about the psychology of the character. The language of Expressionist plays consisted of short sentences, or 'telegraphese'. The set designs also reflected Expressionist tendencies: they 'did not suggest reality but were clearly constructs of the protagonists' mind'.[98]

Some Expressionist writers even sought to go beyond abstraction to express their innermost feelings, plunging instead into 'a totally primitive response to the world'.[99] Episodic *Stationendrama* of abstractionist expressionism gave way to 'the apparent formlessness of kaleidoscopic images'.[100] Language no longer expresses character (naturalism), or the dramatist's ideas (abstractionist expressionism), but raw emotion.[101] Voice turns to scream (Schrei).

Abstraction is relatively more easy to achieve through the text of a play, and in production through set, costume, sound and lighting design. It is much more difficult to achieve in the actor, who always remains concrete and alive. Expressionist plays require a style of acting different from the declamatory style that emphasizes the words of the text, or the realistic style in which the actor was encouraged to search within himself for the emotions that would inform the text.[102] Patterson has defined three related principles of acting relevant for secondary characters in expressionist plays: economy, emphasis on focus and exaggeration. Whereas naturalist actors would attempt to make their characters lifelike by employing apparently superfluous gestures and facial expressions, the Expressionist actor selectively focuses on the character's function in the scene. 'This single-minded concentration makes for the intense stare and absorbed stillness ... characteristic of ... Expressionist acting.'[103] Economy and focus lead to each 'movement and gesture' becoming 'larger than life'.[104] The actor playing the protagonist must stand out among the other actors, and the style has to be different. Again, there are three distinct techniques that characterize the Expressionist style adopted by the actor playing the protagonist: a closer relationship with the audience, an intense expressiveness of the body and the method adopted to deliver his lines. The Expressionistic actor no longer presented a 'pretty or realistic spectacle'[105] to the spectators, but opened himself up, thus providing points of direct communication with the audience. In declamatory acting, the actor's concern regarding his body had been: 'Do I look pleasing to the audience?' In naturalistic acting he would ask: 'Are my postures and gestures psychologically appropriate to the character I am portraying?' The Expressionistic style would lead to a different question: 'Is every part of my body reflecting and projecting my inner emotional state?'[106] Each emotion was depicted in extremes: to represent anger, the actor would create utmost tension in his body, bare his teeth and make his eyes bulge. The outward signs of anger had to be triggered by the inner feeling to avoid empty overacting. The abstract language of the protagonist was presented in telegraphese, characterized by short, clipped sentences and lyrical outbursts, indicated in the written text by numerous exclamation marks.

Bauhaus

Whereas perhaps the majority of theatre artists discussed so far in this book have approached the art of acting from the perspective of the dramatic text and its best transformation on the stage, some based their approach on their interpretation of space. Oskar Schlemmer (1888– 1943), a leading representative of the Bauhaus in Germany, is a striking example. The Bauhaus was an art school, founded in 1919 in Weimar by Walter Gropius (1883–1969), specializing in architecture, painting, sculpture, industrial design and theatre. Space was the starting point for Schlemmer's theatre practice. He took a close look at 'the human figure moving in space'.[107] The human figure is governed by a set of laws which is different from that governing the space in which that figure is placed. The interaction between the two can take different shapes, with different end results. If the human figure dominates, abstract space is adapted to suit the needs and givens of the human figure. In other words, abstract space is 'transformed back into nature or the imitation of nature. This happens in the theater of illusionistic realism.'[108] Alternatively, if space dominates, the human body has to undergo a metamorphosis or transformation to adapt to the laws governing space. This potential of theatre is at the focus of Schlemmer's work and theory. Note that space is conceived by Schlemmer as abstract: thus, the transformation of the human figure to adapt to abstract space involves a process of abstraction. For Schlemmer, abstraction is 'one of the emblems of our time'.[109] In the context of theatre, it means developing a new perspective for, and on, the actor, which takes the actor out of his traditional context (defined as illusionistic, realistic), and places him within a new context of abstract space. Abstraction is of such great importance because of its capacity to elevate acting to its highest potential, or even to result in a new overall conceptualization and view of theatre altogether.

The primary method of abstracting the acting process for Schlemmer is by use of visual means: namely, costume and related movement, both based on mathematical–geometrical concepts and calculations. From the basic situation of an actor in space, with a wall behind him and the audience in front, two 'fundamentally different creative paths are possible. Either that of psychic expression, heightened emotion, and pantomime; or that of mathematics in motion, the mechanics of joints and swivels, and the exactitudes of rhythmics and gymnastics.'[110] The actor merges with the dancer. One, two or three actor/dancers on such an abstract stage, dressed in 'stylized padded tights and papier-mâché masks'[111] in the primary colours of red, yellow and blue, can interact to produce space dance, form dance or gesture dance. In space dance, each actor/dancer has a specific way of walking (slow, normal or tripping), and they measure out the space to the rhythms provided by kettledrum, snare drum and wooden blocks. In form dance, each actor/dancer gets an object, such as a ball, a club, a wand or a pole, and their gestures and movements 'instinctively follow what these shapes convey to them'.[112] If the masks acquire more distinguishing features, such as moustaches or glasses, and if, in addition, more detail is added to costume (not naturalistic, but still stylized), together with some preverbal sounds, a new genre of dance is reached: *gesture dance*. Below is a vivid description of Schlemmer's theatre on the stage by T. Lux Feininger:

> I had beheld the 'Dance of Gestures' and the 'Dance of Forms', executed by dancers in metallic masks and costumed in padded, sculptured suits. The stage, with jet-black backdrop and wings, contained magically spotlighted, geometrical furniture: a cube, a white sphere, steps; the actors paced, strode, slunk, trotted, dashed, stopped short, turned slowly and majestically; arms with colored gloves were extended in a beckoning gesture; the copper and gold and silver heads ... were laid together, flew apart; the silence was broken by a whirring sound, ending in a small thump; a crescendo of buzzing noises culminated in a crash followed by portentous and dismayed silence. Another phase of the dance had all the formal and contained violence of a chorus of cats, down to the meeowling and bass growls, which were marvellously accentuated by the resonant mask-heads. Pace and gesture, figure and prop, color and sound, all had the quality of elementary form, demonstrating anew the problem of the theatre of Schlemmer's concept: man in space.[113]

Lux Feininger continues his observations with the insight that Schlemmer presented on stage a set of fundamental elements of any stage, which were 'assembled, re-grouped, amplified', and which gradually developed into a unity, a kind of 'play', but not in the traditional sense of comedy or tragedy, but in a new dimension of space.

For Schlemmer, the ideal performer in such abstract space was not human, because all human actors are limited by their bodies, but the artificial human figure, either an automaton or the marionette. I have already mentioned that Edward Gordon Craig would have preferred an *Übermarionette* instead of a human actor. Long before him, in a series of newspaper articles entitled *Über das Marionettentheater* (1810), Heinrich von Kleist (1777–1811) argued that the marionette has advantages compared with even the best of human dancers: first, it can achieve an unsurpassed level of grace, because it always moves from the centre of movement. In contrast, in human movement the focus of attention is hardly ever at the centre of movement, but elsewhere in the body. Kleist locates the reason for this human inability to reach unity of centre of movement and focus of attention in the interference of self-awareness, self-reflection. Only if cognition has passed through the infinite does grace return. This is possible in the human body which has no consciousness at all (the marionette) or infinite consciousness (God). The second advantage of the marionette is that it is not subject to the laws of gravity which impede perfect movement of the human performer.

Futurism, Dada and Surrealism

While Germany developed Expressionism as both a way of writing and a style of acting (beginning in 1907 and ending in the mid-1920s), in 1916 a group of refugees from Germany, Romania and France launched the Dada movement in Zurich, Switzerland. The leading figures of the movement were Tristan Tzara (1896–1963), Hugo Ball (1886–1927), Emmy Hennings (1885–1948), Richard Huelsenbeck (1892–1974), Hans Arp (1887–1966) and Marcel Janco (1895–1984). The movement had developed under the direct impact of the war: 'Since insanity seemed the world's condition, the dadaists sought to replace logic and reason with calculated madness.'[114] Performative programmes adopted the format of a cabaret show, initially held at the Cabaret Voltaire, which seated between thirty-five and fifty members of the audience at tables. Dadaist artists wanted to develop a new style of theatre, and, most important, a change in the attitudes of their spectators: 'the passive consenting spectator must give way to a hostile participant, provoked, attacked and beaten by author and actors.'[115] To achieve this effect of shock, the Dadaists used several devices: masks, the concept of simultaneity and experiments with the sound aspect of language (as opposed to meaning), ranging from phonetic poems to noise music. A few examples may serve to illustrate the range of Dada performance. On 23 June 1916, Hugo Ball presented his sound poems. He started with some introductory words, and went on to describe the performance itself:

> With these sound poems we should renounce the language devastated and made impossible by journalism. ... We should stop making poems second-hand; we should no longer take over words (not even to speak of sentences) which we did not invent absolutely anew, for our own use. ...
>
> I had made myself a special costume. ... My legs were in a cylinder of shiny blue cardboard, which came up to my hips so that I looked like an obelisk. Over it I wore a huge coat collar cut out of cardboard, scarlet inside and gold outside. It was fastened at the neck in such a way that I could give the impression of winglike movement by raising and lowering my elbows. I also wore a high, blue-and-white-striped witchdoctor's hat.
>
> On all three sides of the stage I had set up music stands facing the audience, and I put my red-pencilled manuscript on them; I officiated at one stand after another. Tzara knew about my preparation, so there was a real little premiere. Everyone was curious. I could not walk inside the cylinder so I was carried onto the stage in the dark and began slowly and solemnly:
>
> > gadji beri bimba
> > glandridi lauli lonni cadori
> > gadjama bim beri glassala
> > glandridi glassala tuffm i zimbrabim
> > blassa galassasa tuffm izimbrahim[116]

Many of these approaches had been inspired by Futurism, a movement which developed in Italy, led by Filippo Tommaso Marinetti (1876–1944). But whereas the Dadaists were all refugees from the war, and thus from direct experience against the war, the Futurists were decidedly in favour of war and strongly political in a nationalist sense, with many turning fascist in the 1930s. Futurism followed a programme, set down in various manifestos, to achieve a break with 'confining isms of the past', and to reach 'a more liberated future'.[117] Dada, in contrast, while similarly against the legacies of the past, had no programme and was opposed to programmes in general. It was also, in Tzara's words, 'resolutely against the future'.[118]

If there were many things which Dada was against, such as the future, 'anything that smacks of traditionalism in literature and the arts',[119] then there was one aspect which Dada favoured: spontaneity. And it is because acting can be the most spontaneous, short-lived art form, leaving no accounts, no published traces, that Dada favoured theatre as its medium. Such spontaneous acting for Dada was devoid of any aspect of craft or technique. There were no rehearsals, and, as Tzara put it, 'all our sketches were of an improvised nature, full of fantasy, freshness and the unexpected. There were few costumes, little direction, and few sets'.[120] The actors did not play characters on stage, they remained themselves: 'The time is now, the performer is himself.'[121]

A problem with this approach, and those inspired by it, such as happenings, environmental theatre, psychophysical theatre, performance art and theatre of images, may be that the performer gets more out of the performance than the spectator.

After Dada came to an end in Zurich at the end of the First World War, Tzara brought his increasingly influential movement to France, and for a short while his thoughts met with those of Surrealism, whose principal representative was André Breton (1896–1966). Both Dada and Surrealism were not satisfied with the world as it presented itself to them, but they parted company in their individual response to that dissatisfaction. Dada's response was total opposition and no desire to present an alternative. When some of the conditions they had opposed disappeared with the end of the First World War, and when, in addition, the audience had become accustomed to Dada provocation, the movement lost its function. Surrealism, in contrast, took its opposition to the status quo as inspiration to set itself clear tasks. Surrealists wanted to restore imagination to its central role in human life, a position it had lost because of the dominance of the modes of realism and materialism. Language had been considered to be in a crisis since the end of the nineteenth century, and the Surrealists wanted to redeem it. They strove to investigate the potential of the unconscious, and sought a mystical point at which contradiction resolves itself into synthesis.

According to Breton, Surrealism is a pure psychic automatism which is intended to express, verbally, in writing or by other means, the real process of thought. For this automatic process, the subconscious mind in a dream-like state counts as the basis for artistic truth. An artist creating in Surrealistic mode does not mimic nature, and does not allow himself to be restricted by logic or rationality. The true purpose of such creation is to expand our definition of reality until it includes the marvellous. In their work, Surrealist artists ascribed uncommon properties to common objects, even juxtaposed apparently unrelated objects, words or ideas. They wilfully dislocated object and context. Through these methods, the analogical mode of the mind is broken, and imagination is freed. The Surrealist artist is not inspired, but serves as an inspirer of the readers/ spectators. Surrealism owes much to Romantic and Symbolist writers, such as Nerval, Baudelaire, Mallarmé, Rimbaud and Apollinaire. Thus, for example, Surrealism is characterized by a romantic interest in dreams, hypnosis, somnambulism, madness and hallucinations, by a belief in the integrity and significance of emotional response, and by concern with the possibility of some final analysis behind the appearance of heterogeneity. There are striking differences between Romantic and Surrealist thought, though. While Romanticism, for example, held that imagination opens up a path to great abstractions such as God, beauty and truth, Surrealism argued that imagination frees human beings from such abstractions and its related restrictive logic. Romantic artists turned to visible nature for evidence of spiritual forces and analogues of their own state of mind, while Surrealists deliberately closed their eyes to a reality so empty of imaginative insight.

In the theatre, Surrealism had less impact than Dada for several reasons: for one, Breton was not much in favour of this art form. Although much poetry was allegedly written in the automatic mode demanded for Surrealist work, authors later admitted that they had not been able to avoid some element of conscious control in their work. Thus, the plays associated with Surrealism, predominantly those by Jean Cocteau (1892–1963), but also Roger Vitrac (1899–1952), were created following traditional ways of writing, although they did include Surrealist elements, such as a talking horse, or death depicted as a beautiful woman, in Cocteau's *Orpheus*. In fact, the criterion of automatic, unmediated creation had been fulfilled more prominently by Dada.

Brecht

The exaggerated style of heightened expressionistic acting appropriate for portraying protagonists is still firmly rooted in abstractionism, but shows tendencies towards primitivism. Such primitivism was expressly rejected by a growing awareness of the political impact of theatre. While Expressionism had emphasized idealism, liberal humanism, the super-rational, the poetic, subjective and individualistic, placing the regeneration soundly within the individual, and had worked with imagistic settings, the new political theatre in turn focused on materialism, was informed by Marxism, emphasized the scientific, prosaic, objective and collective, saw regeneration happening within society and preferred functional settings.[122] Spearheaded by Erwin Piscator (1893–1966), political theatre in Germany of the 1920s, as with any previous development in theatre, needed an acting style appropriate to its specific concerns. Compared with Expressionism, which was dominated by the actor's 'self-release', in political theatre the actor had to be cooler, 'hard, clear, unsentimental', which Piscator called *neo-realistic*. The term implies the difference of this style from that of late nineteenth-century realism and naturalism. As Piscator put it, 'we demand a performance that is thought through so scientifically that it reproduces naturalness on a higher level'. The actor's intellectual awareness had 'to correspond to the objective content of the role', and rather than being an 'embodiment of individual characteristics', the actor should be 'the carrier of universal historical ideas'.[123]

Brecht's theory of acting has frequently been referred to as constituting the direct opposite of Stanislavsky's approach. Indeed, early in his theatre career Brecht wrote: 'I don't let my feelings intrude in my dramatic work. It'd give a false view of the world. I aim at an extremely classical, cold, highly intellectual style of performance.'[124] Neither the actor nor the spectator should identify with the character's emotions.

To achieve such a distance of both actor and spectator from the character, Brecht developed the concept and practice of the *alienation effect*. According to Knopf, Brecht first used the German term *Entfremdung* in 1930; from 1936 to 1940 he used both *Verfremdung* and *Entfremdung*, and eventually settled for *Verfremdung*.[125] The German term *Verfremdungseffekt* is commonly translated as 'alienation effect'. Alienation properly translates as *Entfremdung*, synonymous, in English, with estrangement. The German *fremd* means unfamiliar, strange. *Verfremdung* thus implies defamiliarization, and in that sense distancing, but not estrangement. Applied to acting, the alienation effect means that the actor 'does not allow himself to become completely transformed on the stage into the character'.[126] Instead, the actor *shows* the character, he 'reproduces their remarks as authentically as he can; he puts forward their way of behaving to the best of his abilities and knowledge of men'.[127] Consequently, the character's emotions have to be externalized, 'developed into a gesture. The actor has to find a sensible perceptible outward expression for his character's emotions, preferably some action that gives away what is going on inside him.'[128]

'Showing' thus becomes multi-perspectival, avoiding dogmatism. Because the actor is not emotionally involved with the character, because the actor does not identify with him, he can include a running commentary on his authentic showing of the character. The actor can 'pick a definite attitude to adopt towards the character whom he portrays, [and] can show what he thinks of him'.[129] Thus the spectator, not asked to identify himself with the actor/character either, can intellectually observe and criticize the character portrayed. The spectator thus reaches the ideal of a 'smoking-observing' status of an 'expert'.[130]

While emphasizing the actor's and spectator's distance from the character, Brecht wanted to avoid mechanical, stylized or abstract acting: 'he aimed for truth to life, naturalness, and close observation of actual behaviour.'[131] Actual behaviour and natural life are characterized to a large extent by emotions. Therefore, Brecht could not do without emotions on the stage; indeed, his epic theatre did employ emotional effects. Their function, however, is not to stimulate the spectator's identification with the particular emotion, but to serve as a 'technique of positive reinforcement for the intellectual message'.[132]

The clue to understanding the difference in the way Brecht treated emotions in the theatre lies in his views on empathy. In psychology, empathy is defined as an individual's ability to 'partially and temporarily suspend the functions that maintain one's separateness from others (usually called ego-boundaries)',[133] leading to an immediate, precognitive experience of the emotional state of another individual as one's own. According to Brecht, the aesthetic assumption that emotion can only be stimulated through empathy is crude and inaccurate. Brecht rejected empathy, because it is identification, which he wished to avoid. He maintained, however, that the 'rejection of empathy is not the result of the rejection of emotions, nor does it lead to such'.[134] What Brecht aimed at, then, is that the actor presents emotions without having to take recourse to empathy while performing on the stage. This means doing more than just getting into the character. Yet the distanced attitude of the actor does not mean that 'if he is playing passionate parts he must himself remain cold'.[135] The actor is allowed feelings, but with an important qualification: 'It is only that his feelings must not, at bottom, be those of the character.'[136] In other words, the actor must not allow empathy – the unity of his and the character's feelings – to arise while showing those feelings, nor may the actor's 'exhibiting of outer signs of emotions' lead him to become infected himself by those emotions.

As a result of such a way of acting, the spectator's empathy should not be stimulated either, allowing the intellect room to critically judge the character, including the character's distanced and empathy-free emotions. In different terms, Brecht's stance resembles Diderot's aims for an actor who is not 'carried away' – subjected to empathy, in Brecht's terms. It also mirrors Stanislavsky's ideal of the actor: he inwardly lives the character, and yet there is the paradoxical second aspect of the actor's consciousness that serves as an uninvolved witness to all emotional involvement, thus ensuring that the actor is not carried away by his emotions.

There are two or three sources for Brecht's concept of the alienation effect: one originates in his interest in Chinese theatre. The Western sources are Russian Formalism and Hegel and Marx. In 1917 Victor Sklovskij defined the term 'alienation' in the field of the arts. In a broader sense, alienation motivates the artistic process and stands behind all acts of theoretical and practical curiosity, not merely as a procedure, but as a noetic principle. As a result, the individual is enabled to recognize voluntary and forced modes of perception and experience, norms and modes of behaviour as 'a pair of glasses' that has placed itself in between unmediated 'seeing' and 'real reality'. Once those glasses have been recognized as such, one can take them off and turn them into an object (no longer only a medium) of perception and reflection.[137] The object of perception is perceived in a non-expected, different context and environment.

Whereas there are those who insist that the Formalists were not much interested in developing an explicit theory of drama or dramaturgy, Hansen-Löve argues that they considered techniques of dramatic alienation as constitutive for modern theatre to such a large extent that they preferred to concentrate on less manifest techniques of literary alienation, taking theatrical alienation as already tolerated and canonized. Hansen-Löve refers to the alienation effects in Meyerhold's stage practice: the mechanization of movements in biomechanics, and the actor distancing himself from his role.[138] The view that Russian Formalism influenced Brecht is refuted by Knopf because Brecht used the concept first in 1930, five years before his visit to Moscow – although the term he used then was *Entfremdung*, not *Verfremdung*.[139] Hilton regards Marx–Hegelian views of history as the source of Brecht's concept:

> Underlying the dynamic of history is the fact that man is alienated, either from God (Hegel) or from the fruits of his labours and from power (Marx). Alienation in the theatre is an aesthetic correlative to economic alienation, a means of showing the historical process at work behind any human action.[140]

Knopf denies that Marx's use of the word *Entfremdung* matches Brecht's concept, but points to some parallels between Hegel's theory of cognition and Brecht's concept of alienation. Hegel argued that the known is not cognized only because it is known: only such things that are not accepted by feeling or faith in an unmediated fashion can be understood. Similarly, Brecht saw the function of the alienation effect to make events and actors on the stage unfamiliar to the spectator so that the spectator might notice them.[141]

The alienation effect is the major technique of Brecht's *epic theatre*, which he regarded as 'the only dramatic means adequate for the elucidation of the complex workings of capitalist society'.[142] Alienation increases the spectator's distance from the events on the stage. As Chaim explains, an increase of distance leads to an increase of the spectator's awareness of the fictionality of the work. This produces a 'dislocation of associations'.[143] The spectator is led to view the events on the stage in a larger perspective, from the outside. The spectator applies critical judgement. Increased distance thus encourages the development of a historical perspective towards one's own time, demonstrating to the audience that events must be viewed within a particular 'historical field'.[144]

Here Brecht clearly shows the influence of Marx. Theatre serves a function in capitalist society: it can help to make the workers aware of 'historical fields', and ultimately aware of their own misery in capitalism, an awareness that will lead to the formation of a class-conscious proletariat, as an antithesis to the dominating, ruling class of capitalists.

The assessment of Brecht's theory of acting has shown that he, too, places emphasis on the actor's dual consciousness of emotionally involved and non-involved, witnessing aspects of consciousness. Brecht, however, shifts the emphasis from emotion to empathy.

Artaud

In their various and differing attempts to improve traditional theatre practice, Diderot, Stanislavsky, Meyerhold, Brecht and Strasberg placed major emphasis on the actor: his techniques and methods of using emotions on the stage to affect the audience. Their innovations, however, remained largely within the frame of tradition: the theatrical production of a pre-written dramatic text. Artaud insisted on the necessity of a revolution of traditional theatre. In his scathing cultural critique, Artaud regarded the theatre of his day as only one aspect of art that is generally inert and disinterested.[145] In contrast, 'true culture acts through power and exaltation while the European ideal of art aims to cast us into a frame of mind distinct from the power present in its exaltation'.[146]

In response to the need for a magic culture, Artaud wished to create a form of theatre that could do justice to the demands of a genuine culture: theatre should be 'magical and violently egoistical, that is, self-interested'.[147] He developed the Theatre of Cruelty, a frequently misinterpreted concept.[148] Artaud took great pains to point out that cruelty was not synonymous with bloodshed. He understood the term from a 'mental viewpoint', implying 'strictness, diligence, unrelenting decisiveness, irreversible and absolute determination'.[149] Artaud regarded any variety of physical violence as merely one minor aspect of cruelty, and emphasized that it is 'very lucid, a kind of strict control and submission to necessity'.[150] Cruelty was for Artaud a 'hungering after life, cosmic strictness, relentless necessity, in the gnostic sense of a living vortex engulfing darkness, in the sense of the inescapably necessary pain without which life could not continue'.[151] According to Artaud, this cruelty needed specific modes of theatre that differed from traditional performance practices. In particular, theatre had to look for different languages than the traditional one of dialogue. Artaud conceptualized language that is physical, 'aimed at the senses and independent of speech'.[152] This physical language, also referred to as 'poetry for the senses',[153] affects primarily the senses, although Artaud pointed out that it might, at a later stage, amplify its full mental effect 'on all possible levels and along all lines'.[154]

The effectiveness of physical language on the stage depends primarily on the actor, on the effectiveness of his acting. In his emphasis on a physical language of the theatre, Artaud compares the actor to a physical athlete, but with one major difference: in the case of the actor, it is not the actual physiological muscles that are trained, but affective musculature 'matching the bodily localisation of our feelings'.[155] For

Stanislavsky, the solar plexus was the physiological seat of the emotions; Artaud regards the rhythm of breathing as the crucial aspect of the actor's physiological counterpart of affective musculature, maintaining that 'we can be sure that every mental movement, every feeling, every leap in human affectivity has an appropriate breath'.[156]

Artaud develops his argument further in demanding that together with breathing, the actor has to have a directly related belief in the soul's flowing substantiality: 'To know that an emotion is substantial, subject to the plastic vicissitudes of matter, gives him [the actor] control over his passions, extending our sovereign command.'[157]

The actor, then, must develop his affective musculature just as an athlete must train his physiological muscles. Such development will enable the actor to do justice to the importance placed on his acting in the performance. However, the actor must also be 'a kind of neutral, pliant factor since he is vigorously denied any individual initiative'.[158] This reflects a paradox in Artaud's theory, still unsolved, despite his vagueness which, according to Innes, is sufficient to 'allow for almost any radical or anti-traditional interpretation'.[159] The paradox of the actor's simultaneous physical presence and neutrality repeats in different terminology, and on the physical level rather than the emotional, Stanislavsky's paradox within the actor: the actor's art of being both deeply emotionally involved (Artaud's physical presence) and yet still in conscious control of the acting through his ability to witness his own acting (Artaud's demand for the actor's neutrality).

According to Artaud, a sufficiently trained actor will affect the anatomy of the spectator, 'first by crude means, these gradually becoming more refined'.[160] Artaud likens this process to the charming of a snake through the vibrations of music through its body. Through violent physical images the audience's sensibility is to be pulverized, mesmerized, 'caught in the drama as if in the vortex of higher forces'.[161] As Martin puts it, the audience is exposed, through Artaud's theatre, 'to its own secret crimes and obsessions'.[162] This helps the actor to rediscover the metaphysical, mystical meaning of life. According to Auslander, 'Artaud adopts the posture of a psychoanalyst in suggesting that if we can recognise and confront our dark impulses we can be free, or at least in control of them'.[163] Innes argues that confronting the spectator with violent physical images 'would release repressed tendencies in an emotional purgation analogous to the classical/tragic effect of catharsis'.[164] In this process, Auslander points out, the actor experiences catharsis before the audience.[165]

Stanislavsky revealed the influence of non-Western, Indian sources in his thought. Brecht was influenced by Chinese acting in formulating his concept of the alienation effect. Artaud owes much of his views on theatre to Balinese performance. In arriving at his concept of Theatre of Cruelty, he was strongly influenced by seeing a performance of a

Balinese dance/theatre company. Artaud apparently attended the performance at the French Colonial Exhibition on 1 August 1931, because he wrote a very enthusiastic letter about this experience to the director Louis Jouvet the next day.[166] Inspired by his experience, Artaud wrote a short article, 'On the Balinese theatre', which was published in *Nouvelle Revue Française* No. 127, on 1 October 1931.

Artaud regards Balinese theatre as different from its European counterpart in its emphasis not on psychology but on 'dance, singing, mime and music'.[167] He describes these forms of theatrical expression further by referring to 'angular, sudden, jerky postures ..., syncopated inflections formed at the back of the throat, ... musical phrases cut short, ... sharded flights, rustling branches, hollow drum sounds, robot creaking, animated puppets dancing'.[168] Hayman notes that most of these images are non-human.[169] Artaud's profound experience of Balinese dance, singing, mime and music led not only to the vivid description just quoted. It set the foundation for the theory that theatre need not exist on the basis of words, of dialogue alone. Rather, the Balinese experience opened his eyes to the potential of a 'new bodily language'[170] based on signs. These signs function on an intuitive level. Because they are so strong and powerful, the spectator who is affected by them does not have to react on the logical, discursive level of language – his or her intuitive reaction is sufficient; indeed, it is this reaction alone that is aimed at in Balinese theatre. Artaud felt that it was possible, through this kind of bodily language practised by the Balinese performers, to 're-establish theatre as pure and independent creativity' on the level of the spectator's consciousness. At the same time, he maintained, Balinese performance is based on realism. The performers skilfully make use of a wide range of theatrical conventions, such as eye-rolling, pouting lips, twitching muscles and horizontal head movements. All these means of histrionic representation produce 'studiously calculated effects which prevent any resorting to spontaneous improvisation'.[171]

Artaud also highlighted the difference between verbal European theatre and total Balinese theatre, a theatre which combines 'everything that exists spatially on the boards or is measured and circumscribed in space, having spatial density (moves, forms, colours, vibrations, postures, shouts)',[172] pointing to the spiritual dimension that is also lacking in European theatre, which Artaud associated with the indeterminable, the dependence on the suggestive power of the mind.

Artaud sets one-sided, dialogue-dominated European theatre against Balinese theatre, in which all theatrical elements are connected in a perfectly ordered fashion. Whereas European theatre mainly serves entertainment purposes, defined by Artaud as 'useless artificiality, an evening's amusement',[173] Balinese theatre takes on the dimension of a religious ritual ceremony. In the Balinese production seen by Artaud, the aim was not to imitate reality. Rather, it aimed at specific experiences in the spectator's consciousness. Artaud seemed unable to pinpoint these experiences clearly, and there is an apparent contradiction in his writings on the matter. In the article for *Nouvelle Revue Française* he had argued that the signs shown on the stage function on an intuitive level. In later comments on Balinese theatre, however, he holds that 'the things this theatre makes tangible are much less emotional than intellectual, enclosing them as it does within concrete, though almost constantly esoteric, signs. Thus we are led along intellectual paths towards reconquering the signs of existence.'[174] Artaud's thoughts about the mechanisms of the effects of Balinese theatre on its spectators do not stop at the contradictory preferences for intellect or intuition or emotion. At times, another level is indicated, when he talks about a trance-like state being induced in the spectator, and he argues that the spectator's thoughts (intellect) and feelings (emotion and intuition) are dissolved and thus returned to their pure state. Artaud here evokes, in poetic language, a state of consciousness beyond intellect, emotions, feelings, intuition, and maintains that this state can be experienced through exposure to Balinese theatre.

A highly controversial point in Artaud's understanding of Balinese theatre is the role of the director. The basis of the controversy lies in the following passage:

> This theatre does away with the playwright to the advantage of what in Western theatre jargon we call the producer. But the latter becomes a kind of organiser of magic, a master of holy ceremonies. And the material on which he works, the subjects he makes thrilling are not his own but descend from the gods. They seem to stem from primal unions in Nature promoted by a double Spirit.
>
> What he sets in motion is MANIFEST
>
> A Kind of ancient Natural Philosophy, from which the mind has never been separated.[175]

This statement was criticized for allegedly misrepresenting facts about Balinese theatre, and thus exposed Artaud's misunderstanding. Indeed, traditional performances in Indonesia as a whole do not have a written text, 'nor are the songs to be played during a show preplanned by the troupe. The genre's set dramatic structure in conjunction with the scenario and rules of type allow performers to generate the text and song sequence in performance.'[176] Improvisation is thus an integral part of Balinese theatre, and the role of the director, central to Artaud's argument, appears minimal. Such a misrepresentation of the elements of another culture led to accusations of cultural imperialism: taking up misunderstood aspects of a foreign culture to form an image of, and an opinion about, that culture, and to misguidedly try to enrich one's own culture with those elements taken from their proper original context.

When Artaud talks about the re-establishment of theatre as pure and independent creativity, he adds that the products of this kind of theatre are hallucination and terror.[177] In a classification of states of consciousness, these would certainly range among maladaptive states, conditions that one would not normally wish to experience. An emphasis on the need for humans to confront and control the darker side of their psyche is generally characteristic of Artaud's theories. In his view, the Balinese theatre allows us to reach such levels of the mind which are located beyond verbal speech.

In 1967, Jerzy Grotowski (1933-1999) wrote that it is impossible to carry out Artaud's proposals for a revolutionary theatre, not because they are wrong, but because of their vague conceptualization in visions and metaphors and the lack of a concrete technique or method. Regarding the influence of Balinese theatre on Artaud, Grotowski points to a major misreading: 'Artaud deciphered as "cosmic signs" and "gestures evoking superior powers" elements of the performance which were concrete expressions, specific theatrical letters in an alphabet of signs universally understood by the Balinese.'[178] On the surface, this criticism is accurate. Whether Artaud knew about the codification of the signs used in Balinese drama or not, he at least does not indicate that he did. However, does the existence of a theatrical alphabet which the Balinese understand intellectually rule out the possibility that the practical use of this alphabet in performance has direct or indirect effects on the spectator's consciousness independent of whether he or she intellectually knows what a particular letter is supposed to *mean*? Artaud attended one Balinese performance without much prior knowledge or any experience of this art form. His direct experience, unmediated by prior knowledge, influenced his thinking, and it is those unmediated experiences that he tried to conceptualize. Lacking any background in specifically Balinese performance aesthetics, he used whatever knowledge he had at his disposal, including Freudian psychoanalysis and the mystic theories of cabbala and gnosticism, and thus arrived at the phrases criticized by Grotowski: for example, 'cosmic signs' or 'gestures evoking superior powers'.

The argument here is that the intellectual level of meaning created in Balinese theatre through signs universally understood by the indigenous spectators can co-exist with a different level on which the signs (which produce meaning on the first level) produce effects that go beyond meaning, intellect.

There is a clear divergence between Artaud's conceptualization of the effects of Balinese theatre on the spectator, perhaps based on his own experience of one performance, and the aesthetics of Balinese theatre itself. Whereas Artaud emphasizes Western concepts dominated by psychoanalysis, the need to confront and control one's dark forces, Balinese theatre aesthetics centre on striving for the spectator's experience of *rasa*. The beneficial end results of the process may be similar, but the paths leading to them are different. These differences lead to an important issue: can aesthetic, psychological and other phenomena of a specific culture (A) be understood, interpreted and used in the terms dominating the critical discourse in different specific culture (B)? If yes, what does it take to translate concepts from one culture to another? Where are the limits, conceptual and ethical?

It is indeed possible to demonstrate, with reference to Artaud's theories, that concepts of one culture may assist in further understanding ideas based in a different culture. Reference to Indian linguistics may prove helpful when examining Artaud's intuition regarding a 'language beyond speech' which the actor should develop. According to Coward, linguistics and the philosophy of language, relatively recent developments in the West:

> were begun by the Hindus before the advent of recorded history. Beginning with the Vedic hymns, which are at least 3,000 years old, the Indian study of language has continued in an unbroken tradition right up to the present day.[179]

The main focus of Indian linguistics is on the relationship of language and consciousness – 'not even restricted to human consciousness'.[180] From among many classical Indian linguists, the grammarian Bhartrihari is of special importance. He distinguishes four levels of language: *vaikhari, madhyama pashyanti* and *para. Vaikhari* 'is the most external and differentiated level', on which speech is uttered by the speaker and heard by the hearer.[181] Its temporal sequence is fully developed. *Madhyama* represents, in broad terms, the thinking level of the mind:

> It is the idea or series of words as conceived by the mind after hearing or before speaking out. It may be thought of as inward speech. All parts of speech that are linguistically relevant to the sentence are present here in a latent form.[182]

The finest relative level is that of *pashyanti*. At this level 'there is no distinction between the word and the meaning and there is no temporal sequence'.[183] Beyond the very subtly manifest level of *pashyanti*, Bhartrihari locates the fully unmanifest level of language, *para*.[184] Bhartrihari associates the *pashyanti* level of language with the concept of *sphota*. It represents meaning as a whole, existing in the mind of the speaker as a unity. 'When he utters it, he produces a sequence of different sounds so that it appears to have differentiation.'[185] The process of differentiation into sounds proceeds from the *sphota* on the *pashyanti* level of language via *madhyama* or inward thought to expressed speech on the *vaikhari* level. For the listener, the process is reversed. Although he first hears a series of sounds, he ultimately perceives the utterance as a unity – 'the same *sphota* with which the speaker began'.[186] The *sphota*, or meaning-whole, thus has two sides to it: the word-sound (*dhvani*) and the word-meaning (*artha*).[187] Sound and meaning are two aspects residing within the unitary *sphota*, which, according to Bhartrihari, is eternal and inherent in consciousness.[188] Meaning is thus not conveyed 'from the speaker to the hearer, rather, the spoken words serve only as a stimulus to reveal or uncover the meaning which was already present in the mind of the hearer'.[189]

Haney points out that the unity of name and form, of sound and meaning, on the level of the *sphota* in *pashyanti* applies mainly to the Sanskrit language. He argues, however, that

> because Sanskrit is considered by orthodox Indians to be the oldest documented language and probably the source of all languages, the same unity of name and form found in it must exist to some extent in other languages when experienced on sufficiently refined levels of consciousness.[190]

Artaud calls the language beyond speech, which he intuits, the language of nature. *Pashyanti* represents the subtlest manifest level of nature, and must thus be assumed to be closest to nature itself. The grammar of this language, Artaud argues, has not yet been discovered. However, in the context of Indian linguistics, experience of sufficiently refined states of consciousness – that is, direct experience of the *pashyanti* level of language – should be able to reveal that grammar. Artaud assigns an 'ancient magic effectiveness to the language beyond speech'. In parallel, Abhinavagupta, the main classic commentator on Bharata's *Natyashastra*, states that it is the poetic experience of *dhvani*, the sound aspect of speech, that brings about the experience of *rasa* 'as a transcendental function of suggestion removes the primordial veil of ignorance from our minds and thereby allows the bliss associated with the discovery of true meaning to be experienced'.[191]

Artaud may well have sensed levels of language beyond speech actively expressed in Balinese and other Oriental forms of dance, though he associated the levels of the mind gained by the spectator through watching such performances with the intellect rather than the emotions, let alone the even subtler level of *pashyanti*: 'Thus we are led *along intellectual paths* [my emphasis] towards reconquering the signs of existence.'[192] Artaud here shows the influence of contemporary science, which positions the intellect above the emotions and has no place for a level of the mind beyond speech. The absence in Western psychology of a model of the mind which takes into account levels of language beyond speech, such as the *pashyanti* level described by Bhartrihari, leads to the vagueness and confusion of terminology in Artaud's argument.

Grotowski

As we have seen, the 'paradox' is the key phrase for Diderot's theory of acting, the 'system' for Stanislavsky, the 'Method' for Strasberg, 'biomechanics' for Meyerhold, 'Theatre of Cruelty' for Artaud and 'alienation' for Brecht. Similarly, there is a heading for Grotowski's theories: 'poor theatre', which he developed while in charge of the Polish Theatre Laboratory. Grotowski sees the 'personal and scenic technique of the actor as the core of theatre art'.[193] Whereas in conventional Western theatre practice the emphasis is on the actor acquiring specific skills,[194] a 'proliferation of signs',[195] Grotowski developed a *via negativa* (way of negation), which 'necessitates the stripping away of "how to do", a mask of technique behind which the actor conceals himself, in search of the sincerity, truth and life of an exposed core of psycho-physical impulses'.[196]

According to Grotowski, the prerequisite that will allow the actor to lay bare the core of his private personality[197] is that he reaches a state of mind characterized by 'passive readiness to realize an active role'.[198] In such a state of mind, the actor is able not to want anything specific; he rather 'resigns from not doing it'.[199]

Grotowski developed various training methods to enable his actors to reach this state of mind. The methods were mainly physical, aiming 'to facilitate the activation of ... body memory: a natural reservoir of impulses to action and expression stored within the physiological make-up of an individual, an intuitive corporeal "intelligence"'.[200] If this body memory is stimulated externally, 'pure and communicable signs of an archetypal nature may be released'.[201] Ideally, the result of such a stimulation of the body memory leads to a state where the actor transcends incompleteness and the 'mind–body split': the 'division between thought and feeling, body and soul, consciousness and the unconscious, seeing and instinct, sex and brain then disappear'.[202] Consequently, the actor achieves totality, 'a certain quality of attention, or consciousness, characterized by a full presence in, and recognition of, the moment'.[203] The actor who has attained this state is free from the 'time-lapse between inner impulse and outer reaction in such a way that the impulse is already an outer expression. Impulse and expression are concurrent.'[204] The process leading to such a 'transcendental state of being', which parallels mystical and transpersonal states, has to be disciplined: undisciplined 'self-penetration is no liberation, but is perceived as a form of biological chaos'.[205]

An actor who has ripened to the ability of enduring the extreme tension involved in completely stripping himself emotionally, psycho-logically and spiritually to 'totally reveal his inner self to the audience',[206] is termed by Grotowski 'holy actor'. A 'holy actor' has been trained through physical exercises and can produce the transcendental state of consciousness described above. Grotowski does not understand the phrase 'holy actor' in a religious sense: 'It is rather a metaphor defining a person who, through his art, climbs upon the stake and performs an act of self-sacrifice.'[207]

Grotowski's terminology – 'holy actor', 'self-sacrifice', 'mounting a stake' – points, however, if not to religion, then to the related concept of ritual. As Kott maintains, 'Grotowski stubbornly and persistently tried to turn theatre back into ritual'.[208] Similarly, Bates claims that for Grotowski acting is a 'ritual testing of the soul, a stretching of the limits of human communication'.[209] This aspect of Grotowski's theory is closely related to his views on the actor–spectator relationship. For Grotowski, theatre originally had a function close to that of ritual. Theatre

> liberated the spiritual energy of the congregation or tribe by incorporat-
> ing myth and profaning or rather transcending it. The spectator thus had
> a renewed awareness of his personal truth in the truth of the myth, and
> through fright and a sense of the sacred he came to catharsis.[210]

In contemporary society, Grotowski maintained, the relation of spectators to myth is different. Therefore, instead of aiming at an identification with the myth, theatre has to confront the spectator with it. Creating a shock makes the 'life-mask crack and fall away'.[211]

The extreme of the actor's gift of his core to the spectator, 'exposure carried to outrageous excess', returns the spectator to a 'concrete mythical situation, an extreme of common human truth'.[212] As Roose-Evans puts it: 'If Brecht wanted to make the spectator think, Grotowski's aim is to disturb him on a very deep level.'[213]

The confrontation with myths is closely related to German psychologist Carl Gustav Jung's (1875–1961) concept of archetypes. At the depth of the human psyche lies the collective unconscious. It is a 'storehouse of latent memories of our human and prehuman ancestry. It consists of instincts and archetypes that we inherit as possibilities and that often affect our behavior.'[214] The archetypes, in particular, are 'themes that have existed in all cultures throughout history'.[215] Jung holds that these collective memories are 'universal in nature because of our common evolution and brain structure'.[216] In confronting spectators with modern versions of myth, Grotowski enlivened archetypes in their collective unconscious.

Different archetypes are not equally developed within the psyche. This accounts for the different effects Grotowski's work has on different spectators. Gilman describes how such deep disturbance, aimed at renewing the spectator, was so forceful that

> the theater ... has felt itself in the presence of something very like a
> redemption. .... Almost every moment and sound is what can only be
> described as 'pure', without precedent or predictability, yet wholly

inevitable, accurate, created, true.... In having passed beyond all hitherto known means of expression and beyond representation, they place us in the presence of emotions and consciousness themselves, in the presence, that is to say, of a creation and not an image of one.[217]

Not every spectator responded favourably to Grotowski's approach: another critic remarked on the performance's infantilism, coarseness, delusion(s) of originality, ugliness and nihilism.[218] Indeed, Grotowski did not present plays for mainstream audiences; he was concerned with a spectator as a spiritual seeker, who wished to improve by self-analysis through 'confrontation with the performance'.[219] Grotowski tried to achieve for the spectator the same 'translumination' that the actor achieves when he is fully and only present in the moment, in the state of transcendence. Grotowski's method here was to minimize, as far as possible, the distance between actor and spectator, both physically and psychologically.[220] Critic Irving Wardle's comment in his review of *The Constant Prince*, a major production of the Theatre Laboratory, points to a difficulty in this approach, noting the 'immense gap between these productions and any common experience. They start on a note of intensity and ascend from there without relief.'[221] Grotowski himself admitted 'that he was impotent to influence directly the spectator's spiritual and psychic responses to the acts witnessed'.[222]

In contrast to Diderot, Stanislavsky and Brecht, Grotowski does not deal explicitly with either the actor's or the spectator's emotions. Innes argues that Grotowski uses 'archetypal ideograms ... to awaken latent emotions in the spectator through subconscious associations'.[223] Reaching the spectator's latent emotions may indeed be one channel through which Grotowski's theatre affects the spectator. However, his ultimate goal for both actor and spectator, the transcendental state of consciousness, or 'translumination' close to, if not identical with, 'mystical and transpersonal states of consciousness and experience',[224] surely lies beyond the already quite subtle level of the emotions. As Kumiega points out, one characteristic of this experience is that the division between thought and feeling disappears.

Frequent scepticism among theatre theorists and practitioners towards concepts such as translumination may be rooted in Freud's and Jung's uneasiness with such concepts. In a letter to Freud, French novelist and mystic Romain Rolland (1866–1944) commented on Freud's views on the 'illusory nature of religion' in *The Future of an Illusion*. He argued that Freud had failed to analyse 'spontaneous religious feelings, or religious sentiments'.[225] A few years later, Freud came back to Rolland's criticism, summarizing his characterization of the religious feeling thus:

> It is a feeling which he would like to call a sensation of 'eternity,' a feeling of something limitless, unbounded – as it were, 'oceanic'. This feeling, he

adds, is a purely subjective fact, not an article of faith; it brings with it no assurance of personal immortality, but it is the source of the religious energy which is seized upon by the various Churches and religious systems, directed by them into particular channels, and doubtless also exhausted by them.[226]

Whereas Rolland stated that he was never without that oceanic experience, and one he presumed existed in millions of people, Freud could not discover this feeling in himself.[227] He intellectually traces the possibility of an oceanic experience back to the early phase of ego-feeling. Originally, the child's ego includes everything, only 'later it separates off an external world from itself'.[228] The feeling in the early, unitary state can be called 'oceanic'. Continuation of such a feeling into adulthood can be explained by the assumption that 'there are many people in whose mental life this primary ego-feeling has persisted to a greater or lesser degree'.[229] In the adult capable of oceanic experiences, the primary ego-feeling co-exists with the 'narrower and more sharply demarcated ego-feeling of maturity'.[230] An oceanic experience is thus characterized by Freud as a 'regression to infantile levels of pre-individuation'.[231]

Jung's model of the human mind differs from Freud's structure of ego, super-ego and id. For Jung, the levels are ego, personal unconscious, collective unconscious and self. The ego is not identical with psyche or consciousness; it is one aspect of the psyche at the centre of consciousness, responsible for 'our feelings of identity and continuity as human beings'.[232] The personal unconscious contains all past and forgotten experience, as well as sense impressions too weak to have become conscious. Material in the personal unconscious is accessible to consciousness in specific circumstances such as, for example, psycho-analysis. The deepest level within the psyche is the collective unconscious, inaccessible to consciousness, seat of archetypes. If the individual is placed in favourable conditions of evolution, of personal development, he or she can reach a state of self-realization, where the ego is replaced by the self as the centre of consciousness.[233]

The paradoxes of acting expressly formulated by, or implicit in, the theories of Diderot (an emotionally uninvolved actor emotionally involving an audience), Stanislavsky (the same actor is both emotionally involved and distanced at the same time) and Brecht (the actor inwardly lives the character, without falling into the trap of empathy) have prepared the way for Grotowski; the paradox that resulted from such a combination, or collage, of elements from various cultural sources was the insight of the creative co-existence of two elements that appear, at first sight, to be opposed and mutually exclusive – spontaneity and discipline: 'what is elementary feeds what is constructed and vice versa.'[234] Grotowski insisted on his actors' physical discipline, which they gained through regular exercise. The idea that the actor can reach the unconscious, the source of archetypes, by stimulating the body memory goes back to the James–Lange theory of emotions and Meyerhold's application of it in his biomechanics. Kumiega has asserted that body memory stimulates the emotions.[235] However, as argued above, Grotowski's ultimate aim is to reach beyond the emotions.

Grotowski closed the Theatre Laboratory in 1970. According to Kott, he realized that his attempts to turn theatre back into ritual 'is sacrilege, pillage of the *sacrum*' for true believers, and 'for non-believers a form of cheating'.[236] In the following years, Grotowski developed paratheatrical activities. Here, he was able to explore fully his role as therapist in a process of social healing. Grotowski had wanted his Theatre Laboratory to have a healing effect on the spectators. However, he had direct access only to the actors, and could only hope that they could produce the desired effect in the spectators. In the set-up of paratheatrical events, there was no longer a distinction between actor and audience:

> Grotowski developed a total concentration on the internal process of self-discovery in groups of the public as participants. In effect they were subjected to an extended session of psychotherapy based on the acting exercises developed by the Theatre Laboratory.[237]

Grotowski had become acquainted with Eastern philosophy early on in his life, and to recover from an illness that interrupted his studies at the State Institute of Theatre Art in Moscow in 1956, he spent two months travelling in Central Asia. Oriental philosophy was the topic of a series of weekly talks which he gave in the Student Club in Cracow, where he trained as a director and directed his first productions in the professional theatre. The talks were about 'Buddhism, Yoga, the Upanishads, Confucius, Taoism and Zen Buddhism'.[238]

The Theatre of Thirteen Rows was founded by Grotowski in 1959, and the second season of the theatre began with his adaptation of an Indian classic, *Shakuntala*. The play originates in the fourth or fifth century AD and deals with love in a highly poetic way. Grotowski's adaptation of this play included major cuts, and the insertion of other Indian texts, including the *Kama Sutra*.[239] Rather than attempting to re-create an Indian production of the play in his theatre in Poland, Grotowski emphasized the difference of this kind of play, the difference of cultural codes, which would free his actors from the expectations of performance associated with any Western literary text presented on stage. Kumiega argues that this production already contained some of the ingredients of Grotowski's later theatre theory and practice: namely, fascination with ritual, experiment with architectural space, the actor–spectator relationship, investigation into a theatrical system of signs and questions of actor training.[240]

Grotowski's fascination with Indian theatre is evident not only from his choice of an Indian classic, in a non-Indian production, but also from his reference to the Indian god Shiva, the Cosmic Dancer, Nataraja, who creates all that exists while dancing: 'If I had to define our theatrical researches in one sentence, one phrase, I would refer to the myth of the Dance of Shiva.'[241] Grotowski defined the essence of what he was searching for by quoting Shiva: 'I am the pulse, the movement and the rhythm.'[242] Byrski, assessing Indian influences on Grotowski, argues that both classical Indian theatre and the theatre created by Grotowski strive to achieve non-ordinary states of consciousness in both actors and spectators. Furthermore, both forms of theatre require a specifically trained audience.

In the early stages of training at the Theatre Laboratory, the actors experimented with training forms and techniques from Oriental and Asian theatre, and practised yoga. However, Grotowski eventually abandoned such experiments, concluding that the non-Western aesthetic was completely alien to him: 'I do not think that we can adopt from them any techniques, or that they could inspire us directly.'[243] He realized that Oriental or Asian theatre forms are characterized by achieving a state of sacred theatre, in which spontaneity and discipline co-exist and mutually reinforce each other. He considered such a state desirable for a Western actor, but felt that techniques that allow, say, an Indian actor to achieve this co-existence, would not work for a Western actor.

Grotowski's problems with intercultural theatre practice are rooted in the way he understands and uses Indian material: *mudras* are first described in the *Natyashastra*. The *mudras* are not isolated means of histrionic representation: in specific situations in a given play, specific means of histrionic representation have to be used to create a specific emotional and aesthetic experience in the spectators. The *Natyashastra* functions on two levels: it is both a description of what a 'perfect' actor, an actor who has reached a state of enlightenment, or *moksha* (liberation), will automatically, spontaneously do to create a specific emotion, a specific aesthetic experience in a specific audience. For an actor who is not yet 'perfect', the techniques described in the *Natyashastra* are a means to achieve perfection, enlightenment, *moksha*, and run parallel to reaching this state through yoga or meditation practices.[244] Thus, though the *mudras* and other means of histrionic representation are apparently fixed codes, laid down and described as such in the text of the *Natyashastra*, they originate in the very moment they are created by the enlightened actor. Grotowski's argument that Indian signs are fixed thus loses its ground.

Grotowski became disillusioned with yoga, believing that it led to an introverted concentration that was harmful to the actor. There are techniques for personal development in India (both physical and mental) that are meant for people who have consciously chosen the way of life of a monk, in a monastery. Renouncing the world, they hope to gain enlightenment. However, this is not the only path to the same goal: there are also methods designed specifically for individuals who have to deal with everyday activities; in this case, the meditative practices do not draw the mind inwards, which would render the individual incapable of ordinary day-to-day activities. Rather, the techniques are geared to produce deep physical relaxation together with refined states of consciousness during the meditation, allowing the mind to access levels of consciousness otherwise not open to experience. Such subtler levels of the mind reverberate with energy, which is then channelled into the activity after meditation. Thus, meditative practices intended for ordinary people as opposed to monks will support their daily activity. Indeed, activity is an integral part of the development to enlightenment: in alternating the meditative experience of *samadhi* with ordinary activity, the nervous system is trained to maintain a state where *samadhi* can co-exist with the ordinary state of consciousness.[245] Such co-existence is not an intellectual understanding, but a profound holistic experience, and is the aim of both the monk and the ordinary person. What differs are the paths adopted to obtain that state of liberation.

When Grotowski found that the practices he used tended to block his actors from activity, then it must be assumed that he employed practices intended for monks, rather than techniques which would indeed support the actor's activities, and lead to the benefits Grotowski had hoped for.

Director's Theatre

In the discussion of twentieth-century approaches to acting, the director has been mentioned quite frequently, and indeed the relation of the actor to the director deserves a chapter of its own. Since the theories of Richard Wagner and Edward Gordon Craig, and the practice of the Duke of Saxe Meiningen, the director has gained increasing importance in theatre production. Some theatre artists deplore this development, such as actress and acting teacher Uta Hagen when she writes:

> since the disappearance of the golden age of the actor-manager in the 1800s, the acting profession as a whole has relinquished its responsibility to the theatre. It has willingly accepted the role of subservient child to a kind of parental control exercised by managers, producers, directors, even its own agents.[246]

Actor Simon Callow also went on record with witty and biting remarks on the crippling effect directors can have on actors.[247] At first glance, this may appear extraordinary if we go through the list of directors whose names we may have come across in books or on course syllabi: Peter Brook, or Jonathan Miller, Ariane Mnouchkine, Peter Sellars and

Giorgio Strehler, to name but a few. All are remarkable directors who have attracted much publicity, most of it praise, and they are associated with important developments of twentieth-century theatre. Theatre implies acting, by definition, and if those directors have achieved much in the theatre, they must have been doing something right with the actors working for them. This assumption is appropriate, as I will demonstrate below when I look at some of the things well-known directors have said about actors and working with them.

Initially, though, it is important to note that indeed not all directors work with actors in a way that helps them to achieve their best level of performance. So if some actors complain, it is not about the function of direction in general. Indeed, most actors acknowledge the benefit for their performances if the direction is appropriate. They complain, rather, about 'bad' directors, or about behaviour in a director that they find unhelpful in their creative work as actors. Sometimes, the directors who come in for criticism are among the 'big' names, but probably in most of the cases, the actors do not even bother to mention the 'bad' directors by name.

What are those characteristics of directing that can destroy rather than support the actor's creative work? Different symptoms will be relevant for different actors, depending on their past experience and personality, but two favourite candidates emerge. First, the director who constantly changes the way a scene is to be played, a sentence or even word pronounced or intoned: 'Let's try this way ... no, let's try that way.' Such an approach destroys any flow of creativity, leaving the actor confused and frustrated. The director guilty of such behaviour probably has little idea himself as to how the textual material should be tackled, and uses the actors as guinea-pigs to arrive at his own best version, rather than working with the actors to achieve a unified performance. Second, and related to this, is the director who not only suggests different modes of acting a specific passage but also extensively demonstrates how the actor should perform, expecting the actor to imitate him.

The director has variously been described in his relation to the actor as

> father figure, mother, ideal partner, teacher, ghost, invisible presence, third eye, voyeur, ego or superego, leader of an expedition to another world, autocratic ship captain, puppet master, sculptor, visual artist, midwife, lover, marriage partner, literary critic, trainer of an athlete's team, trustee of democratic spirit, psychoanalyst, listener, surrogate audience, author, harrower, gardener, beholder, ironic recuperator of the maternal gaze.[248]

Many of these terms imply power, a relationship that is mirrored in the fact that the actor is often said to be playing *for* the director. The director of Shakespeare's *The Tempest* might approach an actor saying 'I want you to be *my* Prospero'. This position of power thus begins, potentially, with casting, is mainly effective during the rehearsal process and extends to re-employability, depending on the reputation spread by the director among his colleagues about the actors he has been working with.

Most directors would agree that it is important to facilitate a creative atmosphere in the rehearsal process. Such an atmosphere is needed to free the actor, to release, stir and maximize the actor's creativity. Differences are, however, apparent when it comes to defining just what constitutes such an atmosphere, and which means should be used to achieve it. Some directors prefer tension among actors, hoping that it will release those otherwise dormant energies which they then intend to channel towards the production. The tension may be on a personal level, or related to the creative work. French director Roger Planchon, for example, provides the actors with freedom of choice to the extent of being lost: 'Being lost, the actor asks himself questions. He becomes curious. He is no longer interested only in his own role but in the whole play.'[249] Ultimately, then, in Planchon's productions, freedom of choice serves as a tool of manoeuvring the actors into recognizing and accepting the framework for the production. Ingmar Bergman, on the other hand, insists that rehearsing 'has to do with contact, with listening, with tenderness, with love, with security'.[250] We should not assume that this implies a 'soft approach', however. As one of his actresses, Ghita Norby, put it, Bergman's 'demands were the greatest conceivable, and his strictness was the greatest conceivable, and he took it as a matter of course that his demands would be met'.[251]

Some directors have referred to their work in rehearsals as teamwork. They allow actors to make suggestions, improvise and disagree.[252] British director Declan Donnellan emphasizes that he, too, learns during good rehearsals, and that his actors should regard his suggestions as useful, but not necessarily true.[253] Russian director Lev Dodin considers the actor as co-author of the production.[254] Neither Donnellan nor Dodin, however (and both are representative for many others of their colleagues), give up their position of power and superiority: Donnellan regards himself in relation to his actors not as a teacher, but as an athlete's coach, and Dodin quickly points out that recognizing the position of the actor as co-author does not imply 'that I am unable to use my will where it is necessary and sometimes where it is quite unnecessary. Sometimes you have to have as strong a will to stir and release an actor's creativity as you would need to strangle it.'[255]

The ratio of power and assumed or real equality between actors and director is thus ambiguous. Maybe the aim – a good production – justifies the means? Maybe the actors will be grateful if the director manages to elicit a very good performance from them, no matter how?

To discuss such issues further, it is important to understand what is believed to hamper free expression, flow of creativity and other desirable characteristics of the actor's art. William Ball, late founding artistic director of the American Conservatory Theatre, provides a detailed analysis of the processes involved in acting. He argues that consciousness is the very source of life, expressed as 'I am'. For most people, it is easy to define themselves by saying, for example, I am a father, or I am a husband: 'The individual's belief in his identities gives a pattern to his reality and a definition to his activity. He limits his belief in order to maintain identities that are manageable, comfy, respectable.'[256] The actor, in contrast to all non-actors, changes his beliefs in identifying with every character he has to play: 'The actor makes a profession of believing in many identities.'[257] When not in role, and that means without a fixed identity, the actor may come across as somehow incomplete, uncertain or vague. The director has to be aware of this condition, and must provide support and strength, instruction and guidance, with great respect and all gentleness.[258] Giorgio Strehler argues along the same line when he insists that the role of the director is to bring the actor 'awareness, help, encouragement and criticism', and that the director's work must 'always be an act of love. Without love, without sharing in this work together, the theatre doesn't exist.'[259] Ball further maintains that any intellectual activity, governed by the left hemisphere of our brains, is detrimental to the activity of the actor:

> Talking, theorizing and intellectualizing must be reduced to an absolute minimum ... emphasis on rationality abruptly shifts the creative process into the left brain. It misleads the actors into thinking that they can make points by using their intellects. Never allow an actor to entangle you in intellectuality. The way to avoid it is to assume an appearance of vagueness. Seem unqualified to enter that realm and say: 'Yes, Yes. Well, when we get into rehearsal, show me. Let me see it. Show it to me. I'm sure it is all very good.' Most discussion is fruitless.[260]

Ball clearly opposes directors who place much emphasis on extensive discussions of the play, such as German Peter Stein or Planchon, who requires that actors 'should appreciate their role rationally, step by step; just as each scene must be analysed in depth, so must each character be considered carefully in its own right'.[261] Instead of left-brain dominated intellect, Ball emphasizes intuition, the domain of the right hemisphere. For him, intuition is perfect, leading, ideally, to spontaneous right thought and automatic right and appropriate action. It is an uncluttered avenue along which perfection makes itself available to human perception. The director's role is to awaken the actor's intuition. It needs awakening, one should add, because our lives today are dominated by left-brain, analytic, intellectual processes. The director should assure, Ball continues, that the intuition is going to be witnessed and used. For this he suggests taking recourse to common principles of the learning process. We discover something new, test the implications and eventually set a pattern. Applied to the theatre, the director should announce to his actors at the beginning of the rehearsal process that he will take up, fully accept, and creatively use the first three ideas suggested by each actor. This is the discovery stage. The actor hears the director's words: this is the phase of the discovery in the learning process. The actor's intuition now tests the claim, and will produce quite bad ideas, challenging the director to stick to his word. If the director succeeds in incorporating uncritically and creatively the bad ideas produced by the actors, the pattern will be set, and the ideas that emerge from the actor's intuition will now be creative and free, independent of the intellect-governed testing phase of the learning process.[262]

Ball's arguments suggest that if the director's attitude towards the actors is informed by such an understanding of the actors' nature, the power implied by the role of the director will be used in measured ways to achieve a clear aim. From his own experience, Ball provides some further suggestions for maintaining the free flow of the actor's creative intuition:

- The director should value the actor's work, and encourage it.
- He should praise aspects of the actor's work that deserve it.
- In battles with the actor, the director should always surrender.
- The director should understand that a question from the actor is not a question, but an innocent bid to draw the director's attention to something that remains unresolved.
- In view of people's attention span, rehearsals should be carefully planned to rehearse between three and seven pages of text in three-quarters of an hour to an hour. At first the actors should present what they remember from the last rehearsal, followed by an intense rehearsal of detail and a run-through of the rehearsed passage, so that the actors get a feeling for the unity of the passage. At each stage, actors should be able to act whatever smaller or larger unit is being rehearsed without interruption.
- In rehearsals, the director should not explicitly show action on the stage to the actor, nor should he read, or even say, the actor's lines. British director Jonathan Miller provides the actor with an example, 'in the hope that they will not copy what you are doing but that they will do a whole series of subsequent actions on their own in accordance with what you have shown them'.[263] Peter Stein takes on 'the movements of the actor that I am watching on the stage and I follow him indicating to him how he should do it. I take his acting design and put something on it.'[264]
- Actors should not be allowed to rehearse on their own. If one of

them begins to make suggestions for improvement to the other actor(s), their equality as fellow-actors has been destroyed, and one has adopted a superior position.

In line with such recommendations based on a director's own experience is the insight by Maria Irene Fornes that secrecy in the rehearsal process is divisive. She refers to the habit of some directors to talk in private to their actors, in an attempt, perhaps, to make them feel special. Fornes argues that everything the director has to say to one actor should be said aloud, because it should indeed be beneficial to all actors in the production.[265]

Acting, Postmodernism and Performance

Philip Auslander has pointed out that possibly all approaches to acting until the last quarter of the twentieth century, despite their obvious and undeniable differences, share one common factor: *logocentrism*. This term belongs to the discipline of philosophy that relates to the question 'what is meaning'. More specifically, the term refers to the tendency among philosophers to posit that meaning exists in itself, as a foundation. French philosopher Jacques Derrida (1930–) has argued that this traditional philosophical approach is faulty, because nothing exists as a foundation. 'Every mental or phenomenal event is a product of difference, is defined by its relation to what is not rather than by its essence.'[266] Theatre is logocentric if and when it implies the dominant power of one of the aspects of theatre. The dramatist's text can be taken as the assumed foundation, or the director's concept. In the context of acting, the important concept is that of the *actor's self*. Stanislavsky, Brecht and Grotowski define that self differently, but they all 'posit the self as an autonomous foundation for acting'.[267] Stanislavsky demands that the actor disguises his own self by means of his

> own emotional experience. Brecht wants the disguise to be separable from the actor's own persona and reflective of social experience ... Grotowski believes that the actor must use the disguise of her role to cut away the disguise imposed on her by socialisation, and expose the most basic levels of self and psyche.[268]

To prove Derrida's point that there can be no logocentric foundation, in this particular case the actor's self, and to demonstrate that all is difference, play, Auslander proceeds to show that the actor's self 'is, in fact, produced by the performance it supposedly grounds'.[269]

According to Derrida, two fundamental reactions are possible to the insight that there are no foundations, that all is the play of difference. Either we are unable to give up the hope and will continue to seek for 'a truth or an origin which escapes play',[270] or we progress towards a response which embraces the concept of play and does not nostalgically seek to trace any kind of foundation which we know does not exist. Many of the avant-garde approaches to acting, in their attempt at achieving *holy theatre* (Grotowski) or *total theatre* (Brook), would fall into the former category of nostalgia. Derrida's approach has been labelled *deconstruction*. Deconstructive theatre might use traditional elements of theatre and simultaneously undermine them.

One of the focal points of the attempts at holy theatre was the human body. Claiming the actor's body as essential in a logocentric sense makes it a 'metaphysical, even a mystical concept: it is asocial, undiffer-entiated, raceless, genderless'.[271] Such traditional approaches can be summarized under the concept of *modernism*. Derrida's demand for deconstruction, along with the critique of the ahistorical view of the actor's body in performance characteristic of modernist approaches to acting, falls into the wider category of *postmodernism*. The concept of postmodernism is ambiguous in at least four main areas: some critics question the legitimacy of the concept, arguing that there are no new phenomena that might justify the introduction of a new term.[272] The next issue is the matter of the term's application. According to Welsch, the term originated in the North American literature debate, then spread to architecture and painting, sociology and philosophy, and by now there is hardly an area 'not infected by this virus'.[273] As far as its origins are concerned, the debate began in the USA in 1959 in reference to phenomena of the 1950s; in 1975, when Europe had caught up with the development, the *New Yorker* wrote that postmodernism was out and there was demand for a post-postmodernism.[274] In the same line of argument, Welsch quotes Umberto Eco's worries that before long even Homer would be considered postmodern.[275] Finally, the contexts of postmodernism are ambiguous: the age of Star Wars technology versus a green, ecological, alternative movement; a new integration of a fragmented society versus increased intentional fragmentation and pluralization.[276]

Welsch attempts to define a common denominator for different approaches to postmodernism: 'We can talk about postmodernism where a fundamental pluralism of languages, models, and procedures is practised, not just side by side in separate works, but in one and the same work, i.e. interferentially.'[277] According to Birringer, 'there is very little discussion about what *postmodern theatre* might be' among 'actors, directors, and writers',[278] and he notices the same reluctance 'among drama critics and scholars who continue to write about a world of texts and performances that seems largely untouched by the debates on the politics of postmodernism or on the technological transformation of late modern culture'.[279] However, more and more theatre artists draw their inspiration from an increasing number of different cultural sources, and they put their source material to practice in different ways. If interpreted as fragmentation, as an active endorsement of intended and precise pluralism, then it is a postmodernist aspect of theatre.

Drawing on a wide, culturally diverse range of source material can be considered postmodern also because it is a strikingly postmodern intertextual activity. Intertextuality can be regarded as a superimposed concept for methods of more or less conscious, and to some extent concrete, references in the text (including the performance text) to individual pre-texts, groups of pre-texts, or underlying codes and complexes of meaning.[280] These methods are already established individually in literary criticism under such terms as source study, influence, quotation, allusion, parody, travesty, imitation, translation and adaptation.[281] Two extreme concepts of intertextuality with different points of departure can be differentiated: the global model of post-structuralism regards every text as part of a global intertext. In contrast, structuralist and hermeneutic models argue in favour of a more conscious, intended and marked reference between a text and a pre-text or groups of pre-texts.[282] Broich and Pfister propose a model of intertextuality that mediates between the two positions: specific criteria for intertextuality can be defined and their intensity evaluated in quality and quantity from case to case. Those criteria are: referentiality, communicativity, autoreflexivity, structure, selectivity, dialogue, density and number of intertextual references, and number and range of pre-texts.[283]

George highlights ambiguity as a postmodern characteristic of performance. He argues that postmodernism 'finds the world hyphenated, elliptical; reversing all established hierarchies and questioning the reduction behind them, deconstruction finds the world doubled, ironic, decentered'.[284] George then asks: 'Beyond roles, masks and other "duplicities", was it not always this which performance already proclaimed: "I ambiguous"?'[285] George extends this argument to the reception process: all spectators (as, indeed, performers) 'are always negotiating between at least two worlds'[286]; that is, the real world of the spectator's life as a spectator in the audience, and the fictional world presented on the stage. Such negotiation leads to doubts. In a non-theatrical context, such doubts would in turn lead to 'existential anguish'. In the theatre, however, the doubts are 'restricted to the realm of the possible', and therefore, they can be 'enjoyed, relished'.[287] This pleasure, an ambiguous phenomenon, has been analysed in Western culture in terms of psychoanalysis, conceptualized as a 'form of retarded climax and therefore ascribed, like all ambiguous phenomena, to the realm of the abnormal'.[288] Because postmodernism does not fear contradiction, because, indeed, it recognizes contradiction as the existential base, ambiguity of performance, in the performative and the receptive aspects, could be an essential feature of a postmodern performance theory. George concludes as follows:

The predominance in post-modern and deconstructionist discourse of terms such as play, game, contradiction, process, performance, suggests that we may be entering an age in which there *are only* media (semiosis, assumptions, paradigms, models) and no ontology, only experiences (and no Self except the one like an actor's career made up of the parts we enact and rewrite), a world in which difference is primordial (no ur-whole) and time endless. For such an age, performance is the ideal medium and model and ambiguity is its life.[289]

In describing postmodernism, George uses the term 'decentred', a reference to Jacques Lacan's theory. Lacan holds that psychoanalysis reveals a split between 'the self, the innermost part of the psyche, and the subject of conscious discourse, behaviour and culture'.[290] This division creates a hidden structure inside the subject – the unconscious. The conditions of human existence, according to Lacan, imply that man is 'essentially a being by and for the other'. The common ground on which individuals 'assert themselves, oppose each other and find themselves again'[291] is the symbolic. To become an individual, accession to the symbolic is necessary. However, such accession is balanced with 'the division of the subject'; in the symbolic, 'the subject can be no more than represented or translated'.[292]

Proposing a decentred self, a split between the self and the subject of discourse, is a postmodern phenomenon. If performances represent the fragmentary, in opposition to 'unitary ambitions',[293] they thus represent what Lacan's postmodern discourse has discovered: the decentred self, the split between self and subject of behaviour and culture.

Regarding performances as postmodern when they show fragmentation of sources and ambiguity, together with a high degree of intertextuality, is in line with critics like Crohn-Schmitt, or George, who research the parallels between contemporary quantum mechanics and the theatre. Crohn-Schmitt distinguishes between Aristotelian theatre and the 'important segment of contemporary theater variously referred to as antitheater, postmodern theater, or simply, new theater',[294] maintaining that new theatre violates 'not only Aristotelian aesthetic principles but also the view of reality that they imply, thus profoundly disturbing many audience members'.[295] From twentieth-century quantum physics, Crohn-Schmitt infers that 'the idea of a single true account of reality is challenged',[296] and together with it the role of the individual:

> Because there is no correspondence between mind and nature, human beings cannot find their unique, essential purpose and pleasure in knowing; like the rest of nature, they have no ulterior purpose. They have no more importance in nature than any other part.[297]

Crohn-Schmitt quotes John Cage's view that art must teach us 'to accept our purposelessness'.[298] In her opinion, contemporary artists do not feel depressed by the fact that neither the self nor the perceived world are 'discrete, inviolable, and constant'.[299] Their excitement with the exploration of this newly discovered world view mirrors the optimistic, even euphoric mode of postmodernism. This view is in line with the reaction to the insight that all life is the play of difference, proposed and preferred by Derrida.

Birringer, however, has quite a different view of postmodernism. He links postmodernism strongly with technological advances and deplores that in 'today's mass market of overproduced images and ubiquitous information circuitries, the imaginary has trouble surviving, since reality seems already always replaced by its simulations'.[300] Rather than accept the fragmented impression of reality conveyed by our senses, especially sight, Birringer argues, theatre should enable a 'radical and unfashionable vision';[301] without forgetting 'the limits and frames of the conditions of its theatricality', performance practices should be developed that 'think of themselves as "acts from under and above" ... – acts that need the limits of the theatre in order to be able to imagine different realities, under and above our normal ways of seeing'.[302] Whatever the precise forms, postmodern theatre understands itself as a response to, and reaction against, modernist theatre, acknowledging the fragmentary nature of the world and the need to 'work within the codes that define the cultural landscape',[303] as opposed to non-historical transcendence of the present.

It is particularly in the development of *performance*, rather than acting in the theatre, that the postmodern paradigm has yielded striking results. Mike Pearson defines performance as

> a 'special world' set aside from everyday life by contractual arrangements and social suspensions, not entirely hermetically sealed, but a devised world, all the elements of which – site, environment, technology, spatial organisation, form and content, rules and practices – are conceived, organised, controlled and ultimately experienced by its varying orders of participant. In such 'constructed' situations, free from the laws and bye-laws of normative theatre practice, other things, real things, can happen. Here, extra-daily occurrences and experiences, and changes in status are possible. All three performance relationships – performer to performer, performer to spectator, and spectator to spectator – can be problematised and renegotiated and conventions and mores reshaped. Performance need not be restricted to the public or monumental zone of the auditorium. It is a locale of cultural intervention and innovation, at once utopia and heterotopia, a place of experiment, claim, conflict, negotiation, transgression: a place where preconceptions, expectations and critical faculties may be dislocated and confounded; a place where things may still be at risk – beliefs, classifications, lives.[304]

The postmodern aspect of fragmentation appears in Pearson's definition of devised performance as 'performance which does not rely on the play-script as its central organizing feature. Instead it uses a series of conceptual, compositional, strategic and tactical devices to collage, montage and juxtapose fragments of dramatic material.'[305] Just as the body was at the focus of holy theatre (see above), the body is central to performance, in the context of *physical theatre*, defined by Pearson as 'performance in which the physical expression of the performers is the primary carrier for dramatic meaning. As such, it shares features with contemporary dance, mime and many non-European theatrical traditions.'[306] The postmodern turn, as suggested by Auslander, is indeed to question traditional assumptions about the body. Pearson describes two models of the human body, one male, the other female, in the Natural History Museum in London, which showed

> how we visualise our own bodies. They had huge hands, huge genitals, huge heads with prominent mouths. The rest of the body was a shrivelled appendage. This image clearly reflects the distribution of our sensory organs and the importance we assign to these centres of response, gratification and communication.[307]

Pearson argues that the performer can challenge this hierarchy

- by placing attention elsewhere in the body, with repercussions for stance, posture, gait;
- by increasing the expressive functioning of the whole body as a three-dimensional entity;
- by creating another body image.[308]

In addition, performance may challenge the conventions of behaviour. 'The performer may engage – in this "special world" – in acts which are socially unacceptable, which then reveal the conventions of everyday life. So we might expect not only virtuoso displays but also vulnerable exposure.'[309] Pearson refers to 'extreme body art', and describes the examples of Annie Sprinkle, Ron Athey and Orlan:

> So, Annie Sprinkle invites audiences to look inside her body using a speculum, Ron Athey who is HIV-positive takes samples of his own blood during performance, allowing the potentially dangerous 'inside' to come 'outside' and perhaps most radical of all, the French female artist Orlan is having her body-shape altered with the addition of horns. She has the operations videoed and then sold as art-works![310]

Related to performance as defined and discussed by Mike Pearson is *performance art*. It is 'also referred to as "live art" and "time-based art"', and 'animates the compositional strategies and procedures of visual art'.[311] Performance art grew out of mainstream theatre, in explicit and intentional opposition to it, and indeed generally in opposition to 'the values traditionally attached to art'.[312] The history of performance art reaches back to the beginning of the twentieth century, with Futurism and Dada. To remind you: Futurism started with the publication of Marinetti's Futurist manifesto in *Le Figaro* in 1909. Subsequently, Futurist evenings were held in Italy, and further manifestos published, advising the performing artist to shock the audience. By the mid-1920s, the Futurists had 'fully established performance as an art medium in its own right'.[313] In the process, performance art had spread to Moscow and Petrograd, Zurich, New York and London. In Russia, artists such as Burlyuk, Mayakovsky and Khlebnikov assimilated Futurist ideas, developing their own forms of performance art in reaction against the Tzarist regime and 'the imported painting styles of Impressionism and early Cubism'.[314]

In 1916, the Dada movement was founded in Zurich by Hugo Ball. He was joined by Jean Arp, Tristan Tzara, Marcel Janco and Richard Huelsenbeck. Appalled by the violence of the First World War, their response 'took the form of an insurrection against all that was pompous, conventional, or even boring in the arts'.[315] Many Dada artists gathered around André Breton from around 1924, giving rise to the Surrealist movement. Surrealism in general represents 'a significant constituent of human feeling, a love for the world of dreams and of fantasy'.[316] For Breton, Surrealism is 'pure psychic automatism, by which an attempt is made to express, either verbally, in writing, or in any other manner, the true functioning of thought'.[317] Inspired by psychoanalysis, Surrealism had a major influence on mainstream theatre's preoccupation with language, whereas post-Second Word War performance art turned to the 'basic tenets of Dada and Futurism – chance, simultaneity and surprise'.[318] In Germany, performance art was pioneered in the 1920s by Oskar Schlemmer at the Bauhaus, a teaching institution for the arts, founded in 1919. In the USA, performance art started to develop following the influx of many European performance artists in the late 1930s. After the Second World War, their individual work and the collaboration between dancer Merce Cunningham and musician John Cage, as well as Allan Kaprov, stand out in the USA as do Yves Klein in France, Piero Manzoni in Italy or Joseph Beuys in Germany.

Performance artists generally did not want to represent a character; instead, they sought to directly confront the audience with a 'real' presence: the worlds of art and real life were merged. Such direct exposure of performers to their audience did not aim at catharsis, though. Performances were single events, not restaged, not rehearsed and not taped. The process of performance was emphasized, not the product. In line with these propositions, performance art was opposed to the commercial value of art.

Mehta provides three motives for the 'anti-illusionistic' nature of performance art.[319] First, the performers' distrust of theatrical conventions of representation: for example, 'debased psychologisms of much realistic theatre';[320] second, performance artists refuse to guide the spectator's experience, thus decentring him or her, leading to a private and subjective experience. Finally, abstraction in performance enables the performer 'to become an object in a formal design'.[321]

The specific use of imagery plays an important role in performance art. Many images are taken from life, but in the context of the performance take on a surrealistic shape. The performing artist's aim will be twofold: first, to seduce the spectators out of their 'quotidian realities into a parallel world of dreams and the subconscious'. The second aim is to intensify the spectators' 'receptive faculties' by shaking them 'out of perceptual ruts'.[322]

Collage is related to imagery in two ways: it constitutes the images themselves, and it exists between different images. The collages are constituted by collisions of media (such as performers versus puppets); or cultures (such as Eastern versus Western); of rhythm and texture (such as movement versus stillness); or of eye and ear (such as 'quoted words distorted through prisms of critical or contrasting visuals'[323]). The difference between the use of these elements in traditional theatre and in performance art is that in the latter 'all linear overlays', such as 'word-and-character-centered through lines', are removed. Performance art thus reaffirms two central quests of modernism: 'to find that which is irreducible in a medium; and to force us to look at art as art and not as life.'[324]

Many pieces of performance art centre on art as their own subject. Mehta proposes three reasons for this tendency: first, an obsession with perspective is characteristic of modernism; second, there is an influence from Formalist painters like Rauschenberg, Johns and Stella; third, breaking new ground is exhilarating.

Since the 1970s, when performance art with its clearly defined function within the modernist framework of opposition against aesthetic tradition reached its peak, there are no longer 'strong political, economic, or aesthetic ideologies, nor any mutual artistic projects'.[325] As a result, performance art has lost many of its distinct characteristics: it has lost its quality of experimentation, either because this has become the way art usually functions, or because it has disappeared as a concept;[326] the body is no longer central to performance art – it has become 'an element of performance art among others';[327] performance art nowadays tends to take place in more traditional places like theatres, galleries, multipurpose halls, rather than some of the original locations like a zoo, a cage or a swimming pool; finally, performance art has become commercial, with an emphasis on the finished product rather than process characteristic of the functional framework of performance art. The loss of function gives rise to performance art as a form, a genre, which, in turn, can 'perform several functions (for example, denuncia-tion, ritual, discourse on the world and the self)'.[328] The original methods of performance art, 'methods of rupture, fragmentation, and repetition',[329] have become the norm themselves. This view is obviously in contrast to that represented by Mike Pearson, among others. It is one of the debates in the relatively new discipline of Performance Studies. However, the differences between acting for traditional theatre and performance remain striking.

ॐ

6

Non-Western Approaches
to Acting

ಚಿಂಡಿ

Having explored the various approaches to acting that have been adapted over the centuries in the West, it is now appropriate to introduce the approaches taken in the non-West. Taking India, Japan, China and the Islamic countries as examples, I shall devote most of the discussion to India, relating the position of the actor in Indian theatre aesthetics to Indian philosophy. Although a similar depth would be possible for the other countries, too, I have decided against it, since delving into four different philosophies and corresponding mind-sets would be too complicated for such an introductory survey.

The previous chapters have shown how closely the theatre in general, and acting in particular, are related to the time and culture in which they develop: the possible origin of drama in its relation to ritual in Greece, the importance of the death cult for acting in Rome and the revival of theatre in the Middle Ages in the context of religion. I have shown the increasing professionalization of acting from the Renaissance onwards, and demonstrated how the different acting styles, located on a scale of formal versus realistic, are always closely related in theory and practice to the predominant philosophical and scientific beliefs of any particular era.

India

Approaches to acting in India are as complex as those in any other culture, but it is probably fair to say that they are even more firmly rooted in the culture's philosophy, forming an integral part of the main body of texts which constitute Indian philosophy, Veda. This term in the classical Indian language of Sanskrit means *knowledge*. In this chapter, I provide the background information on Indian philosophy in two parts: first, I place theatre and approaches to acting in India within the context of the Veda, and second, I explain the Indian model of the human mind, which is essential for the understanding of Indian ideas about acting.

Veda and the process of creation

Traditional scholarship views the Vedic texts in much the same way as the literature of any culture: 'a collection of works by individuals in different historical periods. It [*sic*] has been interpreted from a variety of perspectives, including historical, cultural, philological, and philosophical, depending on the scholar's interest and background.[1] Scholars often refer to concepts of Indian philosophy as 'speculation'. The orthodox conviction, however, is that Vedic literature was not composed by individual 'authors', but cognized on the level of consciousness by the seer (*rishi*) as 'an eternal, impersonal truth'.[2] As Coward describes:

> The *rishi*'s initial vision is said to be of the Veda as one, as a whole, the entirety of Brahman. This is represented in the *Mandukya-Upanishad* by the mantra AUM, which includes within itself the three levels of ordinary consciousness – waking, dreaming, and deep sleep – yet also reaches out beyond to the transcendent where the sound itself comes to an end.[3]

According to Indian philosophy, the basis of all creation is a field of the Absolute, without qualities itself, but the source of all possible qualities of manifestation. It is infinite, beyond space and time. Viewed from different perspectives, it has been called *Brahman*, *Atman* or *Purusha*. Paradoxically, however, within this absolute, unexpressed level of creation, diverse and distinct qualities exist, and they interact. This interaction process is ultimately responsible for the expression of *Brahman* into all aspects of creation as we experience, observe, know and discover it. All aspects of theatre, too, have their origin in this field of *Brahman*.

The first word of the *Rig-Veda*, often considered the most important text in the Veda, illustrates the principles and stages involved in the process of any kind of creation. The first word of the *Rig-Veda* is *Agnim*. The sound of 'A' represents the fullness of the Absolute, *Brahman*, of unmanifest wholeness. The next sound, 'G', represents the collapse of fullness in a point value. There is a gap between 'A' and 'G', and between this first syllable and the next one, etc. The mechanics of the gap is as follows:

1. The sound value collapses into the point value of the gap. This process is called *Pradhvamsa Abhava*.
2. The silent point of all possibilities within the gap, called *Atyanta Abhava*.
3. The structuring dynamics of what happens in the gap, called *Anyonya Abhava*.
4. The mechanics by which a sound emerges from the point value of the

gap, i.e. the emergence of the following syllable. This is called *Prag Abhava*.[4]

It becomes clear that the mechanism inherent in the first two letters of the *Rig-Veda*, 'A' and 'G', is reflected in the mechanism of the gap: in both cases, fullness collapses to point value. *Atyanta Abhava* is a state of absolute abstraction. As such, it is also called *Purusha*. Paradoxically, it would seem, *Atyanta Abhava* possesses qualities within it which make up its nature, *Prakriti*. The aspect of diversity within *Atyanta Abhava* is called *Ayonya Abhava*.

Originally, that diversity within *Atyanta Abhava* takes the form of an interaction of three elements in unity (*samhita*). The elements are *rishi*, *devata* and *chhandas*. *Rishi* here is not the individual human seer of Vedic literature, but an abstract principle of consciousness: the knower, experiencer, observer or subject. *Devata* corresponds to the process of knowing, experiencing, observing or subject–object relationship. *Chhandas* corresponds to the known, the experienced, the observed or the object. The three components of unity (*samhita*) – subject, subject–object relationship and object (*rishi*, *devata* and *chhandas*) – interact with the unity and among each other. This interaction adopts either an emerging mode, leading out of the gap (the process of *Prag Abhava*), or a submerging mode, leading into the gap (the process of *Pradhvamsa Abhava*).[5]

Creation comes about through an intricate pattern of interactions between the components of the Absolute. The interaction of *samhita* and *rishi*, *devata* and *chhandas* begins on the absolute, unmanifest level. This interaction, even though unmanifest, creates a vibration. The varieties of vibration resulting from the different interactions (*samhita–rishi*; *samhita–devata*; *samhita–chhandas*; *rishi–samhita*; *devata–samhita*; *chhandas–samhita*; *rishi–devata*; *devata–chhandas*; *chhandas–rishi*, etc.) create the different sets of Vedic literature. The interactions also have a direction. The table opposite shows the interactions and the resulting parts of Vedic literature.

All transformations of the *rishi* aspect of the *samhita* are shown in the *Itihasa*, the epics of *Ramayana* and *Mahabharata*. All transformations of the *devata* aspect are portrayed in the *Puranas*, and all aspects of the *chhandas* aspect in the *Smritis*.

Veda initially exists on the level of *Brahman* only, as 'laws of nature' structuring the process of creation. The intricate pattern of interactions on the level of *Brahman* ultimately gives rise to manifest creation. To understand the process of how matter arises from consciousness, it is helpful to note that *Brahman* is called *Purusha*. The primal substance of creation, undifferentiated but with latent full potential of creation, is *Prakriti*, nature. Its governing principles are the three *gunas*: *sattva*, *rajas* and *tamas*:

Aspect	Directed towards	Resulting Vedic literature
Rishi	Samhita	Sama-Veda
Devata	Samhita	Yajur-Veda
Chhandas	Samhita	Atharv-Aveda
Samhita	Rishi	Upanishads
Samhita	Chhandas	Brahmanas

The Six Vedangas

Rishi	Chhandas	Shiksha (phonetics)
Chhandas	Devata	Kalpa (rituals)
Devata	Rishi	Nirukta (semantics)
Rishi	Devata	Vyakaran (grammar)
Devata	Chhandas	Chhandas (metrics)
Chhandas	Rishi	Jyotish (astrology)

The Six Upangas

Kalpa	Samhita	Vaisheshika
Nirukta	Samhita	Samkhya
Vyakaran	Samhita	Yoga
Chhandas	Samhita	Karma Mimansa
Jyotish	Samhita	Vedanta

the entire creation consists of the interplay of the three gunas ... born of prakriti or Nature. The process of evolution is carried on by these three gunas. Evolution means creation and its progressive development, and at its basis lies activity. Activity needs rajo-guna to create a spur, and it needs sato-guna and tamo-guna to uphold the direction of the movement. The nature of tamo-guna is to check or retard, but it should not be thought that when the movement is upwards, tamo-guna is absent. For any process to continue, there have to be steps in that process, and each stage, however small in time and space, needs a force to maintain it and another force to develop it into a new shape. The force that develops it into a new shape is sato-guna, while tamo-guna is that which checks or retards the process in order to maintain the state already produced so that it may form the basis for the next stage.[6]

The first state of evolution, indicating that *Prakriti* moves towards manifestation, is called *mahat*. Its emergence is caused by a disturbance of the state of perfect equilibrium between the three *gunas*. *Mahat* proceeds towards individuation, and the individuation principle is called *ahamkara*. The result of the individuation process is *manas*, the cosmic mind. 'In the state of manas, the urge of prakriti towards manifestation becomes clearly defined.'[7]

The cosmic mind is connected with the manifest world of objects by

the ten senses (*indriyas*), the five senses of perception (*gyanendriya*) –
namely, hearing, touch, seeing, taste and smell – and the five organs of
action (*karmendriya*) – namely, language, ability to take hold of, ability
to walk, discharge and procreation. Subtle matter arises in the next
stage of development: the *tanmatras* constitute

> the five basic realities, or essences, of the objects of the five senses of
> perception. They express themselves in the five elements which go to
> make up the objects of the senses, and which provide the material basis of
> the entire objective universe. Thus the essence of sound (*shabda tanmatra*)
> expresses itself in space, the essence of touch (*sparsha tanmatra*) in air, the
> essence of form (*rupa tanmatra*) in fire, the essence of taste (*rasa tanmatra*) in
> water, and the essence of smell (*gandha tanmatra*) in earth.[8]

The elements that constitute material creation are called *mahabhutas*,
and they are space (*akasha*), air (*vayu*), fire (*tejas*), water (*apas*) and earth
(*prithivi*). From the five elements, all matter is formed. *Ayurveda* describes
how this manifestation continues in the human body. There are three
places 'sandwiched between mind and body, where thought turns into
matter; it is occupied by three operating principles called *doshas*'. The
three *doshas* are *vata*, in control of movement; *pitta*, in control of
metabolism; and *kapha*, in control of structure. *Vata* arises from the
combination of space (*akasha*) and air (*vayu*). *Pitta* is associated with fire
(*tejas*) and water (*apas*), and *kapha* has its origin in water (*apas*) and
earth (*prithivi*). Each main *dosha* consists of five sub *doshas*, each located
in different parts of the body. The following table gives a survey.

Dosha	Sub *dosha*	Location of sub *dosha*
Vata	Prana	brain, head, chest
	Udana	throat and lungs
	Samana	stomach and intestines
	Apana	colon, lower abdomen
	Vyana	throughout the body via the nervous system, skin and circulatory system
Pitta	Pachaka	stomach and small intestine
	Ranjaka	red blood cells, liver, spleen
	Sadhaka	heart
	Alochaka	eyes
	Bhrajaka	skin
Kapha	Kledaka	stomach
	Avalambaka	chest, lungs, lower back
	Bhodaka	tongue
	Tarpaka	sinus cavities, head, spinal fluid
	Shleshaka	joints

The next level of concreteness is cell metabolism, dominated by the thirteen forms of digestive fire, *agni*. Their activity leads to tissues, or *dhatus*, *rasa*, *rakta*, *mamasa*, *meda*, *ashthi*, *majja* and *shukra*. Some sources place *ojas* as the first of these – as the most expressed – or as the last – the most subtle. Indian philosophy holds that *ojas* pervades all *dhatus*. From the tissues, all further levels of the body naturally follow – anatomy, functional systems, etc.

The human physiology taken together is thus an expression of *Brahman*. Just as the Veda is an expression of *Brahman* within the realm of the Absolute, so human physiology and all other objects within and beyond the range of human perception are manifestations of *Brahman*.

Theatre in the Context of Indian Philosophy

The aspect of Vedic literature that deals with theatre is *Gandharva-Veda*. The term is a combination of *Gandharva*, divine musician, and *Veda*, knowledge. It is part of a group of four disciplines, called *Upaveda*, which focuses on four major areas of practical life. Apart from *Gandharva-Veda*, this group comprises *Ayur-Veda* (medicine), *Sthapatya-Veda* (architecture) and *Dhanur-Veda* (politics). *Gandharva-Veda* is closely related to *Ayur-Veda*, representing one of its methods of therapy. *Gandharva-Veda* incorporates the major treatises on music theatre, the *Natyashastra*, ascribed to Bharata, the *Narada-Shiksha* by Narada and the *Sangita-Ratnakara* by Sharngadev. All three texts of *Gandharva-Veda* cover, in various scope, three aspects of music: song (*gitam*), instrumental music (*vadyam*) and dance and theatre arts (*nrittam*). Within the concept of *samhita*, *rishi*, *devata* and *chhandas*, *Gandharva-Veda* as a whole is dominated by the *rishi* element. It also represents the *rishi* element in relation to the four *Upaveda*, with *Ayur-Veda* representing *samhita*, *Dhanur-Veda* representing *devata*, and *Sthapatya-Veda* representing *chhandas*. Within *Gandharva-Veda*, the *Natyashastra* represents the *rishi* value, *Narada-Shiksha* the *devata* and *Sangita-Ratnakara* the *chhandas* value. *Sangita* is the total work of art, combining as *rishi* value *gitam* (song), as *devata* value *vadyam* (instrumental music) and as *chhandas* value *nrittam*, dance and theatre arts.

According to *Gandharva-Veda*, dance originally symbolizes the subtle, rhythmical dynamics of transformations from one note to the other, a manifest expression of unmanifest processes in *samhita* on which the entire creation is based. Primordial sounds are qualities of consciousness. Thus the expressed values of consciousness, the individual dance movements, each represent a specific quality of consciousness.[9] Ideally, the performer will automatically, without any time-lapse between impulse and expression, use the gesture, or combination of gestures, that is the manifest equivalent of the quality of consciousness required in a given situation of performance dictated by the contents of performance and the outer conditions of performance: for example, performance space and audience. The inner dynamics of the primordial sound of *nada* begins to vibrate in every cell, gaining such strength that it finally takes hold of the entire body and causes it to dance.[10] The art of dancing was developed into the art of theatre. The intention of this development was, as described in the *Natyashastra*, to enable people who had lost touch with their unmanifest source to gain familiarity with Vedic truths.

The *Natyashastra*

The *Natyashastra* is the oldest and most comprehensive treatise from India to deal with dance-drama. Any past or existing form of dance-drama in India has its roots in the teachings of the *Natyashastra*, and it will, therefore, serve as the focus of the further discussions in this chapter. Since the *Natyashastra* mentions some other texts and their authors, it must be concluded that other sources existed prior to the *Natyashastra* itself, but no manuscripts of these earlier sources have been found so far. The authorship of the *Natyashastra* is ascribed to Bharata. However, there is no historical evidence outside the *Natyashastra* for his existence. Moreover, several critics argue, based mainly on linguistic studies of the text, that the *Natyashastra* is not a homogeneous composition of one author, but a compilation of dramatic theory and instructions for the actor of how to put the theory into practice. Critics disagree as to whether there was one original text by one author which was changed over the years, or whether the text was, from the beginning, the compilatory effort of several authors. Srinivasan finds an irreducible heterogeneity in the text and argues that 'we have every reason to conclude that these disparate materials are not later accretions to the *Natyashastra* known to us'.[11] A major difficulty in textual matters is that there are many manuscripts of the *Natyashastra* which differ considerably in content, numbering of stanzas and chapters, some even in ascribing the author.[12] As uncertain as the authorship of the *Natyashastra* is its date, placed between the first century BC and the eighth century AD.

These issues of authorship and dating are debated among scholars with a specific understanding of history based on concepts firmly placed within the paradigms of Western philosophy and science. It is important to remember that the *Natyashastra* is an Indian text. Are Western concepts of time and history appropriate in establishing data about a text from a culture in which time, and with it history, are conceptualized quite differently? Contemporary Indian sage and philosopher Maharishi Mahesh Yogi writes that the study of history has a very specific aim in the life of the student or scholar: 'Its aim is to educate the mind of the present with information from the past in order to ensure a better present and a better future.'[13] The emphasis of history is on the importance of events, not on chronology, because of the conceptualization of time as eternal. The following passage provides a rather mind-boggling account of how time is conceptualized in Indian philosophy:

> The eternity of the eternal life of absolute Being is conceived in terms of innumerable lives of the Divine Mother, a single one of whose lives encompasses a thousand life-spans of Lord Shiva. One life of Lord Shiva covers the time of a thousand life-spans of Lord Vishnu. One life of Lord Vishnu equals the duration of a thousand life-spans of Brahma, the Creator. A single life-span of Brahma is conceived in terms of one hundred years of Brahma; each year of Brahma comprises 12 months of Brahma, and each month comprises thirty days of Brahma. One day of Brahma is called a Kalpa. One Kalpa is equal to the time of fourteen Manus. The time of one Manu is called a Manvantara. One Manvantara equals seventy-one Chaturyugis. One Chaturyugi comprises the total span of four Yugas, i.e. Sat-yuga, Treta-yuga, Dvapara-yuga, and Kali-yuga. The span of the Yugas is conceived in terms of the duration of Sat-yuga. Thus the span of Treta-yuga is equal to three quarters of that of Sat-yuga; the span of Dvapara-yuga is half of that of Sat-yuga, and the span of Kali-yuga one quarter that of Sat-yuga. The span of Kali-yuga equals 432,000 years of man's life.[14]

Clearly, any attempt at chronology, given this conceptualization of time, would be counter-productive.

The *Natyashastra* itself conceptualizes the origin of *natya*, performance: the golden age (*Sat-yuga*), characterized by fully developed, enlightened people who knew no suffering, gave way to the silver age (*Treta-yuga*) in which people began to be 'afflicted to the sensual pleasures, were under the sway of desire and greed, became infatuated with jealousy and anger and [thus] found their happiness mixed with sorrow'.[15] To counter the influx of negativity and to allow people to return to their lost state of enlightenment, the gods, with Indra as their leader, approached Brahman, the creator, and asked him to create an 'object of diversion, which must be audible as well as visible'.[16] It had to be accessible to members of all castes – an important qualification, since the four main sets of texts in Vedic literature were not open to be listened to by members of the lowest caste. In response to Indra's request, Brahman created the *Natya-Veda*, taking component parts from the four main Vedic texts. Following the instructions set down in the *Natya-Veda*, according to the *Natyashastra*, will be conducive to

> duty (*dharma*), wealth (*artha*) as well as fame, will contain good counsel and collection [of other materials for human well-being], will give guidance to people of the future as well in all their actions, will be enriched by the teaching of all scriptures (*shastra*) and will give a review of all arts and crafts (*silpa*).[17]

In short, the function of the art described in the *Natyashastra* is to restore full human potential, life in enlightenment.

The scope of the material covered in the *Natyashastra* is vast. There are thirty-six chapters, beginning with the origin of drama, and encompassing dramatic theory as well as practical instructions to the actors on how to achieve aesthetic experiences in the spectators. The term *shastra* implies a holy text, and in the *Natyashastra* itself Bharata claims that *natya*, drama, was created by the creator, Brahman, as a fifth Veda, taking recitative from the *Rig-Veda*, the song from the *Sama-Veda*, the histrionic representation from the *Yajur-Veda* and the sentiments from the *Atharva-Veda*.[18] Thus for the orthodox in India the *Natyashastra* has the combined force and authority of a divinely revealed *shruti*, the sage-expounded *smritis* and the broad-based popular tradition of the *Puranas*.[19] It is therefore no wonder that the *Natyashastra* must still be regarded as the primary source for Indian aesthetics, and indeed all the later Indian theorists of dramaturgy expressly refer to the *Natyashastra*.

The Concept of *Rasa*

The key concept in the aesthetic theory presented in the *Natyashastra* is *rasa*. This term occurs frequently in Vedic texts, where it has various meanings:

> In *Rig Veda* the word, *rasa*, is found occurring in the sense of water ..., Soma juice ..., cow's milk ..., and flavour. The *Atharva-Veda* extends the sense to the sap of grain and the taste, the latter becoming very common. In the *Upanishads rasa* stands for the essence or quintessence and self-luminous consciousness though the sense of taste is at places conveyed ... . In Sanskrit other than the Vedic, the word, *rasa*, is used for water, milk, juice, essence, tasteful liquid, etc.[20]

The material aspect of the meaning of *rasa* is emphasized in *Ayur-Veda*, the ancient Indian system of holistic medicine. Here, *rasa* denotes 'a certain white liquid extracted by the digestive system from the food. Its main seat is the heart',[21] and the *Rasayanashastra* is a treatise on chemistry, which 'moves round the pivot of *rasa*. Mercury, which is called *rasa*, plays here a very important part.'[22] The spiritual aspect of the meaning of *rasa* is emphasized in Shankara's commentary of the Upanishadic use of the term: '*Rasa* is here used to mean such bliss as is innate in oneself and manifests itself ... even in the absence of external aids to happiness. It emphasizes that the bliss is non-material, i.e. intrinsic, spiritual, or subjective.'[23] As such, the experience of *rasa* has been likened to the experiences of yogis by Abhinavagupta, the major commentator on Bharata's *Natyashastra*.

In the context of Indian aesthetics, *rasa* is understood as the actor's and especially the spectator's aesthetic experience. In an aesthetic context, *rasa* is translated as 'sentiment'. The *Natyashastra* differentiates eight sentiments: erotic, comic, pathetic, furious, heroic, terrible, odious and marvellous.[24] Some later writers on Sanskrit poetics add one more *rasa* to this number, *santa*. The concept of *rasa* is phrased in the *Natyashastra* in the form of a short statement, a sutra: *Vibhava-anubhava-vyabhicaribhava-samyogad rasa-nispattih*. The translation is '*Rasa* is produced (*rasa-nispattih*) from a combination (*samyogad*) of Determinants (*vibhava*), Consequents (*anubhava*) and Transitory States (*vyabhicaribhava*)'.[25]

Determinants (*vibhava*) are characterized as situations that cause the emergence of *rasa*. For example, the erotic *rasa*

> has two bases, union ... and separation. ... Of these two, the Erotic Sentiment in union arises from Determinants like the pleasures of the season, the enjoyment of garlands, unguents, ornaments [the company of] beloved persons, objects [of senses], splendid mansions, going to a garden, and enjoying [oneself] there, seeing the [beloved one], hearing [his or her words], playing and dallying [with him or her].[26]

Consequents (*anubhava*) are defined as means of histrionic representation. In the above example, the erotic *rasa* in union should be represented on the stage by 'Consequents such as clever movement of eyes, eyebrows, glances, soft and delicate movement of limbs and sweet words and similar other things'.[27]

The *Natyashastra* lists altogether thirty-three transitory states (*vyabhicaribhava*): discouragement, weakness, apprehension, envy, intoxication, weariness, indolence, depression, anxiety, distraction, recollection, contentment, shame, inconstancy, joy, agitation, stupor, arrogance, despair, impatience, sleep, epilepsy, dreaming, awakening, indignation, dissimulation, cruelty, assurance, sickness, insanity, death, fright and deliberation.[28] In the example of the *rasa* of love, the *Natyashastra* states that 'Transitory States in it do not include fear, indolence, cruelty and disgust'.[29]

To the concern of critics, the *rasa-sutra* on its own appears not to mention all elements that work together to create *rasa*. It does not mention, that is, dominant states (*sthayibhava*) and temperamental states (*sattvikabhava*). The *Natyashastra* lists eight dominant states: love, mirth, sorrow, anger, energy, terror, disgust and astonishment.[30] There are eight temperamental states: 'Paralysis, Perspiration, Horripilation, Change of Voice, Trembling, Change of Colour, Weeping and Fainting.'[31] The text explains the relationship between *rasa* and determinants, consequents, dominant states, transitory states and the temperamental states through an analogy: just as various ingredients such as vegetables and spices, when mixed, produce a flavour, so the combination of the 'Dominant States (*sthayibhava*), when they come together with various other States (*bhava*) attain the quality of the Sentiment'.[32] All the eight sentiments, the eight dominant states, the transitory states and the temperamental states are described in the *Natyashastra* in detail with reference to the determinants, the consequents and their relation to the sentiments.

The *Natyashastra* places much emphasis on the means of histrionic representation (*abhinaya*). They are the techniques used by the actor to portray the consequents: 'From the point of view of the playwright or the character it is *anubhava*, and from that of the actor it is *abhinaya*.'[33] Four kinds of *abhinaya* are differentiated: gestures (*angika*), words (*vacika*), costume and make-up (*aharya*) and the representation of the temperament (*sattvika*). To each of these aspects the *Natyashastra* devotes several chapters. Gestures are treated in chapters on the movements of minor limbs, hands, other limbs, dance movements and gaits. The movements are also specifically related to the space of the stage.[34] *Vacika abhinaya*, representation through words, is covered directly in chapters on prosody, metrical patterns, dictions of play, rules concerning the use of languages, and modes of address and intonation; more indirectly in chapters on the construction of the plot. Yet more chapters provide details about costume and make-up, thus referring to *aharya abhinaya*, while others describe the representation of the temperaments (*sattvika abhinaya*). The means of histrionic representation (*abhinaya*) are variously combined to give rise to four different styles of dramatic performance (*vritti*): the verbal (*bharati*), the grand (*sattvati*), the graceful (*kaisiki*) and the energetic (*arabhati*). Finally, the practice of representation in a dramatic performance is twofold: realistic (*lokadharmi*) and theatrical (*natyadharmi*). The means of histrionic representation, *abhinaya*, belong to the category of *natyadharmi*.

The Actor in the *Natyashastra*

Within this broad scope of material covered in the *Natyashastra*, the actor is regarded as the agent responsible for creating an aesthetic experience, *rasa*, in the audience, which he achieves by his acting skills; thus, the traditional view is that the majority of chapters in the *Natyashastra* represents a 'how-to-do-it' manual for the actor, describing in minute detail all the different techniques of the *abhinaya*, the means of histrionic representation, especially those involving gestures (*angika abhinaya*), costume and make-up (*aharya abhinaya*), representation of the temperament (*sattvika abhinaya*) and the particulars of verbal representation (*vacika abhinaya*). The text contains repeated instructions on how to combine elements of those four performance categories to convey the emotions of the characters to the spectators, to arouse the adequate *rasa* in the spectators.

In the *Natyashastra*, the focal point of the actor's emotional involvement with the character he plays is indeed the representation of the temperament (*sattvika abhinaya*). This mode of representation has its special function in conveying the temperamental states (paralysis, perspiration, horripilation, change of voice, trembling, change of colour, weeping and fainting).[35] In ordinary life, such states are involuntary and would be classified by contemporary Western psychology as directed 'mostly by the effective motor region of our nervous system'.[36] The *Natyashastra*, however, explains that this way of acting is accomplished by concentration of the mind: 'Its nature ... cannot be mimicked by an absent-minded man.' This statement appears to imply that the actor has to fully identify with the character he plays. Identification could then be understood to be equivalent to the concentration of the mind requested in the *Natyashastra* for a satisfactory performance of the temperamental states. However, the *Natyashastra* states in the same paragraph that 'tears and horripilation should respectively be shown by persons who are not [actually] sorry or happy'.[37] This contradicts the requirement of a concentrated mind; it is difficult to understand how the actor's mind can be so concentrated to produce 'real' tears, horripilation, etc. without his involvement in the character's emotions, when it is those emotions that are shown to the spectators as the cause for the tears or horripilation.

This contradiction between involvement and non-involvement has been variously discussed by later commentators and critics of the *Natyashastra* up to the present day. Abhinavagupta, for example, summarizes the positions of Bhatta Lollata and Srisankuka before presenting his own view of the nature of *rasa* and the actor's role in achieving it. According to Bhatta Lollata:

> the aesthetic experience ... is a matter of mere appearance occasioned by false identification. It is analogous to the experience of a man who experiences fear because he erroneously takes a rope for a snake. ... The actor creates an illusion; he is a master of *maya*. The spectators are subject to his *maya* ... [which] is productive of *rasa*.[38]

In creating this illusion, or *maya*, the actor, according to Bhatta Lollata, is identified with the hero, and *rasa* is a characteristic of the character.[39] Srisankuka disagrees with this opinion. Using popular plays about Rama, hero of the Indian epic *Ramayana*, as an example, Srisankuka argues that the actor does not identify with the character, because

> an actor who appears on the stage as Rama is obviously not identical with the real Rama. Nor is he 'non-Rama'. Since the spectators take him to be Rama, he is not different from Rama either. He cannot be said to be 'similar' to Rama since the spectators do not know the real Rama. The cognition involved in the experience 'enacted' Rama is unique.[40]

Abhinavagupta himself regards the actor as an instrument for conveying *rasa* to the spectators. The actor is not involved in the emotions of the character he plays. Moreover, 'the moment he starts enjoying himself and the emotion he is playing he ceases to be an actor and becomes a *sahridaya* [connoisseur of art]'.[41] Abhinavagupta analyses the Sanskrit term for actor, *patra*, to substantiate this point. It means both 'character' and 'carrier-pot'. The first meaning refers to the actor proper. The latter meaning implies that the actor, just as the pot, is only the carrier of relish: 'the kettle does not know the taste of the brew.'[42] Starting with the contradiction in the *Natyashastra*, we find that Bhatta Lollata appears to defend, if vaguely, an identification and involvement, whereas Srisankuka and Abhinavagupta argue against such an involvement. Among contemporary critics, Jhanji points out that 'to say that the actor does not feel anything *qua* himself does not imply that he does not imaginatively reconstruct the emotive experience of the character he portrays'.[43] In support of this argument he mentions Bharata's emphasis on the *sattvika abhinaya*, the means of histrionic representation dealing with the temperamental states. He interprets these means as the 'internalisation of emotive experience on the part of the actor'.[44] This view presents a compromise: Jhanji accepts Abhinavagupta's idea of the actor's non-involvement. He then explains the actor's ability to get his body to function in a mode that is the domain of the involuntary nervous system by reference to the 'internalisation of emotive experience'. However, this concept would need a thorough explanation in itself as to how it might be able to account for the phenomenon it has been used to explain.

In her study of the technique of *abhinaya*, Pandya attempts to explain the actor's ability to present temperamental states with reference to the term *sattvika* and the concept of *sattva*. Thus, she defines *sattva* as 'the capability of an individual to bring into being the pleasures and pains experienced by others, making them his own'.[45] This capability applies to the author, the actor and the spectator. Through *sattva* the author experiences the pleasures and pains of the character he creates and is thus able to draw the character. 'The actor ... with the help of *sattva* makes these experiences his own and presents them on the stage while the sympathetic spectators enjoy the representation through the same medium, i.e. *sattva*.'[46] Dalal interprets *sattva* similarly. Referring to Dhanika, a later Sanskrit theorist of drama and poetry, he states that *sattva* 'is a mental condition which is highly sympathetic to the joys and sorrows of the others'.[47] She adds that this mental state arises when the mind 'is in a state of composure'.[48] Bhat takes both the mental and the physical aspect into account when he defines *sattvika abhinaya* as 'a physical manifestation of a deep mental state'.[49] Marasinghe defines *sattva* as 'a certain law (*dharma*) which governs the expression of the inner state of a person'.[50]

Western critical views of the *Natyashastra*

It has only been in the last half of the twentieth century, following the seminal first full translation of the text into English in 1950, that many Western theatre theorists and artists have discovered the *Natyashastra*. Richard Schechner argues that because it is so 'full of details, of exact descriptions and specifications', it can only be a 'how-to-do-it manual, collectively authored over four or five centuries'.[51] Schechner points out that some theatre 'needs an audience to hear it', while some theatre needs 'spectators to see it'. Indian theatre, however, needs 'partakers to savour it'. Schechner derives this image from the main concept of the *Natyashastra*, *rasa*, which is traditionally translated as flavour or taste: '*Rasa* happens where the experience of the preparers and the partakers meets.' In the context of Schechner's differentiation between transformation and transportation, both performers and spectators are transported; that is, they return to their ordinary state after their shared experience has passed. They are not transformed in the sense of a change that continues after the performance.[52] Schechner also addresses the mechanism of acting, arguing that the practice of proper gestures described in the text arouses the corresponding feelings in the performer; this interpretation is in line with the views developed by Meyerhold in his biomechanics, and with Ekman's research on facial movement and the arousal of autonomous nervous system reactions.

Grotowski had been interested in Eastern philosophy since childhood and first visited India in 1956. He was later influenced by Eugenio Barba, who, when already an unofficial member of Grotowski's Theatre Laboratory, travelled to India in 1963 with 'the vague agenda of finding something of value for his colleagues'.[53] In India, Barba came across the dance-drama form of kathakali, visited the major kathakali training academy in Kerala, the Kalamandalam in Cheruthuruthy, and 'was so impressed by what he saw that he wrote what was then one of the first technical descriptions of the form by a European'.[54] As a result, Grotowski introduced kathakali-based exercises in his training. For Barba's later development, it was not only the exercises themselves that proved important; he was also influenced considerably by the 'dual ethics of intense discipline and regarding theatre as a vocation rather then merely a profession'.[55]

Throughout their intercultural experiment, both Grotowski and Barba avoided merely mimicking kathakali aesthetics. Rather than adopt a foreign system which they understood as completely codified and thus rigid, they aimed to incorporate some of the techniques they found in the 'other' theatre aesthetics to enable further development of their Western actors along the lines they found useful.

Barba derived one of the major concepts of his theatre anthropology from the theatre aesthetics of the *Natyashastra*. The *Natyashastra* differentiates between *lokadharmi* and *natyadharmi*, realistic and theatrical forms of representation; on this basis, Barba developed his concepts of daily behaviour (equivalent, in his view, to *lokadharmi*), and extra-daily, performative behaviour (equivalent, Barba argues, to *natyadharmi*). A close look at the *Natyashastra*, however, shows that this parallel is limited. In the text, both terms refer to practices of representation which can be employed in performance. The realistic style, *lokadharmi*, is defined as follows:

> If a play depends on natural behaviour [in its characters] and is simple and not artificial, and has in its [plot] professions and activities of the people and has [simple acting and] no playful flourish of limbs and depends on men and women of different types, it is called realistic (*lokadharmi*).[56]

These two verses are followed by twelve verses on *natyadharmi*, providing a detailed description of the particular circumstances in which theatrical representation is appropriate. The emphasis on *natyadharmi* might lead to the conclusion that it is more important in *natya* than *lokadharmi*, and indeed all the numerous descriptions of the means of histrionic representation (*abhinaya*) in the *Natyashastra* belong to the category of *natyadharmi*. However, whatever the emphasis, *lokadharmi* is part of the actor's theatrical practice. Although it is thus possible to differentiate daily from extra-daily behaviour on the basis of the concepts of *lokadharmi* and *natyadharmi*, the important difference is that in Barba's theory, daily behaviour lies outside the realm of performance; even more, it is the kind of behaviour that the performer has to *overcome* to become a good actor. In contrast, *lokadharmi* and *natyadharmi* both pertain to the performance.

Grotowski eventually became disillusioned with non-Western theatre practices, concluding that 'their aesthetic is completely alien to me. I do not think we can adopt from them any techniques, or that they could inspire us directly'.[57] In this context, Brook seems to have shifted in a similar direction. At the time of producing *The Mahabharata*, he referred to it as the 'great history of mankind', informed by the concept of *dharma*. During a talk in London some years later, he characterized the epic as an instruction manual for a young prince about the skills of being a good ruler.[58]

Kramer has tried to compare the theatre aesthetics of the *Natyashastra* with Stanislavsky's system, acknowledging that drawing such parallels makes no claim at establishing direct influence. According to Kramer, the determinant (*vibhava*) causes a specific emotional state (*bhava*), which in turn causes a consequent (*anubhava*). This, according to Kramer, parallels Stanislavsky: 'given circumstances cause emotions cause behavior.'[59] The assumptions on which Kramer bases his parallels, however, require a reassessment. The causal chain 'determinants–

emotional state–consequents' is not appropriate. Rather, the mechanism is as follows: in specific situations laid down in the play (determinants), the actor has to use specific means of histrionic representation (consequents) to create specific dominant emotional states (*sthayibhava*). These dominant emotional states combine with transitory states (*vyabhicaribhava*) and temperamental states (*sattvikabhava*). The end product of this combination process is the aesthetic experience, *rasa*. Although Stanislavsky comes close, the parallel as argued by Kramer cannot be maintained.

Kramer links the temperamental states *sattvikabhava* to Stanislavsky's 'magic if' and 'sense of truth', since *sattva* can be understood, he argues, as 'the mental capacity of the actor to identify himself with the character and his feelings'.[60] Similarly, the 'magic if' or 'sense of truth' allows 'the actor to convince himself that the circumstances are real to the character, even though, as an actor, he knows that they are not'.[61] The discussion of the concept of *sattva* has shown, however, that, whatever its exact definition, it certainly refers to a state of mind that is beyond the emotions, the field of operation of the 'magic if'.

The comparison of aesthetic concepts and theories of acting in the *Natyashastra* and in Stanislavsky's system was inspired by the apparent influence that Indian philosophy had on Stanislavsky. Kramer's essay highlights the difficulties of this approach: scholarship currently lacks a consistent model of human consciousness, of the human mind, that allows a precise understanding of the assumptions of consciousness informing the aesthetics of the *Natyashastra*, and thus enables a coherent comparison with Stanislavsky's concepts.

The majority of current attempts at making sense of Indian theatre aesthetics, especially the concept and experience of *rasa*, are based on Western concepts of the mind. In the next part of this chapter, the Indian concept of the mind is introduced to provide an appropriate background against which it is possible to further understand Indian theatre aesthetics. In particular, the following issues have to be addressed:

1. Is the actor to be emotionally involved or not while acting? On the current understanding – that is, without taking the Indian model of the mind into account, the *Natyashastra* is not conclusive on this subject. In requesting the actor to be of utmost concentrated mind, it appears to suggest involvement. In stating that the temperamental states (*sattvikabhava*) should be shown by persons (i.e. actors) who are not actually feeling the emotions that cause those states, the text appears to suggest emotional non-involvement on the part of the actor.

2. How exactly does the actor achieve (the process of *sattvika abhinaya*) the histrionic representation of those temperamental states? The problem here is that the temperamental states belong to the domain of the autonomous nervous system. This part of the nervous system is in charge of involuntary neuro-muscular activities, commonly understood to be beyond the influence of the will. How could an actor influence this domain, irrespective of whether or not he is emotionally involved in the emotions of the character he is portraying?

3. A brief survey of previous attempts to clarify the problem raised in item 2 suggests that major importance will have to be placed on an adequate interpretation of the concept of *sattva* in its different occurrences in the technical terms used in the *Natyashastra* and later Indian aesthetics, such as *sattvika abhinaya* and *sattvikabhava*.

4. In this context, the frame-concept of the entire *Natyashastra*, *rasa*, has to be reassessed, especially regarding the following sub-areas of interest:

   (a) What is the nature of the aesthetic experience called *rasa*?

   (b) What importance does the number of *rasas* have on the understanding of the *rasa*-concept in general, and with reference to items 1 to 3 stated above? In detail this means an investigation of

   - whether there is a difference in concept between the eight sentiments (erotic, comic, pathetic, etc.), originally found in the *Natyashastra* and the ninth sentiment later added to that enumeration;
   - whether there is a difference in concept between the eight or individual sentiments in the *Natyashastra* and later additions, rendered as *rasa*-s, and the eight or nine *rasa*-s and one *rasa* in the singular, on a different (possibly hierarchically higher) conceptual level.

   (c) Is the spectator's aesthetic experience as described by the concept of *rasa* like, equal to or unlike the spiritual experience of a yogi? Is there any parallel between an actor's experience while acting and the spectator's? Is there a spiritual dimension involved in acting that mirrors the yogic practices that lead to yogic experiences?

Based on a thorough discussion of items 1 to 4, the meanings of the crucial terms in the *rasa-sutra* – *samyogad*, traditionally rendered as 'combination', and *nispattih*, traditionally rendered as 'produced' – have to be subjected to a reassessment.

The Model of Consciousness in Indian Philosophy

From our own experience we can distinguish three states of consciousness: waking, dreaming and sleeping. They are the 'normal' states of
consciousness. The term 'normal' needs further explanation, however.
What is 'normal' is 'defined by society and it is society's standards of
perceptual normalcy that are part of an individual's personality'.[62]
Normal states of consciousness, then, are what society agrees to be the
norm, the ordinary. Non-ordinary states of consciousness are referred to
as 'altered states of consciousness' (ASC). In one of the first attempts to
account for ASC, Ludwig describes their general characteristics. They
include alterations in thinking, a disturbed time sense, a loss of control,
changes in emotional experiences, a change of body images, perceptual
distortions, changes in meaning or significance, a sense of the ineffable, a
feeling of rejuvenation, and hypersuggestibility.[63] Ludwig also lists
major ways of inducing ASC, and discusses their functions.[64] It is
revealing that he supports seven maladaptive expressions by empirical
evidence, but mentions only three adaptive expressions (healing,
avenues of new knowledge and experience, social function).[65] This
emphasis on the negative attributes of ASC is in line with Tart's claim
that orthodox psychology regards ASC as 'a temporary reorganization
of brain functioning', and holds that 'our ordinary state of consciousness
is generally the most adaptive and rational way the mind can be
organized, and virtually all ASC are inferior or pathological', that going
into ASC spontaneously is a sign of mental illness, and 'deliberately
cultivating ASC is also a sign of psychopathology'.[66] This view,
formulated in 1975, is supported by the choice of contents in an
annotated bibliography on 'States of Awareness', which lists articles on
subjects such as depersonalization, sleepwalking, amnesia, anaesthesia,
thyroid disorders, near-death experience, déjà-vu, out-of-body experiences and sensory deprivation, many of which would feature in
psychopathology.[67]

However, serious attempts can be found to account for and explain
desirable and adaptive ASC. Clark constructs a map of mental states,
similar to a map in geography. His incorporation of states of mental
illness necessitates the inclusion of some extra variables such as 'Anxiety;
Obsessions; Compulsions; Phobias; Irritability; Hallucinations; Delu-
sions; Pain; Disorientation; Anger; Fear; Guilt; Repugnance; Boredom;
Depersonalization; Derealization'.[68] However, as opposed to other
researchers writing about states of consciousness, Clark also incorporates
desirable, 'higher' mental states in his map. For this purpose, he
discusses mysticism, which 'concerns an unusual kind of experience
obtained other than by the senses'.[69] Clark identifies seven main ideas in
the content of mystical states, and relates those to some faculties of the
mind:[70]

Seven main ideas (aspects of mind)		Faculty
K	Knowledge, significance	
U	Unity, belongingness	
E	Eternity, eternal now, being	Cognition
L	Light, exteroception	
B	Body sense, interoception	Perception
J	Joy	Emotion
F	Freedom	Volition

Clark also extracts certain recurrent comments on mystical states from the writings by the mystics. They are intensity, certainty, clarity, ineffability, sudden onset and change of personality.[71] Finally, he differentiates between an average state, a state of peak experience (expressly borrowing the term from Maslow) and the mystical state proper (which is more intensive than the peak experience, but still possible to describe in words).[72] The climax of a transition from average state to peak experience to mystical experience proper is referred to as the 'Void'. Clark describes it as ineffable, and 'a place of sudden transition',[73] and associates it with the Buddhist concept of *Nirvana*.

The attempt to provide consciousness with a basis is found in studies of the phenomenon of pure consciousness, the mystical state proper in Clark's terminology. The term 'pure consciousness' is similar to that used by Stace to describe the extraordinary state of consciousness reported by saints and sages throughout the ages: 'pure unitary consciousness'.[74] Also in the context of mysticism, Forman edited a collection of essays explicitly dealing with 'Pure Consciousness Events (PCE)', defined as 'wakeful though contentless (nonintentional) consciousness'.[75] Placing the PCE within Stace's framework, Forman considers them as a form of what

> W.T. Stace called 'introvertive mysticism', which he distinguished from 'extrovertive mysticism'. In extrovertive mysticism one perceives a new relationship – one of unity, blessedness, reality ... – between the external world and the self. In introvertive mysticism there is no awareness of the external world *per se*; the experience is of the Self itself.[76]

Forman describes the current 'received view' on all kinds of mystical experiences, including PCEs, as 'constructivism', which argues that

> mystical experience is significantly shaped and formed by the subject's beliefs, concepts and expectations. This view, in turn, emerged as a response to the so-called perennial philosophy school. Perennialists – notably William James, Evelyn Underhill, Joseph Maréchal, William Johnston, James Pratt, Mircea Eliade, and W.T. Stace – maintained that

mystical experience represented an immediate, direct contact with a (variously defined) absolute principle. Only after that immediate contact with the 'something more', according to this school, is such a direct contact *interpreted* according to the tradition's language and beliefs.[77]

In the book, Forman assembles articles that argue in favour of the existence of PCEs, by looking at yoga, Buddhist philosophy, the writings of Meister Eckhart and Jewish mysticism. The articles in the second part of the book argue that 'constructivism has not, and cannot plausibly account for these experiences'.[78]

Forman also provides two descriptions of the experience of pure consciousness. The first recounts the experience of a subject who has just received instruction in the transcendental meditation technique:

> I distinctly recall the first day of instruction [in the transcendental meditation technique], my first clear experience of transcending. Following the instruction of the teacher, without knowing what to expect, I began to drift down into deeper and deeper levels of relaxation, as if I were sinking into my chair. Then, for some time, perhaps for a minute or a few minutes, I experienced a silent inner state of no thoughts; just pure awareness and nothing else; then again I became aware of my surroundings. It left me with a sense of deep ease, inner renewal, and happiness.[79]

Forman comments: 'It is striking that the subject notes that he did not "know what to expect", for this tends to support the claim that one may have a PCE even without the purportedly shaping expectations.'[80] The second report demonstrates how the experiences deepen in the course of time:

> After about two years, my experience of the transcendent started to become clearer. At that time, I would settle down, it would be very quiet . . . and then I would transcend, and there would be just a sort of complete silence void of content. The whole awareness would turn in, and there would be no thought, no activity, and no perception, and yet it was somehow comforting. It was just there and I could know when I was in it. There wasn't a great 'Oh, I am experiencing this'. It was very natural and innocent. But I did not yet identify myself with this silent, content-free inner space. It was a self-contained entity that I transcended to and experienced.
>
> Then, with increased familiarity and contingent on the amount of rest I had, the process of transcending became more and more natural. The whole physiology was now accustomed to just slipping within, and at some point it would literally 'click', and with that, the breath would almost cease, the spine would become straight, and the lungs would cease to move. There would be no weight anywhere in the body, the whole physiology was at rest. At this point I began to appreciate that this inner space was not an emptiness but simply silent consciousness without content or activity, and I began to recognise in it the essence of my own self as pure consciousness. Eventually, even the thin boundary that had

previously separated individuality from unbounded pure consciousness began to dissolve. The 'I' as a separate entity just started to have no meaning. The boundaries that I put on myself became like a mesh, a net; it became porous and then dissolved; only unbroken pure consciousness or existence remains. Once I let go of the veil of individuality, there is no longer 'I perceiving' or 'I aware'. There is only that, there is nothing else there. In this state the experiencer is not experiencing as it normally does. It is there ready to experience, but the function has ceased. There is not thought, there is no activity, there is no experiencer, but the physiology after that state is incredible. It is like a power surge of complete purity.[81]

The theory and practice of Indian philosophy maintains that the human nervous system enables the direct experience of pure consciousness at the basis of creation as the *samhita* of *rishi*, *devata* and *chhandas*. In asserting this possibility, Indian philosophy is in line with the mystics and those who, like Forman, accept their experiences as real and natural. Unlike the mystics, Indian philosophy holds that through mental techniques which can be learned easily, everyone can have this experience, not merely a few isolated individuals.

Gelderloos and Beto argue that the characteristics of pure consciousness as defined by Indian philosophy are similar to the characteristics of 'pure unitary consciousness' as described by Stace:[82]

1. EGO QUALITY: refers to the experience of loss of self while consciousness is nevertheless maintained. The loss of self is commonly experienced as an absorption into something greater than the mere empirical ego. Indian philosophy differentiates between self – the individual ego, the core of personality – and Self – or pure consciousness. When pure consciousness is experienced, the self 'is not lost; it rather becomes expanded toward a higher dignity ...'.

2. UNIFYING QUALITY: refers to the experience of the multiplicity of objects of perception as nevertheless united. Everything is in fact perceived as 'One'. Pure consciousness is experienced as one field of consciousness underlying all manifestations. Pure consciousness is beyond any perception. Therefore, Indian philosophy holds that the perception of unity in diversity is not characteristic of the experience of pure consciousness on its own. Rather, only when the unity of pure consciousness 'becomes carried over into the field of diversity' will the resulting experience be that of perceiving 'the multiplicity of objects of perception as nevertheless united'.

3. INNER SUBJECTIVE QUALITY: refers to the perception of an inner subjectivity to all things, even those usually experienced in purely material forms. Pure consciousness is regarded as inner subjectivity. After it has been experienced on the transcendental level – that is, in its pure form without any contents – it is afterwards

sequentially experienced 'in more and more expressed levels of consciousness, feelings, thinking, senses'.

4. TEMPORAL/SPATIAL QUALITY: refers to the temporal spatial parameters of the experience. Essentially both time and space are modified with the extreme being one of an experience that is both 'timeless' and 'spaceless'. Pure consciousness is experienced as being beyond time and space. In parallel to the unified field described in quantum physics, it is timeless, unbounded, omnipresent and the source of all diversification.

5. NOETIC QUALITY: refers to the experience as valid knowledge. Emphasis is on a non-rational, intuitive, insightful experience that is nevertheless recognized as not merely subjective. Indian philosophy takes up a concept developed by Patanjali in his definition of *samadhi* (pure consciousness) in his *Yoga Sutras*. This implies that a fully developed person can function from a level of consciousness termed *ritam bhara pragya*, 'the level that knows only the truth'. It is a level just this side of pure consciousness, on the finest level of manifestation. Knowledge gained on this level is gained 'directly, without the intermediacy of *indriyas* [senses] or *manas* [mind]'.

6. INEFFABILITY: refers to the impossibility of expressing the experience in conventional language . The experience simply cannot be put into words due to the nature of the experience itself and not to the linguistic capacity of the subject. Indian philosophy fully agrees with this finding: 'although pure consciousness can be experienced daily, it cannot be expressed in words, it is beyond speech and thoughts.'

7. POSITIVE AFFECT: refers to the positive affect quality of the experience. Typically the experience is of joy or blissful happiness. Indian philosophy classifies affect as an expressed form of consciousness. Because pure consciousness is unexpressed, it cannot be 'appreciated by emotion'. The experience of pure consciousness is nonetheless later described in terms of 'bliss or ultimate contentment'.

8. RELIGIOUS QUALITY: refers to the intrinsic sacredness of the experience. This includes feelings of mystery, awe and reverence that may nevertheless be experienced independently of traditional religious language. Indian philosophy explains that 'for many people an experience of the highest magnificence like the experience of the Absolute is appreciated with awe and reverence'. Such an experience is then likely to be described and interpreted in religious terms. Indian philosophy appreciates the religious quality of the experience. In agreement with Stace's assumption that the religious quality 'may be experienced independently of traditional religious language', Indian philosophy 'highlights the universal

nature of the experience of pure consciousness, emphasizing the scientifically verifiable reality of the Vedic perspective'.

Indian philosophy proposes 'an architecture of increasingly abstract, functionally integrated faculties or levels of mind'.[83] This hierarchy ranges from gross to subtle, from highly active to settled, from concrete to abstract, and from diversified to unified. The senses constitute the grossest, most highly active, most concrete and most diversified level of the mind, followed by desire, the thinking mind, the discriminating intellect, feeling and intuition, and the individual ego. Indian philosophy, in this context, uses the term 'mind' in two ways: 'It refers to the overall multilevel functioning of consciousness as well as to the specific level of thinking (apprehending and comparing) within that overall structure.' Underlying the subtlest level, that of the individual ego, and transcendental to it, is the Self, 'an abstract, silent, completely unified field of consciousness'. Each subtler level is able to 'observe and monitor the more expressed levels'.[84]

Indian philosophy does not stop at describing the interrelationship of the elements of consciousness and pure consciousness as their source. In answer to the question 'What are the highest possible forms of human development?',[85] Indian philosophy proposes that it is possible not only to have occasional experiences of higher states of consciousness as described by the mystics, or called 'peak experiences' by Maslow, but also to systematically develop such more advanced states of consciousness as phenomena of permanent daily experience. The exploration of adulthood has only recently attracted 'significant attention from developmental psychologists'.[86] The focal point of the emerging theories is the relationship of proposed models of higher stages of human development to the seminal theory of cognitive development advanced by Jean Piaget. He differentiated distinct developmental stages, leading to an endpoint termed 'formal operations':

> For him [Piaget], formal operations is the culmination of cognitive development: there is no further development of the organisational form of thought beyond this stage; remaining changes are in terms of increased competence with formal operations and their more comprehensive application in the accumulation of greater knowledge.[87]

The developmental stage of formal operations is normally attained, according to Piaget, during the teen years. It thus belongs to 'preadult development, even though full facility in this mode of thinking may not develop until adulthood – or may never develop'.[88]

Alexander holds that assessing the possibilities of adult development beyond Piaget's stage of formal operations involves three related issues: 'Does development towards the endpoint proceed through qualitatively distinct stages? What mechanisms underlie this development? What major areas get developed (e.g. cognition and affect), and how do they interrelate?'[89] Alexander differentiates non-hierarchical and hierarchical theories, theories of advanced moral development, and theories of consciousness and self-development.[90] The concepts of adult development proposed by Indian philosophy fall into the last category.

Based on the proposition to regard pure consciousness as a fourth state of consciousness next to the commonly known and experienced ones – waking, dreaming and sleeping – Indian philosophy describes three further stages of consciousness development. Termed 'cosmic consciousness', a fifth state of consciousness is characterized by the co-existence of waking, or dreaming, or sleeping, and pure consciousness. In cosmic consciousness, the level of pure consciousness, which is never overshadowed in daily experience by the activities and experiences of the individual psyche, becomes a 'stable internal frame of reference from which changing phases of sleep, dreaming, and waking life are silently *witnessed* or observed'.[91] The following is a description of witnessing dreaming:

> Often during dreaming I am awake inside, in a very peaceful, blissful state. Dreams come and go, thoughts about the dreams come and go, but I remain in a deeply peaceful state, completely separate from the dreams and the thoughts. My body is asleep and inert, breathing goes on regularly and mechanically, and inside I am just aware that I am.[92]

This double nature of experience – pure consciousness witnessing the activities of waking, dreaming and sleeping – is not equivalent to an uncomfortable dissociation or split personality, as evident, for example, in Thoreau's description in *Walden* of occasionally 'witnessing' his own thoughts and feelings:

> I only know myself as a human entity; the scene, so to speak, of thoughts and affections; and am sensible of a certain doubleness by which I can stand as remote from myself as from another. However intense my experience, I am conscious of the presence and criticism of part of me, which, as it were, is not a part me, but spectator, sharing no experience, but taking note of it: and that is no more I than is you. When the play ... of life is over, the spectator goes his way. It was a kind of fiction, a work of imagination only, as far as he was concerned.[93]

Referring to a contemporary woman athlete, Billie Jean King, Alexander points out that 'witnessing' as an experience characteristic of cosmic consciousness is not limited to quiet moments. King experienced 'witnessing' during a tennis match and describes it in relation to 'its value for spontaneous right action and personal fulfilment':

> I can almost feel it coming. It usually happens on one of those days when everything is just right. ... It almost seems as though I'm able to transport myself beyond the turmoil of the court to some place of total peace and calm. Perfect shots extend into perfect matches. ... I appreciate what my

opponent is doing in a detached abstract way. Like an observer in the next room. ... It is a perfect combination of [intense] action taking place in an atmosphere of total tranquility. When it happens I want to stop the match and grab the microphone and shout that's what it's all about, because it is. It's not the big prize I'm going to win at the end of the match or anything else. It's just having done something that's totally pure and having experienced the perfect emotion.[94]

The next stage of development, according to Indian philosophy, is called 'refined cosmic consciousness'. In cosmic consciousness, the field of pure consciousness is permanently experienced together with waking, or dreaming or sleeping. This level of functioning is maintained in refined cosmic consciousness and 'combined with the maximum value of perception of the environment. Perception and feeling reach their most sublime level'.[95] The British poet Kathleen Raine's description of her experience of seeing a hyacinth is suggestive of this state of refined cosmic consciousness as predicted by Indian philosophy:

I dared scarcely to breathe, held in a kind of fine attention in which I could sense the very flow of life in the cells. I was not perceiving the flower but living it. I was aware of the life of the plant as a slow flow or circulation or a vital current of liquid light of the utmost purity. I could apprehend as a simple essence formal structure and dynamic process. This dynamic form was, as it seemed, of a spiritual not a material order; or of a finer matter, or of matter itself perceived as spirit. There was nothing emotional about this experience which was, on the contrary, an almost mathematical apprehension of a complex and organised whole, apprehended as whole, this whole was living; and as such inspired by a sense of immaculate holiness. ... By 'living' I do not mean that which distinguishes animal from plant or plant from mineral, but rather a quality possessed by all these in their different degrees.[96]

The final level of human development according to Indian philosophy is called 'unity consciousness'. In this state of consciousness, 'the highest value of self-referral is experienced'. The field of pure consciousness is directly perceived as located at every point in creation, and thus 'every point in creation is raised to the ... status' of pure consciousness. 'The gap between the relative and absolute aspects of life ... is fully eliminated'.[97] The experiencer experiences himself and his entire environment in terms of his own nature, which he experiences to be pure consciousness. Gustave Flaubert describes a transient experience that suggests this state in the 1849–1858 version of his novel *The Temptation of St Anthony*:

It is true, often I have felt that something bigger than myself was fusing with my being: bit by bit I went off into the greenery of the pastures and into the current of the rivers that I watched go by; and I no longer knew where my soul was, it was so diffuse, universal, spread out. ... Your mind itself finally lost the notion of particularity which kept it on the alert. It was like an immense harmony engulfing your soul with marvellous palpitations, and you felt in its plenitude an inexpressible comprehension of the unrevealed wholeness of things; the interval between you and the object, like an abyss closing, grew narrower and narrower, until the difference vanished, because you both were bathed in infinity; you penetrated each other equally, and a subtle current passed from you into matter while the life of the elements slowly pervaded you, rising like a sap: one degree more, and you would have become nature, or nature become you ... immortality, boundlessness, infinity. I have all that, I am that! I feel myself to be Substance, I am Thought! ... I understand, I see, I breathe, in the midst of plenitude ... how calm I am![98]

Consciousness and the Actor

Theatre, in the sense of dance-drama, functions not only on the level of symbolism of theatrical action but also through language (*vacika abhinaya*), costume and make-up (*aharya*) and representation of the temperament (*sattvika-abhinaya*). Costume and make-up will function mainly through the sense of sight, affecting the emotions. The symbolic nature of theatre affects mainly the intellect. Gestures (*angika abhinaya*) function through the sense of sight, and language through the sense of hearing. Both gestures and language arise from the level of pure consciousness, and will ultimately affect the spectator on that very same level of pure consciousness. The fully developed actor, then, achieves his effects on the spectator by stimulating the spectator's senses, intellect and emotions; both through stimulating all these, and unmediated, the actor reaches to the spectator's Self, pure consciousness, which is the ultimate target of his art and skill. In meditation, the aim might be to reach the experience of pure consciousness on its own. However, as we have seen, Indian philosophy holds that the ultimate aim of meditation is not pure consciousness on its own, but the co-existence of pure consciousness with waking, or dreaming or sleeping, a state called cosmic consciousness, which develops further to refined cosmic consciousness and ultimately unity consciousness. What theatre in the Vedic sense aspires to is to provide the spectators with experiences of at least cosmic consciousness, initially only lasting for a short time, eventually longer. Repeated exposure to Vedic theatre will train the mind to experience naturally pure consciousness together with sensory impressions.

One of the characteristics of pure consciousness, or *sat chit ananda* – absolute (*sat*) bliss (*ananda*) consciousness (*chit*) – is bliss. Any experience of pure consciousness will have that quality. Thus the specific experience in the theatre, an aesthetic experience, if it allows the spectator's mind to reach pure consciousness, will suffuse the impressions gained by the senses with the underlying quality of bliss. Neither the sensory impressions nor the bliss, however, will overshadow the Self: when the spectator experiences temporary cosmic consciousness while watching a play, his Self is separate from the sensory impressions, and bliss is a quality of the Self itself. In cases of temporary experiences of unity consciousness through the stimuli of the performance, the spectator will experience the events acted on the stage, the actors and even fellow-spectators as expressions of the same pure consciousness that also forms his own basis. There is an experience of unity, all in terms of the Self, which is not overshadowed.

The nature of the aesthetic experience, *rasa*, is thus the experience of pure consciousness together with performance-specific theatrical contents of the mind (in the broad definition of Indian philosophy). Through repeated exposure to the experience of pure consciousness, brought about by the actor's art, the spectator's consciousness is trained to uphold pure consciousness for longer periods of time, ultimately indefinite, not only in subsequent theatrical performances but also in daily life outside the theatre. The *Natyashastra*'s claim of its original purpose, to restore the golden age which had given way to the silver, thus becomes more than a rhetorical claim for usefulness.

Rasa has been redefined from the spectator's perspective as a combination of blissful pure consciousness and the specific impressions on the mind provided by a theatrical performance. Abhinavagupta held that the actor does not experience *rasa* himself. From the point of view of Indian philosophy, this assumption needs a reassessment. What affects the spectator are the actor's means of histrionic representation: gestures, words, representation of temperament and costume and make-up. For the enlightened actor, gestures and words, it has been shown, will proceed spontaneously from his pure consciousness, transforming themselves without time-lapse into objective expression, which is then subjectively experienced by the spectator, affecting his senses, intellect, emotions and, through those, his pure consciousness. Pure consciousness has been shown to be a field that connects all individuals. If the actor, then, operates from the level of pure consciousness, he will affect the spectator not only on the expressed levels of the mind but also directly on the level of pure consciousness. The enlightened actor has the continuous experience of the bliss characteristic of pure consciousness. If he produces from within that pure consciousness the expressed means of histrionic representation, he combines bliss with expressions of *abhinaya*, which make up the experience of *rasa*. Thus the actor establishes *rasa* within himself in the process of stimulating the experience of *rasa* in the spectator.

In Bharata's *Natyashastra*, eight *rasas* are mentioned: the erotic, comic, pathetic, furious, heroic, terrible, odious and marvellous.[99] A ninth *rasa* is added to this list by later theorists, *santa rasa*, whose characteristics match the descriptions of pure consciousness as contentless: the individual experiencing *santa rasa* feels 'the same', i.e. nothing, 'towards all creatures'. There is no pain, no happiness, no hatred and no envy. The effects that experiencing *santa rasa* bring to the spectator are 'happiness and welfare', 'highest happiness', 'stabilization of the Self'. The ingredients leading to the experience of *santa rasa* are also related to the process of gaining liberation (*moksha*): the dominant emotion (*sthayibhava*), the determinants (*vibhava*), the consequents (*anubhava*) and the transitory states (*vyabhicaribhava*).

Santa rasa is called the natural state of the mind, in the sense that it is the basis of all other states. Seen from the perspective of Indian philosophy, *santa rasa* is equivalent to the experience of pure consciousness evoked in actor and spectator through theatre; the other eight *rasas* represent the influence of the expressed stimuli of theatre, leading to an aesthetic experience dominated by love, mirth, sorrow, anger, energy, terror, disgust and astonishment.[100] The fully developed actor is best able to create *santa rasa* and a specific expressed *rasa* in the spectator. Again the assumption applies that the actor, too, not only the spectator, experiences *rasa*.

These considerations necessitate a reassessment of the *rasa-sutra*: *Vibhava-anubhava-vyabhicaribhava-samyogad rasa-nispattih*. The translation provided by Ghosh is: '*Rasa* is produced (*rasa-nispattih*) from a combination (*samyogad*) of Determinants (*vibhava*), Consequents (*anubhava*) and Transitory States (*vyabhicaribhava*).'[101] Ghosh translates the term *vibhava* from the expressed context of the theatrical situation as 'determinant', given situations found in the playtext in which specific means of histrionic representation have to be used. In view of the fact that *santa rasa* is pure consciousness, and taking into consideration that *vibhava* also means 'pure consciousness',[102] the use of the term *vibhava* in the context of the *Natyashastra* refers to situations structured as possibilities in the dynamism of pure consciousness. Such latent situations, present as potentialities on the level of pure consciousness, take their shape in the theatrical context as *anubhava*. Ghosh again renders this term on the expressed level as 'consequent', means of histrionic representation doing justice to the 'Determinants'. *Anubhava* also means the experience of multitude after arising from pure consciousness.[103] In other words, the potentialities of *vibhava* are experienced by the actor and in turn by the spectator as taking a specific shape in the theatrical context. Manifestation progresses further by 'adding the ingredient' of *vyabhicaribhava*, translated by Ghosh as 'transitory states [of emotion]'. Indeed, *vyabhicaribhava* means the spreading and the expression of that experience of multitude implied by *anubhava*.[104] *Samyogad* has been translated by Ghosh as 'combination', taking recourse to the illustration provided by the *Natyashastra* itself, which compares the functioning of the different elements in creating *rasa* to adding diverse ingredients to cook delicious food. *Samyogad*, however, means not so much a combination, an adding together, but implies a unity.[105] Only when pure consciousness (*vibhava*), the experience of the multitude after coming out of pure consciousness (*anubhava*) and the spreading, or expression of that experience, form a unity will *rasa* be produced in actor and spectator alike.

To summarize: *rasa* is an aesthetic experience for both actor and spectator, consisting of the co-existence of pure consciousness with aesthetic, theatre/performance-specific contents, sensory impressions, stimuli for the mind, the intellect and the emotions. As time is non-existent on the level of pure consciousness, the basis of theatrical activity in the case of the enlightened actor, the creation of *rasa* in the actor will be simultaneous with the stimuli emitted by the actor that create *rasa* in the spectator. The time-lapse between the onset of those stimuli and their taking effect in the consciousness of the spectator, and the degree to which they take effect, depends on the 'openness' of the spectator's consciousness. Repeated exposure to such experiences will train the spectator in responding to *rasa*-inducing stimuli faster, and to a more intense degree. In due course, experiences of pure consciousness together with other (that is, not necessarily aesthetic) contents of the expressed mind will be the natural consequence of the training process.

So far, this chapter has shown the relation of the roots of Indian theatre, as discussed in the *Natyashastra*, to Indian philosophy in general, and Indian philosophy of consciousness in particular. Compared with the majority of Western approaches to acting, a striking picture emerges. Through acting, the actor himself may achieve a state of enlightenment and perfection not only in his art while performing but also in everyday life. Through the actor, the spectators, too, are trained in maintaining a higher state of consciousness not only for the duration of the performance (transportation) but also in daily life before and after the performance (transformation). The minute details of acting technique presented in the *Natyashastra* function on two levels: they represent a description of what an enlightened actor does to create specific aesthetic-spiritual experiences in the audience, and they provide a training guide for the non-enlightened actor (apprentice) to gain enlightenment himself.

According to Subrahmanyam, all existing forms of performance in India have their origin in the *Natyashastra*.[106] Differences can be explained by the varying emphasis on any one or several of the four elements of histrionic representation: namely, gesture, voice, costume and make-up and representation of temperament. Socio-political factors have contributed to a temporary diminishing of dance-drama activities, which has led to some forms dying out completely. Significant events include the introduction of Islam as the state religion under the Mogul empire (fifteenth century) and the virtual abolition of temple dancing (the basis of the currently popular dance form of bharata natyam) under British rule at the end of the nineteenth century. Thus, any reference to the traditions of Indian dance-drama has to be taken with caution: often, whatever is called 'traditional' is in itself a restoration of an almost extinct or entirely extinct art form on the basis of the recollection of a few individuals or even on the basis of written documents only.

The plots for dance-dramas, no matter which particular style, were usually taken from the great epics of Indian/Vedic literature, *The Mahabharata* and the *Ramayana*, as well as stories revolving around Krishna. The duration of performances is unlike anything known in the West. In kathakali, for example, performances would often begin in the evening, around 9 or 10 p.m., after about two to three hours of an elaborate percussion overture and preliminaries performed by apprentices. The performance would then last for some eight hours, finishing around 6 a.m. *Krishnattam* begins at 9 p.m. and ends at 3 a.m., and *Kutiyattam* performances last for several days. Westernization has influenced performance duration. Productions of Indian dance-drama intended for touring abroad to the communities of the diaspora, or intended for consumption by tourists visiting India, will be severely cut to suit the two-and-a-half to three-hour slots common in Western theatres. It is more than likely that much of the impact of the original performance is lost in these truncated versions.

It is not only the duration of performances that has been subjected to the Western influence. Artists firmly rooted in their 'tradition' believe that through invoking a Hindu god in or through their performance the god will bestow blessings on themselves and the audience. Thus, they continue to develop new choreographies of dance depicting those traditional plots and characters, and write/direct plays based on the material of the epics. For more secularized artists who do not share this belief, the issue of *relevance* arises. Many 'modern' Indian artists, perhaps a larger percentage from among the communities of the diaspora than from India itself, query the plotlines involving heroes and events from the great epics. They ask themselves what the relevance is today, for themselves and their audience, of depicting Krishna as a child stealing butter from the milkmaids. They abandon 'tradition' in favour of intercultural exchanges, combining, say, kathak with Spanish flamenco, or use their performance idiom to explore Western music or themes and plots they develop themselves. Especially interesting are artists who return to Indian themes derived from the epics after excursions to other material, in an attempt to trace their own roots.

Japan

As in the West, the origins of theatre, and with it acting, in Japanese history are difficult to trace. There are indications that rituals existed in the Jomon period (until 250 BC), in which earthen masks were used, possibly in connection with fertility rites, exorcism or the cure of illnesses. Some of the oldest written sources point to the ritual disrobing of a female shaman. Evidence for rituals and shamanism grows for the Yayoi period (250 BC to 300 AD). It was during those centuries that tribal communities settled down, forming agricultural, rice-growing communities. With the ownership of land, a class system developed. We find records of rituals connected with the seasons and the planting, transplanting and harvesting of rice. At the same time, evidence shows the importance of magic and sorcery. During the Kofun period (250–710), rituals, especially for the dead, became more elaborate.

In the eighth century, we find mythical stories related to dance and theatre, as described in the first chapter of this book on the origins of the theatre. In the Shinto religion, the worship of a deity took place in three phases: 'summoning the deity, entertaining the deity, and bidding the deity farewell'. Entertaining the deity was performative in nature, encompassing 'possession, role-playing, and the enactment of a story'.[107] From various ritual sources, popular song and dance, as well as elements of Buddhist ideals, one of the most well-known and still extant forms of drama in Japan, Noh, was developed primarily by two artists, Kiyotsugu Kan'ami (1333–84) and his son Zeami Motokiyo (1363–1444). For centuries, Noh was kept alive and taught only in the context of a family tradition, and many of the aspects of the art remained the families' secret. Only in 1909 were Zeami's writings discovered and made publicly available. From the writings it becomes clear that Noh is placed firmly within the religious traditions of the main temples of the country.

The Noh actor is expected to dedicate himself fully to his art, to the exclusion of all other arts except poetry. Sensual pleasures, gambling and heavy drinking are prohibited. In Noh performance, four principles are of major importance (similar to the dominant importance of *rasa* in Indian approaches to acting). They are *monomane*, *yugen*, *hana* and *kokoro*, and I will describe them one by one and in their relation to each other. *Monomane* is the equivalent of what we could today, in the Western theatre, call realistic acting. An emphasis on *monomane* in Noh implies that the emphasis on elegance in dance and singing over drama, characteristic of the precursors of Noh, is no longer applicable. *Monomane* comprises five elements:

1. IMITATION. In performance, the actor will have to portray characters from real life, such as a young girl, or an old woman or old man. The actor should carefully observe the objects of imitation to achieve accuracy in their portrayal; if the actor does not have access to those objects, he should seek advice from expert witnesses.

2. TRUTHFULNESS. If the object of imitation – a young girl, for example – has the characteristic of elegance, the actor's performance achieves the level of elegance only if the actor imitates the elegant person truthfully. This result is not achieved if the actor tries to play 'elegance'.

3. IDENTIFICATION. The actor should fully identify with the character he plays, so that the two become one.

4. ESSENTIALIZATION. This aspect of *monomane* is related to identification. Ideally the actor should identify not with the entire object of imitation, should not, that is, try to bring out all kinds of characteristics, but should, instead, focus on the true intent, interior essence and inmost nature of the character.

5. LIMITATION. This concept relates to both the nature of Noh plays and assumed audience expectations. Not all kinds of poeple existing in the world should serve as objects of imitation. Unsightly appearance or menial occupations, for example, might be considered unpleasant. For the same reason, horror and vulgarity are excluded from presentation on stage.

Zeami's use of the term *yugen* shifted in emphasis over his career. Initially it refers to the performer's elegant beauty. Later it implies a combination of elegance with depth and a touch of cosmic truth. In the latter meaning, it is clearly related to *monomane* in its emphasis on the interior essence and inmost nature of the character. *Hana* translates as flower. It is an aesthetic effect within the performer that is transmitted to the audience by an excellent performance. The achievement of *hana* is the ultimate aim of training the Noh actor. The young actor is able to achieve temporal *hana* as a result of his natural beauty and youth, not from training. However, only years of rigorous training will enable the actor to achieve true *hana*, which culminates in the 'mysterious flower of the miraculous that sublimely unites actor and audience in a unique experience of the Absolute'.[108] This unique experience relates to the cosmic truth of *yugen* and the essential interior of *monomane*. *Kokoro* is the most abstract concept in Zeami's aesthetics. It comprises four levels:

1. Emotion and feelings. On this level, *yugen* arises.

2. The mind, which is self-conscious and knowing, centres on objects and makes decisions. On this level, the actor is aware of good and bad in the performance.

3. The heart of the unconscious. This is a void. The performer on this level of consciousness is no longer aware of himself, of good or bad, or of the art itself. The distinction-making, self-conscious mind has disappeared; the art becomes *mushin* (literally: nothingness-heart). All division is overcome in a unity with the source (the Absolute of *hana*, the cosmic truth of *yugen*, the essential interior of *monomane*). Once the actor has reached that level of consciousness, the

performance becomes sublime, mysterious, numinous and indescribable. Here *hana* of the miraculous has become the instinctive, spontaneous, free-flowing mind of the master actor that has reached unity with nothingness and emptiness.

4. The all-encompassing, deep and spiritual heart is the highest level of all. This is the real *kokoro*, the true essence of all things, or the all-encompassing, unchanging, pure Buddha-nature. At this level of consciousness, only unity, totality, exists, and the differentiation of *kokoro* into four levels becomes a fiction. This view is similar to that in Indian philosophy, where the attainment of unity consciousness, the highest level of human development according to *Vedanta*, unifies all the differences in perception characteristic of less highly developed states of refined cosmic or cosmic consciousness. In Zeami's terms, reality remains the same: the artist, and through him the spectator, passes through phases or stages of skills and realizations (each with its own view of reality), until he eventually becomes one with the heart of everything, spontaneously following the rhythms of the One, the Absolute, the primordial Energy. Just as the puppet is moved by the strings, the supreme master of Noh is governed in each step by the invisible heart that holds the forms and techniques of the Noh together and unites all powers in his masterful performance, in his life and in his audience.

In contrast to the deeply religious origins of Noh theatre, the other well-known traditional form of theatre in Japan, kabuki, is secular in origin. In 1603, the establishment of the Tokugawa regime (in power until 1868) ended over a century of political chaos. Society under the new regime was isolated from the West, and organized in a strict hierarchy, with Edo (today's Tokyo) as its capital, and Kyoto providing a home for the powerless emperor. The warrior-administrators (samurai) were below the rulers, followed by peasants, artisans and merchants. Even lower down were the old court nobility in Kyoto, the priests of Buddhism and Shinto, and finally outcasts, including prostitutes.

In that society, *kabuku* was the term used for anti-establishment action that defied the conventions and proper rules of behaviour. *Kabuki-mono* were people who expressed their anti-conformism through a series of protests, such as unusual ways of dressing, shocking hairstyles, wearing extravagantly decorated, oversized swords, and smoking tobacco from 4-foot long pipes. They would roam the streets, engaging in violence. For the rulers, kabuki meant subversion, heresy and danger. For the people, they were heroic, because they dared to express their protest.

The first kabuki performer, Okuni, mixed sacred and profane elements in an existing dance form, *nembutsu*, to create *kabuki*, implying anti-conformism in the art. For example, she dressed in Portugese pants, a foreign-style hat or men's clothes, and sometimes had a cross hanging from her neck. The topics depicted in her dances were the exploits of famous *kabuki-mono*.

Many prostitutes of the time imitated Okuni, emphasizing in their dances comical scenes and clowning, and performing comical soliloquies and pantomime. True to their profession, they wore exotic, revealing costumes. Their kabuki came to be known as *onna kabuki* (women's kabuki) or *yujo kabui* (prostitutes' kabuki). However, fights often developed among spectators favouring the same prostitute, and women's kabuki was banned. Instead, young boys aged between eleven and fifteen, before their foreheads had been shaved as a sign of coming of age, now played kabuki, but as with the women, fights and scandals developed, and boys were prohibited from acting kabuki as well. Blatantly sexual scenes were censored, and as a result, actors had to develop the dramatic element of their shows. Only men with their foreheads shaved were allowed to perform. In the social hierarchy, kabuki actors ranged among the outcasts, together with prostitutes. Not surprisingly, kabuki theatre rose in the off-limits red-light districts of Edo. There the merchants, socially inferior in official society, could serve as patrons to the arts. Actors were restricted to where they were allowed to live and the people they were allowed to mix with, and outside their territory they had to wear a wicker hat so that other people could recognize and avoid contact with them.

The period from 1688 to 1703 witnessed a great public demand for plays: day-long performances were held in three major cities of Japan, in at least ten major theatres. Since the dramatists were relatively inexperienced, however, the impression we have today of the majority of plays, whose material was taken from traditional myths, folk legends, episodes of Japanese history and scandals of the day, is that of complicated, melodramatic plots hastily and arbitrarily put together. There is abundant use of fantastic interventions of spirits and gods, mixed with more realistic scenes. In the second half of the eighteenth century, kabuki became a recognized art form, and among the brilliant performers there were even some samurai. The economic crisis of the Edo period led to the prohibition of luxury for all except the samurai, and a new type of kabuki play developed, depicting the poor, the wretched and the underworld. With the onset of the Meiji period, Tokyo became the capital of Japan and the country was swept by a wave of modernization and Westernization. All aspects that might give offence were removed from kabuki, and the former red-light district entertainment was granted the status of a dignified national theatre.

China

The origins of theatre in China have been traced to the period between 2600 and 207 BC, where it took the form of songs of praise to rain gods, the dragon in the depths of the ocean, the phoenix (whose cries were considered a lucky omen) and the tortoise (the lines on whose shell were used to predict the future). Music occupied a place of special importance among the Chinese arts, since it was thought to be identical with the universe. Dance and song thus contributed to maintain order and balance, and were considered influential for human success in politics and business, as well as for health. However, since the music of those ancient times was not noted down, what exactly it may have sounded like remains guesswork. As in other cultures, the performers of music and dance eventually became professionals, at first in a religious context, later in employment for the entertainment of the rich.

From 206 BC to about AD 588, dance served both ritual and entertainment functions. A poetic *Ode to Dance* survives from the first century:

> Sixteen enchanting girls before the emperor.
> How noble in their elaborate robes,
> how beautiful and enchanting they are
> with rosy cheeks.
> Their glowing hair decorated with jewels,
> their brows raised high,
> elaborate patterns embellish the fabrics;
> When they straighten the folds of their garments in the dusky light,
> the wind carries the fragrance of their scattered perfume.
> Opening their lips, with brows raised high,
> they begin their song in a high pitch.
> And now the dance also commences:
> they raise their head and soar up,
> stride back and forth:
> gently, but almost as if in melancholy,
> an image which almost defies description.
> And on they dance, accompanied by the sound of music,
> with agile fingers and talking glances.
> The long robes fly in the wind,
> the wide sleeves meet
> when they glide to and fro.
> Their bodies are light swallows,
> and move like a swan in a storm,
> of fragile elegance,
> and fast as a dart.[109]

In due course, vaudeville-like entertainment appeared, including acrobats and animal tamers, and eventually, the forerunners of plays combined dance, music and song. During the Tang dynasty in China

(618–906), the first theatre school was founded, and choric dance and vaudeville-like entertainment continued. While the Chinese Middle Ages saw an emphasis on poetry, the novel and the essay, leading to the creation of many stories which would later serve as inspiration for dramatic writing, during the Sun dynasty (960–1276), drama proper developed. Initially, stories were dramatized in breaks between dances and songs; later, the dramatization of stories was combined with dance and music. Such dramatic entertainment proved popular not only at court but also with the people, since many plots were based on folkloric motifs. The first differentiation of character types is recorded in this period: the less important, virtuous, bearded man who starts the play off (*fu mo*); the 'painted face' (*fu ching*), a rough character who causes laughter and fights the *mo*; and *chuan ku*, appearing as the emperor.

During the Yuan dynasty (1277–1367), north China was conquered by Mongols (Kublai Khan), and in the development of drama, greater emphasis was placed on plot elements. More character types were added: *cheng mo*, the bearded main character; *wai mo*, the old man; *hsiao mo*, the young man; *ching*, the 'painted face'; and *ch'ou*, the clown. For the first time in Chinese theatre, there are important female character types: the old woman, the young, virtuous woman and the lively and fighting type. Note that all such female roles were played by men. Song, spoken dialogue and expression through gesture were combined, with minor characters speaking and major ones singing.

During the Ming dynasty (1522–1735), theatre enjoyed the freedom to develop, without any restrictions. Regional styles emerged, as did the increasing importance of southern drama. The form of theatre most readily associated with China, *jingju*, developed under the Qing dynasty (1644–1911). The popular rendering of the term *jinju* is *Beijing Opera*. In fact, however, the form does not have much in common with Western opera, and the term literally translates as 'theatre of the capital'.[110] Many of the plays in this category deal with patriotism, or the love for one's children. They may represent attacks against superstition, and may be fantastical or sentimental. The subgenres are not tragedy and comedy, as in Western drama, but civil or military plays. A civil play would deal with the domestic problems of everyday life, centring on the conflict of good and evil. A good person suffers at the hands of a villain, and the conflict is resolved by the intervention of a third person, either a high official or a supernatural power. In the end, the evil person is always punished. The conflict of good and evil is also predominant in military *jingju*, with some cunning act of war leading to the victory of the good.

The plays in Chinese Opera or Beijing Opera employ colloquial language. Thus, this form of theatre, supported by the popular plots, has been defined as art for a mass population. This popular appeal is reflected by the staging conventions: the stage was placed in tea houses, where people would drink tea, chew watermelon seeds and talk. The price of tea included the performance, for which no special fee was levied. The stage was placed on painted columns, with entrances to the left and right and a large curtain at the back. The musicians were situated in full view of the audience on the right-hand side of the stage. During the performance, stage managers and friends and relations of the performers would come on stage and serve tea to the performers. In due course, the musicians were hidden from the stage, and during performances, access to the stage was restricted to all but the actors. In addition, longer operas were cut down. Strict rules of conduct were followed backstage, with stars allocated a small cubicle for make-up, while the other performers used one room with a large table.

The character-types were developed from the precursors of Beijing Opera, and included four major types: male, female, comic and painted face. Among the men, there were the following sub-categories: warrior, intellectual, young man and old man. Young warriors were agile and strong in battle. Older generals appeared full of dignity and noble bearing. Then there were those fighters who did not sing or speak but merely fought, at times serving as comics. The intellectual was a quiet gentleman, highly stylized with symbolic actions which required a trained audience to recognize and appreciate. The young man was a youthful hero, either a poor student, a prince or a playboy. The old man was often the central character, always honest, noble and faithful. He could be a general or an intellectual. Apart from the young man, all characters have beards; indeed, Beijing Opera features eighteen standardized varieties of beards to choose from depending on the character: a full, white beard, long to the waist, is appropriate for an old man; a long beard in five strands is used to characterize the god of warriors; a three-strand beard indicates scholars; a moustache is reserved for the clown; red beards signify rough characters, while purple red is for generals.

Female characters have six sub-categories. The 'flower' charms with cunning sensuality and enchanting gracefulness, supported by an elaborate, colourful costume. The ideal woman complies with the philosophy of Confucius (551–449 BC). The behaviour is refined, the gestures restricted. The eyes are cast down, but a repertory of more than fifty set movements of the sleeves allows her to express her feelings. The costume, in moderate colours, consists of a long, white, shirt-like robe with a high-collared black tunic, often with a wide band around the waist. Young innocent girls are dressed simply in tight-fitting jackets over trousers. Older, noble women, rich or poor, are dressed in darker silk robes and support themselves on strong cane sticks. Their songs are dark and mournful, but strong. Evil and sometimes comic women of lower social status are often involved in intrigues. Finally, there are women who are masterful in handling the sword and display many acrobatic feats. All female characters, except the old woman, use a similar pattern of make-up: face and neck are covered with matt white paste and accentuated with rouge, starting from deep red under the eyes to light pink in the lower part of the face. The eyes are elongated and lifted up by a band which is wound tightly round the forehead.

For 'painted faces', the colour of the make-up indicates the character traits: black is used for an honest, robust warrior, white for cunning and energy, red for righteous generals, blue for cruelty, while a wild mixture of colours indicates a disdainful villain, a ghost or a supernatural creature. The clown has a white dot of paint on the nose and uses colloquial language. Military clowns are good at using the sword, while civil clowns are renowned for their wit.

In *jingju*, the family tradition is of great importance. As I will demonstrate in more detail in the chapter on actor training, traditionally, actors trained within families, of which they were either natural members, or into which they had been sold. Each apprentice would learn the entire role from his teacher, who in turn had been taught by his own teacher, and so on. Thus, 'each performer embodies a whole family tradition of professionals who have gone before him'.[111] If the actor makes a mistake during a performance, he is said to have 'disturbed the ghosts/spirits', as if 'the actor had offended these presences'.[112] Added to the ancestral heritage of a role is the history of its interpretation by members of other families. The close family tradition of *jingju* actors gives them a very strong sense of identity. Through exposure to performances at village temples, martial arts training and performance, spectators were well acquainted with the style of theatre they were about to watch, and this implied an awareness of the training undergone by a well-known performer. Use of the past tense here is intentional: in the course of the Cultural Revolution in China (1966–76), performance, training and spectating traditions were ultimately cut off, leaving only remnants of their original richness.

In India, as we have seen, theory and practice of acting are covered extensively in the *Natyashastra*, and from Japan we have Zeami's writings about Noh. There is no comparable textbook dealing with *jingju* aesthetics. Tradition is carried in the actor's body. Despite the lack of textbooks, however, *jingju* is just as informed by complex philosophical concepts as are Indian dance-drama or Noh. In *jingju*, they relate to the actor's presence, or *qi*. This term literally translates as 'air', 'spirit', 'energy' or 'breath'. Applied to *jingju* performance, the term may be applied to several levels. On a technical level, *qi* refers to breath control: 'In singing and moving, the performer must ensure he has the right quantity of breath at all times.'[113] In relation to the actor's body, *qi* resides in the centre, the solar plexus. From this centre, *qi* must flow throughout the body, and the body's movements must be such that the flow remains at will within the limits of the body, and is released only intentionally. To achieve this, 'the basic pose positions of performers of all role categories depend on the roundedness of arms never being fully extended but always describing a curve'. For example, when 'holding the arms out from the body, the backs of the hands face the chest. When the leg is raised, the toes are turned back towards the ankle, or the sole is hooked inwards.'[114] *Qi* is not randomly released to create the actor's presence, but at special, carefully chosen moments of punctuation, or frozen poses, in a performance. With the choice of the rhythm which governs the moments of the release of *qi*, the actor sets the beat, which is then picked up by the drummer in the orchestra and determines the entire rhythm of the performance.

A second concept, related to *qi*, is that of Yin/Yang. Yang is the male principle, representing creativity, light; Yin is the female principle, representing the imagination and darkness. Since *qi* is a Yang element, Yang provides life or presence in the theatre. The imagination (Yin) needs an infusion of Yang to come to life. Thus the actor in *jingju* brings

> opposing elements of Yang and Yin together to interact and provoke presence, or *qi*. That is to say, it is the *interaction* between the opposing qualities Yin and Yang, female and male, dark and light, death and life which is the cause of presence.[115]

In performance, the *jingju* actor expresses Yin and Yang through bringing his body in 'congruence with the aesthetic idea of Yin and Yang through pose, movement and text'.[116]

The *jingju* actor's movement in space is conceptualized and carried out in line with the Luo diagram. Its origin is mythological, like the origins of theatre in India and Japan. Yu the Great is a mythological figure 'who was given a special document known as the Luo diagram, inscribed on the back of a tortoise which rose out of the Luo river. With it he could stop the great flood and create the world.'[117] The Luo diagram takes the form of a grid made up of nine cells of equal size. Each cell in the grid is allocated a number, from 1 to 9, arranged in such a way that the sum of numbers in cells across a straight line is always 15. 'The matrix represents the philosophical (Daoist) idea of life as change in constancy.'[118] Besides the numbers allocated, the Luo diagram shows a cosmological scheme, the five elements, the five seasons and the four orientations. In each of those cases, four or five elements are grouped around a centre.

The use of the Luo diagram in performance implies a conceptualization and embodiment of space different from that known in the West. Thus, in training, the student learns to create any role he learns on the basis of such a grid, knowing precisely where each movement should be placed in relation to the grid. He will be able to adapt to any size of stage, narrowing down or enlarging the scope of movements accordingly. The grid implies that the actor does not orient himself towards the

4 wind wood spring South-east	9 fire fire summer South	2 earth earth Indian summer South-west
3 thunder metal autumn East	5 Centre 	7 vapours wood spring West
8 mountain earth Indian summer North-east	1 water water winter North	6 heaven metal autumn North-west

audience. It also enables the actor to use his body creatively to move in other dimensions: for this we must imagine a grid that is not only superimposed on the floor of the stage but one that is also vertical and takes the body itself as its axis.

At the nine junction points of the cells on the floor grid, the actor will pause for poses which serve to express *qi*. Movement sequences within various levels of grids (floor, vertical body) will relate to the various implications of the cells. Well-educated spectators understand the implications and their appreciation of the performance is thus heightened. The question arises whether a performance of *jingju* which adheres to, and makes use of, the intricacies of the Luo diagram will have an effect on spectators independent of their detailed intellectual understanding of what is happening.

Islamic countries

Orthodox Islam refused to condone theatrical performance, because of its imaginary reality. Nevertheless, dramatic art continued to exist in Islamic countries in the forms of puppet drama, storytelling, religious drama and comic drama improvisation, many examples of which have survived into the twentieth century. Islamic dance is mainly known from the Whirling Dervishes in the mystical tradition of Sufism. Towards the end of the twentieth century, the freedom enjoyed by theatre mainly depends on the openness of the respective governments.

Puppet theatre, or Karagöz, is mainly performed with shadow

puppets. The stages for shadow puppet theatre consist of a frame covered with white, translucent cloth. The puppets themselves are made from thin leather, which allows light to shine through. Since they have many holes in them, they no longer represent animate beings, and thus do not infringe on the Islamic prohibition against representing people on stage. The puppets are between 35 and 60 cm high, and are manipulated by the puppeteers by a horizontal rod affixed to the back of the puppets. A second rod allows for the movement of various distinct parts of the body. The typical puppet theatre play consist of three parts: a prologue, a dialogue and interlude, and the main story. One of the main characters, called Hacivat, first gives a long speech or religious invocation; then the chief comic character appears, the Karagöz, from whom this kind of theatre derives its name, and who is characterized by a black eye. Hacivat and Karagöz have an argument and beat each other. The dialogue may not be related thematically to the main story, but often takes the form of a contest of wits or an exercise in insulting. The main story involves many traditional stock characters, including young and old women, and a young man who is usually in love with a young woman of higher birth and has to overcome difficulties before being allowed to marry her. Shadow puppet theatre flourished especially in the Ottoman empire (1498–1926), where it enjoyed royal patronage. In Iran, royal patronage is not evident, but there were individual puppeteers who toured the country until the 1976 revolution. In the twenty-first century, the popularity of puppet theatre continues, both as mere entertainment and also as a means of expressing political protest.

Islam strongly features sermons and public recitations. Some specialists argue that the tradition of dramatic storytelling in the Islamic world has its origins here. By the ninth century, a famous storyteller, ibn al-Magazili, is reported to have introduced a dramatic element into his art. In the Ottoman empire, narrative drama was called *meddah* (eulogy), and in Iran *naqqali* (recounting). Over the centuries, the art of dramatic storytelling used more and more parody and satire, so that it was eventually subjected to strict censorship. The venue for such narrations was usually the coffee house.

Religious drama was originally limited to Shi'a communities concerned with the events of the death of the Shi'a martyr Imam Husain (died AD 680). At the beginning of the twentieth-first century, religious drama is still performed in countries with a large Shi'a population, such as Iran, Iraq, Bahrain and Lebanon. The performance is not really experienced by the spectators as theatre, but as a ritual of mourning. Performances may be long or short, sometimes preceded or followed by processions and religious chanting as part of communal mourning ceremonies. Good characters in the plays – those who follow Imam Husain – chant their lines in the mode of classical Persian music, whereas the bad characters declaim their lines. The good characters wear the colour green, the bad ones red. Female characters are played my men, wearing black and veiling their faces. Although these religious performances are still popular at the beginning of the twenty-first century, there is some uneasiness from religious and political officials towards this practice.

Comic improvised drama was known, under different names, throughout the Islamic world. The two principal forms are *ru-howzi* and *orta-oyunu*. They enjoyed wide royal patronage. The performers would create laughter by imitating the accents and manners of well-known local people. The central figure of the plots is the clown, often called Rajab in *ru-howzi*, where he is often a servant, and is distinguished from the other characters by his black face. In *orta-oyunu*, he is often called Tosun Efendi, and wears red trousers, a yellow gown and a multicoloured hat. The other characters in comic improvised drama clearly resemble those in Karagöz, suggesting that it may well have developed from puppet theatre. Despite their name, however, these performances are not entirely improvised. From a common pool, the different troupes take up stock plots, which they change in their performance practice.

Although dance is discredited in orthodox Islam, it was always practised in Islamic countries as part of the mystical traditions of Sufism, which represents the Christian wing of Islam. The tradition of Sufism is organized in brotherhoods (*tariqa*), in which a chain of masters and disciples, through generations, constitute a school of thought and practice. The son of the great Sufi poet Rumi (d.1273) founded the brotherhood of Whirling Dervishes (Mevlevi). Music and the whirling dance are used to create a mystic, ecstatic state of mind. At its peak, it would lead to an experience of unity with God. Whereas this ultimate religious aim was beyond doubt, different Sufi brotherhoods disagreed about whether dancing in ecstasy, where the dancer loses self-control, is permissible as a means to achieve a religious state characterized by perfect self-control. Another urgent question is whether the ultimate experience of unity with God can be mechanically achieved through specific modes of dancing, or whether it is a gift of God. In Turkey, the dances of the Mevlevi Dervishes and other brotherhoods were banned by Atatürk in 1925; since 1954, however, they have been allowed to perform on the anniversary of Rumi's death, on 17 December.

Following the decline of the nineteenth-century empires at the end of the First World War, the new nations became oriented towards the USA and Europe in all things, including the theatre. In Turkey, a national theatre was established in 1908, and its most important director was Muhsin Ertugrul (1892–1979), who supported productions both of Western classics and new Turkish playwrights. Muslim women were allowed to appear on stage. Today, the heavily subsidized state theatres employ some 450 actors nationwide, Istanbul's municipal theatres about 110, and there are many privately owned theatres as well. The National Theatre of Egypt was founded in 1957, and there are some fifty registered free theatre companies in Cairo, and more than a hundred outside the capital. After the First World War, with the rise of an independent director (whose function had, up to then, been taken up by the leading actor), distinct acting methodologies developed. George Abyad emphasized a melodious delivery with a strong voice; Abdul Rahman Rushdie was in favour of deep and heavy emotion; whereas Yusuf Wahbi emphasized absorption into the role in the line of French actor Coquelin.[119] After the Second World War, the influence of Stanislavsky became evident, and in the 1960s that of Brecht. 'By the 1990s, it can be said that the Egyptian theatre was a mélange of styles representing virtually all the forms of acting and genres of drama that exist, from the most realistic to the most exaggerated elements of musical-comedy.'[120]

Government funding is available for theatre in many other Islamic countries, such as Kuwait, Syria and Iran. In Saudi Arabia, theatre, in the European sense, did not exist until 1974, and since then state support has been growing; there are, however, hardly any women involved in the theatre. In Jordan, there is a strong emphasis on Theatre in Education, whereas the actors appearing in private companies do not earn their living from acting, but have to take other jobs; rehearsals and performances have to be arranged around the professional commitments of those involved. The development of theatre has been severely hampered by countries involved in war. In Lebanon, the war that lasted from 1975 to 1990 destroyed any infrastructure; there is no state funding, and all theatrical activity takes the form of private enterprises. In Iraq, war and the UN sanctions have also had an adverse effect on the theatre scene, which manages to survive, though.

The Arab-speaking part of the Islamic world has been dominated in the twentieth century by developments in Egypt. Many important playwrights emerged. However, the years of war with Israel and the assassination of Sadat in 1981 led to economic difficulties and an increase in Islamic religious fundamentalism, which made theatre productions difficult. In Iran, a National Theatre was established in 1911. Under the reign of Reza Shah Pahlavi from 1925 to 1941, theatre was subjected to strict censorship, although during this period women appeared on the stage in Iran for the first time. In the 1960s and 1970s, Mohammad Reza Pahlavi sought to develop the arts along European lines. Among other developments, a School of Dramatic Arts was founded. Since the revolution in 1978–9, public theatre in Iran has been restricted to four venues in the capital, Teheran.

கை

7

Approaches to Acting in the Intercultural Paradigm

ಖು೧೮

Now that the basic information on approaches to acting in non-Western cultures is available, it is possible to address a development in the late twentieth century in the West: intercultural theatre. Typically, a Western theatre director takes material of plot, philosophy or acting techniques from a non-Western culture and uses that material in some way in his own production, often with a Western, sometimes with a multicultural, cast of actors. Such a directorial approach has implications for acting, which I discuss in this chapter.

So far, we have discussed approaches to acting within more or less clearly defined geographic boundaries, from the West (Europe and USA), to India, Japan, China and the Islamic countries. When the theatres of more than one culture meet, we can broadly talk about *intercultural theatre*. Initially, we have to be clear about the meaning of the terms 'culture' and 'intercultural theatre'. The concept of culture is as heterogeneous as the phenomena of the theatre commonly termed 'intercultural'. Set against nature, culture may be defined as 'the mediation that appears to rob a man of his nature and locate his action and practices within an endowment of socially produced symbolic forms'.[1] Historically, in the critical thinking following the Industrial Revolution, culture could also be viewed as mediating between man and machine. In the context of the arts, high culture is often differentiated from low, or popular, culture. The concept of high culture goes back to the German Romantic view that 'culture specified the pinnacle of human achievement'.[2] High culture is traditionally associated with an elite, a minority, which, according to F.R. Leavis, writing in 1930, can be described as follows:

> In any period it is upon a very small minority that the discerning appreciation of art and literature depends: it is (apart from cases of the simple and the familiar) only a few who are capable of unprompted, first hand judgment. There are still a small minority, though a larger one, who are capable of endorsing such first hand judgment by genuine personal response. ... The minority capable not only of appreciating Dante,

Shakespeare, Baudelaire, Hardy (to take major instances) but of recognising the latest successors constitute the consciousness of the race (or of a branch of it) at a given time. ... Upon this minority depends our power of profiting by the finest human experience of the past; they keep alive the subtlest and most perishable parts of the tradition. Upon them depend the implicit standards that all of the finer living of an age, the sense that it is worth more than that, this rather than that is the direction in which to go. In their keeping ... it is language, the changing idiom upon which fine living depends, and without which a distinction of spirit is thwarted and incoherent. By culture I mean the use of such language.[3]

Popular culture has been regarded as inferior to high culture, and Gans has identified four main areas of criticism:

1. The negative character of popular culture creation. Popular culture is undesirable because, unlike high culture, it is mass produced by profit-minded entrepreneurs solely for the gratification of a paying audience.
2. The negative effects of high culture. Popular culture borrows from high culture, thus debasing it, and also lures away many potential creators of high culture, thus depleting its reservoir of talent.
3. Negative effects on the popular culture audience. The consumption of popular culture content at best produces spurious gratifications, and at worst is emotionally harmful to the audience.
4. Negative effects on the society. The wide distribution of popular culture not only reduces the level of cultural quality – or civilisation – of a society, but also encourages totalitarianism by creating a passive audience peculiarly responsive to the techniques of mass persuasion used by demagogues bent on dictatorship.[4]

This dichotomy of high and popular culture is not at all generally accepted today, but subject to much controversial discussion. The principle of dichotomy, however, features strongly in practical applications of the term culture, such as in the binary opposites of first world versus third world; developed culture versus undeveloped culture; complex versus simple culture; advanced versus backward culture; literate versus traditional culture; or conscious versus unconscious culture.

Patrice Pavis, one of the first to theorize intercultural theatre, defines culture generally and globally as a system of creating meaning, a signifying system, 'thanks to which a society or group understands itself in its relationship with the world'.[5] Pavis applies this general definition, and more specific ones taken from Camilleri, to the theatre. The group or culture in which we live influences all aspects of our psyche and our body. We can predict these influences.[6] Similarly, Pavis argues, all aspects of the theatre are subject to cultural determination. In this sense, culture does not necessarily extend to national differences, differences in the culture of Britain and France, for example. Pavis takes up a further idea from Camilleri: cultural determination 'is common to members of the same group'.[7] Theatre artists represent such a group. The most striking example is the actor's body. It is characterized by the techniques of training the body that are culture-specific and can thus be quite different: training for three to four years at, say, the Royal Academy of Dramatic Art in London, or from the age of four for all the performer's life in traditional theatre in India.

On the basis of this brief view on the relationship of culture and theatre, it is possible to argue that the phenomenon of intercultural theatre exists when different cultures meet in the theatre. In this definition, culture can be understood on several levels: potentially referring to national differences, certainly referring to theatre-specific differences.

First of all, it is necessary to demarcate the term intercultural from the closely related neighbours in the word field. Pavis defines intercultural as 'an exchange of civilities between cultures'.[8] Intercultural theatre is thus a form of theatre in which the aim is a true exchange of material from at least two cultures. Pavis presents the model of the hourglass in his attempt to theorize intercultural theatre thus defined:

> In the upper bowl is the foreign culture, the source culture, which is more or less codified and solidified in diverse anthropological, sociocultural or artistic modelizations. In order to reach us, this culture must pass through a narrow neck. If the grains of culture or their conglomerate are sufficiently fine, they will flow through without any trouble, however slowly, into the lower bowl, that of the target culture, from which point we observe this slow flow. The grains will rearrange themselves in a way which appears random, but which is partly regulated by their passage through some dozen filters put in place by the target culture and the observer.[9]

In the theatrical context, the hourglass consists of three levels, each with its own sub-categories:

Level 1
The source culture before the process of theatrical adaptation
   begins:

(a) cultural modelling, sociological, anthropological codification, etc.
(b) artistic modelling.

Pavis acknowledged the necessity of accounting for our ways of gaining knowledge about different cultures, so as to avoid ethnocentrism. These problems continue on the second level:

Level 2
The theatrical production:

(a) perspective of the adapters
(b) work of adaptation
(c) preparatory work by the actors, etc.
(d) choice of theatrical form
(e) theatrical representation/performance of culture
(f) reception-adapters

On this level, Pavis locates increased dangers of ethnocentricity, in the form of projections of 'ways of thinking, schemas and categories belonging to the target culture on to the source culture'.[10] He also points to the need of the theatre to make the foreign culture material accessible and comprehensible for the target culture's theatre audiences, which are described in Pavis's model on Level 3:

Level 3
Reception by the audience and target culture:

(a) readability
(b) reception in the target culture
     (i)   artistic modelling
     (ii) sociological and anthropological codification
     (iii) cultural modelling
(c) given and anticipated consequences

Pavis introduced the hourglass concept as a model for what he defines as intercultural theatre. The prefix *inter* suggests, as does, indeed, Pavis's definition, an exchange of cultures. However, the hourglass allows only for a one-way flow of culture, from source (foreign) to target (own) culture. In addition, each member of the target culture is determined by his own culture, which will be projected onto the source culture. Pavis recognizes this deficiency in his model when he argues that intercultural transfer would have to be seen 'as a process whereby the target culture appropriates the source culture'.[11]

The relationship of the theatres of more than one culture can be one of exchange, although practical theatre productions that would meet this description seem to be rare, possibly non-existent. The term intercultural can be used as a generic term to indicate the relationship between theatre and cultures, but would appear to be a contradiction in terms if we take it literally to indicate genuine exchange between cultures on a theatrical level. Therefore, it would be more appropriate to call 'cross-cultural' any relationship between culture(s) and theatre in which Pavis's model applies, i.e. in which the source culture is appropriated by the target culture.

The rest of this chapter is based on the following initial terminological assumptions: all theatre in which clearly more than one culture is expressed shall be referred to as intercultural theatre. Theatre in which we can define a clear exchange of two or more cultures will represent intercultural theatre in the narrower sense. Intercultural theatre which can be reduced to the act of appropriation of source culture material by a target culture will be called cross-cultural. In Pavis, these concepts are blurred.

Pavis differentiates intercultural from 'intracultural', referring to the 'traditions of a single nation'.[12] It is interesting to note that here he equates culture and nation. Pavis points out that traditions of a single nation are 'very often almost forgotten or deformed, and have to be reconstructed'.[13] Could the theatre perform the function of reconstructing this national-cultural identity? Does the theatre extend beyond reconstructing past national-cultural identity into actively shaping the present national-cultural identity? The latter might well be one function, for example, of Athol Fugard's *Valley Song* (1996) in helping to shape the new, post-apartheid South Africa.

In intracultural and intercultural theatre we are dealing either with specific cultures, possibly identical with nations, and the theatre reflecting or shaping one particular nation-culture, or the interaction, or exchange, between theatres of at least two distinct nation-cultures. According to Pavis, it is possible to deal with culture in a less specified context. *Transcultural theatre* transcends 'particular cultures and looks for a universal human condition'.[14] *Ultracultural theatre* is closely connected to this: whereas transcultural theatre strives for the element that links contemporary humans, ultracultural theatre is on a 'somewhat mythical quest for the origin of theatre', searching for 'a primal language in the sense of Artaud'.[15] Pavis mentions Brook's production of *Orghast* (1970) as an example (see page 149).

The search for a universal language is the third of three main categories for intercultural theatre proposed by Fischer-Lichte, who also points out that attempts to achieve it have failed to date, and are bound to fail, because language is always culture-bound, never universal.[16]

The 'precultural', according to Pavis, 'would be the common ground of any tradition in the world, which affects any audience, "before" (temporally and logically) it is individualized and "culturized" in a specific cultural tradition'.[17] This concept is closely linked to the transcultural and ultracultural dimensions. Indeed, it may appear difficult to see the differences. They all appear to search for, or attempt to describe, human states of being that are not defined, or conditioned, by culture. The difference lies in the 'area' where the 'beyond' is conceptualized: for the transcultural dimension this area is the universal human condition, a somewhat vague concept, but still within the grasp of reason. For the ultracultural dimension, the area of beyond is mainly that of language, less in the grasp of reason, as indicated by Pavis's use of the terms 'mystical', 'quest' and 'primal language'. The precultural dimension, finally, is the least precise and most poetic in its nature, and is associated with Barba's poetic concepts of the *pre-expressive* or *tradition of traditions*.

The three dimensions of transcultural, ultracultural and precultural are thus closely related concepts that allow more precise differentiation of theatrical productions. All three have in common a theatre which tries to appeal to and operate on a level of the spectator's consciousness which reaches beyond any culture-specific human characteristics. The difficulty in accepting the existence of human experiences that are not culture-specific is twofold: first, such experiences are not common, everyday experiences, but involve altered states of consciousness. Second, all experiences are described in language, and language is culture-specific. Each culture will have its own specific concepts to describe or explain any human experience, including the non-common experiences of ASC. Thus the description of the experience of altered states of consciousness, proposed as not culture-specific, will vary from culture to culture, and cultural relativism will argue that because no two descriptions in two different cultures are alike, no such state of consciousness exists that could lay claim to be not culture-specific. With reference to the theatre, the questions arise whether the theatre can stimulate experiences of non-ordinary ASC in performers and/or spectators, and whether these experiences may legitimately lay claim to universality, to being not culture-specific. If so, what may be the function of the induction of such states of consciousness?

Pavis returns to apparently more solid ground in the next differentiation: he defines the 'postcultural' dimension as applying to the 'postmodern imagination, which tends to view any cultural act as a quotation of restructuring of already known elements'.[18] Finally, Pavis introduces the 'metacultural' dimension as referring to the 'commentary a given culture can make on other cultural elements, when explaining, comparing and commenting on it [*sic*]'.[19] As an example, one might mention those Canadian plays that deal with the cultural-political relationship between Canada and the USA.

Jatinder Verma, artistic director of Tara Arts in London, adds the category of *multicultural* theatre, which he defines, broadly, as a theatre production which uses a cast from many cultural backgrounds.[20] This category points to a differentiation of modes of interaction between culture and theatre according to the field of theatre concerned: namely, rehearsal, production, performance and reception.

To summarize, culture and theatre can combine in the following modes:

1. *Intracultural*, referring to the traditions of a single nation-culture. The function of the theatre might be to reconstruct the deformed

or almost forgotten traditions and to develop new structures for national-cultural identities.

2a. *Intercultural* theatre in the wide sense includes all theatre which clearly draws on, makes use of, refers, alludes to or aims at an exchange with at least one other different culture.

2b. *Intercultural* theatre in the narrower sense exists when there is an exchange between the two theatres of two cultures.

3. *Cross-cultural* theatre refers to the kind of theatre described by Pavis in his hourglass model, in which a target culture appropriates a source culture, whether intentionally or not. As no real exchange takes place, the term intercultural, whose prefix *inter* suggests exchange, would not be an appropriate choice for this phenomenon.

4. *Transcultural, ultracultural* and *precultural* theatre practice share a search for the conceptualization and experiences of non-ordinary altered states of consciousness which are not culture-specific. Transcultural theatre would appeal to a generally universal human condition; ultracultural theatre would try to present and/ or access the origins of theatre in the form of a primal language; whereas precultural theatre, in line with Barba's concept of the pre-expressive, would attempt to access the common ground of any tradition in the world.

5. *Postcultural* theatre practice is informed by the postmodern imagination in being intentionally fragmented, regarding any cultural act as a quotation or restructuring of already known elements. Where theatre is in search of universality, however, it leaves the postmodern imagination behind.

6. The *metacultural* dimension refers to the commentary of one culture on another and is closely linked with cross-cultural theatre. However, metacultural theatre is limited, according to Pavis's definition, to commentary, whereas cross-cultural theatre is characterized by the appropriation of a source culture by a target culture, which implies a comment on the source culture, and which in turn may or may not be explicit in the theatre production.

7. *Multicultural* theatre, according to Verma, refers to any theatre production, with a cast drawn from many cultures, independent of whether or not the play is more than intracultural.

After this somewhat lengthy exercise in definition, it is now possible to address the implications of intercultural theatre on approaches to acting. In recent years, two theatre artists, in particular, have been closely associated with intercultural theatre both in theory and practice: Eugenio Barba and Peter Brook. Barba spent some years at Grotowski's Theatre Laboratory in Poland, and continued his teacher's research into the psycho-physiological basis of acting.[21] Barba founded the Odin Teatret in Norway in 1964, moving to its permanent home in Holstebro, Denmark, in 1966. In the early 1970s, non-Scandinavians joined the group, and it has since included members from Italy, the USA, Britain, Canada, Germany, Spain and Argentina. The Odin Teatret became the centre for the government-funded Nordisk Teaterlaboratorium,[22] inspired by Grotowski's Theatre Laboratory. Its activities reach beyond Barba's direct theatrical activities at the Odin Teatret: it is a major teaching centre, and arranges performances for international companies in various parts of Scandinavia; publishing and selling theatre books, it also makes and rents films on the theatre, and is the umbrella organization for several groups associated with the Odin.[23] In 1979, the activities of the Nordisk Teaterlaboratorium culminated in the foundation of the International School of Theatre Anthropology (ISTA), which 'is a most unusual school that has no classrooms or students, meets only periodically, has no curriculum, and has no graduates. Nevertheless, it is one of Europe's most important theatre research institutions.'[24] Holstebro functions as the administrative centre of ISTA; its primary work takes place, as Watson describes, at public sessions 'held from time to time at the request of particular funding bodies'.[25] At these sessions, Eastern and Western master performers share their expertise with 'relatively young, inexperienced' Western actors and directors. These practitioners are joined by 'intellectuals including theatre scholars, anthropologists, psychologists, biologists, and critics'.[26]

Theatre anthropology is the key concept in Barba's theatre theory and practice, and it subsumes a variety of concepts. Barba emphasizes that the term 'anthropology' is not used 'in the sense of cultural anthropology'.[27] Rather, it 'is a new field of study applied to the human being in a performance situation'.[28] Theatre anthropology incorporates both Western and Eastern theatre theory and practice and intends to provide 'bits of advice' to the actor, rather than looking for universal principles or laws.[29]

The actor is at the centre of theatre anthropology. Barba was inspired to set this priority by Grotowski and his interest in the actor's *presence* on stage: 'I am interested in a very elementary question: Why, when I see two actors doing the same thing, I get fascinated by one and not by the other.'[30] Barba also uses the terms *body-in-life* or *bios* when analysing presence.[31] He distinguishes between daily behaviour – i.e. mainly unconscious 'processes through which our bodies and voices absorb and reflect the culture in which we live'[32] – and extra-daily behaviour – i.e. the specific codes of movement pertaining to specific performance forms, which, in their aesthetic function, differ from daily behaviour.[33]

Closely related to the notion of extra-daily behaviour is the concept of the *pre-expressive*, which Barba defines as 'the level [of performance] which deals with how to render the actor's energy scenically alive, that is with how the actor can become a presence which immediately attracts the spectator's attention'.[34] Research has led Barba to differentiate three principles that govern the pre-expressive level of performance: 'alterations in balance, the law of opposition, and ... coherent incoherence'.[35] Whereas in daily behaviour, all movements of the body tend to follow the principle of least action, leading to a 'minimum expenditure of energy for standing, sitting, and walking',[36] extra-daily behaviour of performance requires shifts in balance, which in turn lead to more energy being required for movement, for remaining still or for retaining balance. The second principle, the law of opposition, is closely related to the alterations of balance. In both cases, daily behaviour patterns have to be distorted. In Western classical ballet the dancer maximizes the opposition between body weight and gravity in 'soaring feats of lightness and grace'.[37] The dancer expends much energy in the attempt to free himself from the force of gravity. The surplus of energy needed in performance is incoherent, because it 'makes no sense from a practical, daily life, point of view'. However, it is also understandable, and in that sense coherent, that the actor spends this much more energy in extra-daily, performative activity, because the excessive energy expenditure is a major source of the dynamic in each of the performance genres.[38]

Barba suggests a sequence of development of proper (extra-daily) technique for the actor: the actor first has to distance himself from 'incultured' spontaneity. He has to understand the difference between himself in daily mode of behaviour and the techniques which characterize the extra-daily mode of performance.[39] It is as if the actor has to learn all movements on the stage anew: he undergoes a process of physical acculturation. However, the more conscious the actor is of his extra-daily movements, the more he becomes blocked. The actor has to aim for accultured spontaneity rather than incultured spontaneity.

In the process, Barba pinpoints a paradox at the centre of the actor's art and methodology: it is located in the actor's interaction with his role and with the audience. Barba argues that an actor does not merely present the fictional world of the play, nor does his activity end in his own experience of portraying a fictional character. For Barba, performance is a 'dialectic between the two' – what he calls 'the anatomical theatre'.[40] In the performance, the actor portrays the fictional score – i.e. the 'physical actions and vocal delivery decided upon in rehearsal and repeated in each performance'[41] – and his meeting with it. This meeting will vary from performance to performance, depending on several factors:

the audience's reaction to the piece, the actor's psycho-emotional responses to events on stage as well as in the theatre, and the actor's personal associations with particular actions and/or situations in a work s/he has developed with his/her colleagues over a period of some eighteen months to two years.[42]

The relationship between (rehearsed) score and (unrehearsed, spontaneous) meeting with the score is characterized by tension. Barba maintains that it is through the convergence of these opposing forces that our personal experiences can reach others, and be transformed into a social experience through theatre.[43]

Here Barba's theatre aesthetics differ substantially from Grotowski's: for Grotowski, the convergence of opposing forces of score and the actor's experience was 'the means by which the actor instigated a process of self-revelation that affected the spectator'.[44] This implies that the performer's catharsis leads to catharsis in the audience. For Barba, the convergence of score and the actor's experience enriches the 'relationship between the performer and his/her audience directly'.[45]

It is in this relationship between actor and spectator that Barba's paradox is located: the actor's 'articulate actions' on the stage are perceived by the spectator as objective signs. These objective signs, however, result from subjective processes within the actor. Barba raises the question: 'How can the actor be this matrix and be able, at the same time, to shape them into objective signs whose origin is in his own subjectivity?'[46] This paradox, the simultaneity of inner subjectivity and objective outer expression and reception of that subjectivity, closely resembles the paradox of acting formulated by Diderot and taken up with different shifts of emphasis by the other theorists discussed so far. Barba's position combines the paradox in the actor–spectator relationship with the paradox in the actor himself. Indirectly, Barba also argues in favour of an actor's dual consciousness.

The externalization of subjectivity, i.e. emotions, has to be disciplined. In Barba's theatre anthropology, discipline is closely related to training: 'Training is a process of self-definition, a process of self-discipline.'[47] The emphasis on training is an emphasis on the body, which in turn is in line with the general tendency among contemporary theatre theorists and artists to stress the importance of the actor's body. Training thus appears outwardly physical, but, as Barba points out.

> it is not the exercise in itself that counts – for example, bending or somersaults – but the individual's justification for his own work, a justification which, although perhaps banal or difficult to explain through words is physiologically perceptible, evident to the observer.[48]

What Barba appears to imply here is that the actor's physical performance as perceived by an outside observer will differ depending on the mental attitude that lies behind the actor's physical expression.

Body technique is only one component of the 'theatre's body'. The second is 'the organ of *u-topia*', of 'non-place', residing in the actor's viscera and his right hemisphere. 'It is the super-ego which the presence of a master or masters has imbued us with during the transitions from daily technique to extra-daily performance technique.'[49] This organ transforms technique and raises it 'to a social and spiritual dimension'.[50] Barba describes the third organ as the 'irrational and secret temperature which renders our actions incandescent'.[51] Whereas the body and the 'super-ego' can be trained, the elusive third organ is 'our personal destiny. If we don't have it, no one can teach it to us'.[52] A unity of the three organs of the 'theatre's body' allows the actor to radiate energy and establish 'presence', thus attracting the spectator's attention.

The other major theatre personality associated with an intercultural approach is Peter Brook. In 1942, Peter Brook (born 1925) directed his first production, Marlowe's *Doctor Faustus*. He continued directing in major mainstream theatre in Britain, including the Royal Shakespeare Company (RSC), as well as opera and film. Inspired by Artaud, Brook mounted a short Theatre of Cruelty season in 1964, and continued what Williams calls a phase of 'theatre of disturbance',[53] with Genet's *The Screens*, Weiss's *The Marat/Sade*, a public reading of Weiss's *The Investigation*, about the atrocities at Auschwitz, in 1965, followed in 1966 by *US*, centring around the Vietnam war. Williams argues that these projects all aimed at confrontation, 'comprising abrupt tonal transitions and jarring clashes of style, to create the impression of a continually shifting and mutable reality'.[54] From 1968 to 1970, Brook directed *Oedipus* at the National Theatre in London, *The Tempest* at the Théâtre des Nations and *A Midsummer Night's Dream* at the RSC. In 1968, his seminal book, *The Empty Space*, was published.

In 1970, Brook left Britain for Paris, from where he founded the Centre International de Recherche Théâtrale (CIRT; the name was changed to Centre International de Créations Théâtrales, or CICT, in 1974), and from where he has conducted his theatre research and projects since, including journeys to Africa, the USA and India, and projects such as *Orghast*, *Conference of the Birds*, *The Ik*, *La Tragédie de Carmen* and *The Mahabharata*.

Commenting on Peter Brook, Jacqueline Martin argues that his ideas about acting provide a synthesis of several acting theories of the nineteenth and twentieth centuries:

> From Stanislavsky he has learned that an actor must practice how to be insincere with sincerity – how to lie truthfully; from Brecht he has learned the value of distancing oneself from the work by stepping back and looking at the results; from Artaud he has learned that by abandoning the text and working through improvisation one can return to the roots of physical expression; ... and from Grotowski he has learned that actors are mediumistic.[55]

Brook's main interest in the theatre is concerned with the 'possibility of arriving ... at a ritual expression of the true driving forces of our time'.[56]

The various phases of his career are nothing but different approaches to reaching this aim. Whereas Grotowski tried to turn theatre back into ritual, Brook turns ritual into theatre.[57] His ultimate aim is a 'totality of theatrical expression',[58] a theatre that transcends 'the surface of reality'.[59] This may be achieved by shocking the audience, as in Brook's experiments with Artaudian *Theatre of Cruelty*; by working with an international cast; by forays into anthropology (*Conference of the Birds*); by creating (or re-creating?) a new (ancient) language (*Orghast*); by making the elitist genre of opera accessible again (*The Tragedy of Carmen*, seen, worldwide, by at least 200,000 people[60]); by bridging the gap between theatre and storytelling (*The Mahabharata*), or the gap between theatre and science (*The Man Who*). In addition to these new approaches of 'transcending the surface', while working at CICT, he directed two plays from the more traditional theatrical canon: *The Cherry Orchard* (1981 and 1988) and *The Tempest* (1991).

In our problem-ridden society, according to Brook, transcendence is difficult to achieve; however, he maintains that despite all movement, destruction, restlessness and fashion, there are 'pillars of affirmation', rare moments when during a theatre performance actors, play and spectators merge collectively in a 'total experience, a total theatre'.[61] Brook further characterizes such experiences: 'At these rare moments, the theatre of joy, of catharsis, of celebration, the theatre of exploration, the theatre of shared meaning, the living theatre are one.'[62]

Grotowski reduced the theatre, leaving, as Brook puts it, 'a solitary man playing out his ultimate drama alone'.[63] In contrast, for Brook, theatre leads 'out of loneliness to the perception that is heightened because it is shared'.[64] If the theatre tries to 'slavishly recapture' such experiences of sharing through imitation, however, once they are gone, theatre will become deadly.

Stages on the way to total theatre are rough theatre and holy theatre. Both 'feed on deep and true aspirations in their audience, both tap infinite resources of energy, of different energies'.[65] Rough theatre is down-to-earth and direct; its energies are militant – anger and hatred – but are also fed by lightheartedness and gaiety. Holy theatre, Brook maintains, could also be called 'theatre of the invisible-made-visible'.[66] The invisible contains all the hidden impulses of man. Brook's view mirrors Barba's position on the function of theatre: 'rendering the invisible visible', implying an investigation of the process 'by means of which mental energy (invisible) becomes somatic energy (physical)'.[67] Although he uses the same terms here, Brook's understanding of the function of theatre is different from Barba's. Brook's point of departure is the religious implication of the pair of opposites: although the invisible is visible all the time, seeing it is not automatic, but requires certain conditions, either a mental state or a certain understanding. Meeting such conditions is not easy and it takes a long time: 'In any event, to comprehend the visibility of the invisible is a life's work.'[68] Theatre that deserves to be called holy theatre 'not only presents the invisible but also offers conditions that make its perception possible'.[69] Once total theatre is experienced, however, the divisions into deadly, rough and holy theatre disappear.

Rough theatre, holy theatre, and, above all, total theatre need a highly trained actor. For Brook, training first implies physical training, leading to a body that is 'open, responsive, and unified in all its responses'.[70] Second is the training of the emotions, leading to the actor's 'capacity to feel, appreciate and express a range of emotions from the crudest to the most refined'.[71] While the actor experiences the emotions, however, although he is sincere, he has to be detached at the same time. Brook here reflects Stanislavsky's and Brecht's paradox.

The achievement of total, transcendental theatre has remained Brook's 'grail-like quest'[72] throughout his career. The actor applies his physical and emotional efforts to achieve Brook's aim of simple forms of theatre that are both understandable and simultaneously 'packed with meaning'.[73] In *Orghast*, Brook commissioned the poet Ted Hughes to develop a new language, also called Orghast, which was based on the concept of total identity between sound and meaning.[74] The intention, according to Innes, was

> not only ... to reflect the sensation of a half-barbaric world, but to affect 'magically' the mental state of the listener on an instinctive level in the same way as a sound can affect the growth of plants or the patterning of iron filings.[75]

Innes points out, however, that *Orghast* worked only with intellectually sophisticated spectators, whereas a 'supposedly more primitive (and therefore in theory more receptive, even more susceptible) audience on Brook's African tour apparently found those dark primordial cries hilariously funny'.[76]

I now focus on Brook's controversial production of *The Mahabharata* to reveal the implications of an intercultural approach to acting, which has to be discussed and understood in a wider political and philosophical context. French cultural politics allowed British theatre director Peter Brook to come as close to fulfilling his theatrical dreams as can be imagined. His adaptation for theatre, film and television of the Indian epic *The Mahabharata* has become, for many, the prime example of intercultural theatre. The arguments exchanged in the course of the controversy surrounding Brook's production, documented in a purpose-published reader,[77] and perhaps most eloquently shaped by Rustom Bharucha,[78] have recently been fielded against the intercultural movement in general; Pavis, among others, claims that the intercultural approach, the dominant critical and theatrical approach of the 1990s, has reached a dead end, and argues in favour of a re-Occidentalization of Western theatre practice and theory.[79]

I would like to argue that the theoretical approaches adopted by a majority of critics do not do justice to the work of art almost by definition, because they approach the production with tools and concepts inappropriate to its own aesthetic. Predominantly political (politically correct?), postcolonial and superficially psychological approaches cannot do justice to a source (*The Mahabharata*) *and* a production that *both* aim to tell the story of humankind and to reach into a common human ground beyond cultural diversity, a state of freedom characteristic of 'total theatre', in Brook's theatrical context, and liberation (*moksha*) in the philosophical context of *The Mahabharata*. I propose a way out of this dilemma, taking recourse to the currently booming debate in science and philosophy on the nature of human consciousness, which is steadily expanding into the field of the humanities and the arts, and includes interesting views on the relation between theatre and consciousness. Once the theory of intercultural theatre integrates relevant aspects of the current consciousness debate, the dead-end position may need revision.

Since the majority of the critical debate surrounding Brook's *Mahabharata* has revolved around Bharucha's essay 'A view from India', I will in turn focus on the argument he presents. It is useful to differentiate several levels of discourse in his critique. According to Bharucha, Brook fails to expressly make clear the implications of various important philosophical concepts informing the action and motivation of *The Mahabharata*'s characters. *Dharma*, for example, Bharucha insists, is mainly absent in Brook's conception of character, or else, it is

> travestied through:
> a mish-mash of cultures with an overriding aura of 'Indianness';
> a total avoidance of historicity, or social transformation underlying *The Mahabharata* from a tribal to a brahmin-dominated caste society;
> a monochromatic presentation of characters with no sense of their evolution through different stages in life;
> a failure to suggest that this life is just part of a series of rebirths, relivings of past transgressions, that can cease only through *moksha*.[80]

The implications of the caste system, especially those surrounding *kshatrya* (inadequately rendered as 'warriors'), are not made clear, neither is 'a sense of time that transcends chronology'.[81] The unsatisfactory characterization of the god Krishna annoys Bharucha and other commentators, both regarding his personality and the rather short coverage in Brook's production of the *Bhagavad-Gita*, frequently considered the key section of the entire *Mahabharata*.

Several traits of the major characters in *The Mahabharata* are not included in the production text, although it would have been easy, Bharucha maintains, to do so. Here, the issue is one that is pertinent to any adaptation of a literary text for the theatre: which elements to choose, which to foreground and why. Choices have to be made, and they are open to critical discussion. However, these are no longer central only to intercultural theatre. The choice of an international cast for the production of *The Mahabharata* is criticized by Bharucha for its lack of purpose. He asks: 'But what is the point of that if most of the actors' voices, rhythms and performance traditions have been homogenized within a Western structure of action, where they have to speak a language unknown to most of them?'[82]

Indians assert that the characters of the epic, and the various stories it contains, are very familiar to all Indians, independent of their background and social status. This level of familiarity is expressed, for example, by Mallika Sarabhai, who played Draupadi in Brook's adaptation of *The Mahabharata*, when she says:

> if there is one child in a school who is very strong or very large, the other children will compare him with Bhima. In India when you talk of Draupadi or Krishna or Bhima in the middle of a completely contemporary conversation, you still know exactly who you are talking about. And that is the extent of *The Mahabharata*'s contemporaneity in India today.[83]

Mishra's argument supports Sarabhai's view, and he goes on to distinguish several 'texts' of the epic. First, there is the edited text, a result of scholarship. Second, the one Sarabhai refers to, which is 'passed on from mother to child'. Third, the text 'as it exists through folk, theatrical and filmic representations'. Finally, *The Mahabharata* in translation, 'both in Indian vernacular and in major world languages'.[84] In India and throughout South-East Asia, Williams points out, *The Mahabharata* has become 'the common source of the bulk of the dramatic material of dance drama, storytelling, popular folk players, puppet shows, films and even strip cartoons'.[85] There has also been an adaptation by Indian television, in many parts, which was later shown on British TV.

This deep-rootedness of Indians in *The Mahabharata* must be accepted as at least one, and perhaps the initial reason, why Indian critics have, on the whole, voiced their reservation about Peter Brook's adaptation of *The Mahabharata* for stage, screen and television. Bharucha points out that his own criticism of Brook's work does not imply a fundamentalist attitude: Western theatre artists, Bharucha argues, should not be 'banned from touching our sacred texts'. Instead, he demands that *The Mahabharata*

> must be seen on as many levels as possible within the Indian context, so that its meaning (or rather, multiple levels of meaning) can have some bearing on the lives of the Indian people for whom *The Mahabharata* was written, and who continue to derive their strength from it.[86]

A production based on Indian material and directed by a Western director, then, according to Bharucha, has to pay its respects to the source material by leaving the material taken up for the production as much as possible within its cultural context. This has to be a potential benefit for the audiences in the source culture, who produced the cultural material taken up in the Western performance in the first place, and for whom this material is supposed to have beneficial effects. This demand echoes Bharucha's criticism that none of the intercultural theatre artists in the West have turned 'to India out of the faintest concern for its present socio-cultural tradition. Rather they have been drawn almost exclusively to our "traditional" sources.'[87]

In preparation for the production, Brook and his company travelled through India to get a first-hand impression of the country and its culture. A number of the people with whom Brook interacted on this journey later complained about his inappropriate behaviour, such as humiliating his hosts, being insensitive to the conditions they were able to offer, suspicious about the moderate fees charged by companies that had been booked to perform for the company, promising parts in the production to local people and then forgetting about it, and so on. Such anecdotes serve very well to stir (understandable) resentment against Brook. Some or all of these points of criticism are then usually subsumed under the umbrella of neo-colonialism, neo-imperialism, cultural theft and orientalism. Thus, Bharucha categorically states that Brook's production of *The Mahabharata* 'exemplifies one of the most blatant (and accomplished) appropriations of Indian culture in recent years'. Its neo-colonialist tendencies emerge in 'its appropriation and reordering of non-Western material within an orientalist framework of thought and action, which has been specifically designed for the international market'.[88]

The critique of Brook's *Mahabharata*, triggered mainly by Bharucha's essay, is certainly complex. The level of discourse adopted (consciously?) by Bharucha and other Indian and Western commentators on Brook's production is clearly set within the confines of the Western mind-set with its predominance and superiority of reason, the intellect, concepts, historicity and understanding over levels of the mind that in this context are considered inferior, such as intuition, anything that cannot be expressed clearly in words, hunches, myth, archetypes, the spiritual, the universal. It may be expected that Western critics adopt 'their' Western paradigms in critical approaches to Brook's production. Thus, Shevtsova argues that Brook's *Mahabharata* 'obliges performers and spectators alike to review routine assumptions about their own culture through its prism of cultures',[89] and Williams appears puzzled at *The Mahabharata*'s 'claim to be a beneficial poem' when he writes: 'all who hear it will be somehow "better" ', and he can only interpret 'better' in a political-intellectual way as 'empowered'.[90]

What is more striking is that even the arguments 'from India' against Brook's production are clearly located within a Western mind-set. Thus, Bharucha considers what Brook could or could not *understand* about *The Mahabharata*;[91] he assumes that an Indian, brought up with *The Mahabharata*, can transform even an unsatisfactory representation of the epic into 'a deeply spiritual experience'.[92] Bharucha does not expect such a transformation to take place in Brook or his Western audience, who do not have the knowledge of the various concepts informing the philosophy of *The Mahabharata*. Bharucha is highly critical of Jean-Claude Carrière's decision to enter the deepest places of the characters 'without imposing our concepts, our judgements or our twentieth-century analysis, in so far as that's possible'.[93] For Bharucha, Carrière's argument implies that the characters' deepest places can be appreciated without the use of the intellect, without 'a critical consciousness'.[94] The further implication of this understanding of Carrière's view for Bharucha is that it is as if '*The Mahabharata* lies beyond questioning and that its "story" can be told only through some mystical communion with the work itself'.[95]

All these examples serve to demonstrate that Bharucha and others clearly favour the aspects of intellect over and above those which go beyond the intellect's capacity. Such a preference is characteristic of the majority of views proposed until very recently in the current Western debate in science and philosophy, on the nature of the human mind and consciousness. The study of human consciousness has become a major focus of research in a number of disciplines such as philosophy, psychology, cognitive science, neuroscience, computer science and physics. Numerous publications in the field – in general as well as two specialist journals, *Consciousness and Cognition* and *Journal of Consciousness Studies*, and in a book series published by Oxford University Press and MIT Press, among others – indicate this development. In 1997, the British Psychological Association approved the establishment of a new section dedicated to consciousness and experiential psychology, and the Fetzer Institute provided a grant of $1.4 million to the University of Arizona to establish a Center for Consciousness Studies at their Tucson campus. This centre hosted major conferences, entitled 'Towards a Science of Consciousness', the most recent of which attracted some 1,000 delegates from all over the world.

The emphasis of the debate has been focused on the scientific study of consciousness, fully established in the Western, science- and objectivity-oriented mind-set. By definition, this approach has to cancel out subjectivity, precisely those areas of the mind which, in the debate surrounding *The Mahabharata*, have come in for attack or ridicule. It is striking that in 1998, one of the first major projects run under the auspices of the Center for Consciousness Studies was designed to specifically address the issue of dealing with human subjectivity in a scientific context. Not surprisingly, the strongest arguments in that debate came from scholars whose thought has been influenced by non-Western philosophy, in which a more holistic, all-encompassing view of consciousness is not only theorized, but where numerous physical and mental techniques are provided which may well serve as the scientific tools of the future.

Brook's own comments on his *Mahabharata* have been dismissed as lacking the level of precision required to make them useful in the intellectual debate on the production. He is not interested in politics or historicity. He did not want to imitate India. Rather, most of Brook's comments refer to the experience of *The Mahabharata* on levels of the mind beyond the intellect. He expressly insists that we should not come to the production with our 'own set of notions about Hinduism, Christianity, comparative religion, mythology, the relative nature of different types of epic or non-epic storytelling', in order to encounter something 'never encountered anywhere else, which cannot be received on a theoretical basis, which can't be received other than as a direct experience'.[96]

For the following discussion, we have to remind ourselves of the model of the mind proposed by Indian philosophy, with its hierarchy of senses, desire, mind, intellect, emotion, feeling and intuition, ego and underlying pure consciousness. Viewed from the level of the intellect alone, devoid of the experience of subtler levels, especially that of underlying pure consciousness, Brook's statement seems suspicious at best. The experience aimed at must appear as unmediated, and, as Carlson points out, critical theory has revealed the possibility of unmediated experience as illusory.[97] What Brook is in fact describing as the aim of engaging with *The Mahabharata* is a state of mind in which the mediated (processes on the levels of senses, desire, mind, intellect, intuition and feeling, and ego) and the unmediated (pure consciousness) co-exist. In the context of the *The Mahabharata* production, Brook is unable to put into words,[98] to name, the envisaged experience. All he can say is that the intellect alone (as the agent responsible for notions, theories, concepts, etc.) is not sufficient as a *means* or *tool* of gaining access to this more comprehensive state of mind, which is *beyond* language. Thus, what *is* illusory, or a 'dangerous, or self-deceptive vision, denying the voice of the Other in an attempt to transcend it'[99] *only* if considered from the isolated perspective of the intellect, becomes the *potential* of theatre practice at subtler, more comprehensive levels of experience.

How does Brook go about achieving his aims in practice? His *Mahabharata* appeals to all levels of the mind. Many commentators have noted the appeal of his production to the senses, with their display of fireworks and the extraordinary setting in a quarry or an impressive old theatre. The intellect is stimulated by concepts, by reasoning, by thought experiments. Some of these are found in Carrière and Brook's adaptation, such as the story told by Bhishma on his deathbed about the significance and implications of death. Indirectly, the debate caused by Brook's production is an indication of its effectiveness on the intellectual level. The key method he used to access the subtler levels of the mind, such as intuition and especially pure consciousness, is suggestion. Philosophical concepts or customs are hinted at, are implied, but never didactically presented. Set and costumes create a sense of India without being museum replicas. Brook calls it 'a flavour of India'. Similar to the experience of *rasa*, which is at the centre of Indian theatre aesthetics as described in detail in the *Natyashastra*, it is an aesthetic experience that is created within the spectator while watching the performance.

A particularly striking (and controversial!) example of suggestion is Brook's treatment of what many consider to be the most important episode of the entire *Mahabharata*, the *Bhagavad-Gita*. A close look at the actual text of that brief passage in the production reveals, however, that Brook captures its essence: in the course of a long conversation, Krishna in his divinity leads the hero, Arjuna, to the state of full enlightenment. In the structure of the dramatization chosen by Brook, with its emphasis on action and linear narrative, the long spiritual discourse of the *Bhagavad-Gita* does not offer itself for any other rendering: it is in line with the overall concept. A separate production altogether might choose to deal with the *Bhagavad-Gita* only: attempting to fathom its depth in dramatic form is likely to be quite a challenge. Thus, it only appears that Brook did not do full justice to Hindu philosophy and Indian society. He may not have done so on the intellectual level, to which the criticism by Bharucha and others is limited, but by taking the Indian epic and adapting it for an audience (irrespective of its culture or nationality), he did make its essence available to all involved, facilitating the development of higher states of consciousness. Not everyone may *understand*, immediately or even after reflection, 'what it is all about'. Deep philosophical concepts may be lost *intellectually*, because they have not been mentioned, described, analysed, brought out clearly (enough) in the production. However, all structures, elements, aspects and facets that may be revealed in the text through any means possible (scholarship, intuition, cognition) exist in every part of it, and it is on this level that the efficacy of *The Mahabharata*, and with it Brook's production, lies. Every part contains the whole, which is always active on all levels of the mind.

Thus, Bharucha's argument that Brook's production failed because it did not provide the main audience of the production with sufficient *information* about *The Mahabharata* through the way the epic was dramatized is again limited to (although accurate on) the level of the intellect: it is not necessary to *know* and *learn about* Indian philosophy to benefit from the deep aspects of that philosophy contained in Brook's production. These aspects are part of the production because it is based on *The Mahabharata*, and because they are suggested in the specific adaptation created by Carrière and Brook. This epic was not merely a great literary creation, as, for example, Shakespeare's plays, so it is thus not appropriate to refer to it as an 'artistic product'.[100] Rather, *The Mahabharata* was cognized by Vedic *rishis* on the level of the Absolute, Brahman. Thus, each of those units on its own, and taken together, will affect the reader's or spectators' consciousness in line with the general effect ascribed to Veda and Vedic literature: eliminating blocks from the system, and thereby facilitating the development and permanent experience of higher states of consciousness in all those subjected to it in any possible form of production and reception.

A further aspect of the production's strength relates to the international cast with whom Brook worked both in Paris and on tour. It is an essential factor in this suggestive approach to the text. The performers bring their own individual cultural backgrounds, languages, etc. to their parts, naturally and unobtrusively, neither emphasizing their traditions nor by any means hiding them. Critics have noted the variety of accents and styles of acting: Yoshi Oida, for example, is clearly influenced by his classical Japanese Noh training. However, despite this diversity, which is all the intellect can perceive, by integrating the intellect with the subtler levels of the mind, Brook manages to bring out an underlying unity. Ultimate unity exists only on the level of pure consciousness. The aesthetic experience created by Brook's *Mahabharata* is thus one which comprises unity in diversity.

Part of the success of Brook's *Mahabharata* production in affecting all levels of the mind and creating the aesthetic experience of unity in diversity is due to the fact that the source, *The Mahabharata* itself, is universal in a very special sense, which includes but also transcends intellectual discourse: reading the text, or watching excerpts performed, will produce effects on the whole range of the mind. They are found on the level of the ego, when people identify (themselves) with the heroic characters. On the level of the intuition and feelings, when even repeated narration of major episodes never fails to move, or when generations of artists in various genres find their artistic inspiration in the epic. On the level of the intellect, when generations of scholars come up with new and fascinating interpretations. On the level of the senses, finally, when episodes of *The Mahabharata* are enacted on the stage, or sung about accompanied by music. Most importantly, *The Mahabharata* has a direct influence on the level of pure consciousness, facilitating its experience in the reader's or spectator's mind. It is important to note that the causes for this multi-level effect of *The Mahabharata* are not restricted to the contents of the epic, or to the characteristics of its heroes and villains – that is, to any concept or construct which the intellect could isolate in the text.

The effect of *The Mahabharata* in general, and of Brook's theatre adaptation in particular, on all the levels of the mind, may be, statistically, most obvious in India, because the text originated in that country and is kept alive in its traditions of storytelling, dance, theatre and folklore. The effect is, however, not *restricted to* India. No matter what the background of someone who comes in contact with the epic, its texture is so rich that everyone will benefit on at least one level of the mind. The more of those levels that are developed, the richer the resulting experience of the epic will be, the more nuances may be picked up, the more links to one's own previous experience can be established.

An Indian person may resonate more directly with the characters and events, because of their familiarity with them. But who is 'the Indian?' What about the Indian who is not familiar with *The Mahabharata?* Does it make a difference where the Indian was born and lives? Will any Indian (familiar or unfamiliar with the epic, born and living in India or elsewhere) be more familiar on some collective unconscious level than any non-Indian, no matter how familiar with the epic the non-Indian may have become through study, life in India, friendship with or marriage to an Indian person? It is quite possible to extend such questions even further, and their purpose in my argument should be clear: the critics' references to the deep-rootedness of *The Mahabharata* in India is poignantly limited to the political discourse, based on the level of the intellect devoid of the experience of pure consciousness. Bharucha's criticism is accurate on that level alone, ignoring (by definition) subtler levels of functioning.

As an exposition of knowledge of intellectual contents and concepts, intercultural theatre is limited both in theory and in practice. To a large extent, the practice has attempted to reach beyond the intellect to create an aesthetic experience characterized by universality, by unity in diversity. To an equally large extent, theatre researchers are trapped in the current Western, intellect-dominated mind-set. For this very reason, there are only a few projects developing suitable research methodologies to establish whether the theatre artists' use of intercultural theatre to reach beyond the intellect, beyond the emotions, even beyond the ego into the universal level of pure consciousness and on towards higher states of consciousness (as described by Indian philosophy) has been successful. Looking at intercultural theatre from the perspective of the intellect *alone* can only lead to the conclusion that it has failed, for the very reason that it is an inappropriately limited approach because it is the level most theatre artists want to get *away* from through their choice of intercultural theatre.

What is the way ahead? Certainly, not to abandon intercultural theatre practice, or the main tendency of interculturalism in theatre research.[101] The reorientation demanded by Pavis is indeed needed, but not towards a further strengthening of the exclusively intellectual approaches of our own critical tradition that he suggests such as

Freudianism, Marxism or socio-critics. The reorientation needs to take note of the crucially important debate in consciousness studies regarding subjectivity. Such an approach will bring new insights within the intellectual domain. With reference to intercultural theatre, it means approaching intercultural theatre practice on its own terms to develop a research methodology that accounts for subjectivity in the production and reception processes, not as an unwanted parameter to be excluded (following the paradigm of science), but as a fully valid component of human experience, one that might be worth saving from years spent in an undeserved and ultimately unjustifiable position of marginality. In the final chapter of this book, I take the opportunity of coming back to the intercultural debate in relation to acting.

ஓ<u></u>

8

Training the Actor, Past and Present

ଌⲒଓଔ

In our survey of approaches to acting over the centuries and across the world, we have already briefly come across actor training on several occasions. It is now time to provide a fuller picture. In Greece, as we have seen, the training of the chorus was spread over the eleven months prior to the performance. Initially, the dramatist himself trained and choreographed the chorus, but in due course, professional trainers took over, probably working closely with the dramatist. Training is said to have been intense, long and arduous, involving special diet, exercise and disciplined practice. In return, members of the chorus were often pampered and given special treatment, remarkable in view of rather spartan treatment of soldiers.

In Rome, many actors were originally slaves. When considered talented by their masters, they were given for training to established actors, and, on completion of training, were hired out to managers. The profit was shared between master and teacher. Since actors were expected to speak, dance and sing, we must assume that they were trained in these three fields. There is evidence that special emphasis was placed on the angle of the head, the placement of feet, the use of hands and vocal intonation to convey their characters' emotion in given situations of the play. Movements, for which there were strict codes, were exaggerated. The great actors, such as Roscius and Aesopus, listened to the great orators of their time to improve their vocal delivery and gestures.

With the rise of professionalism in European theatre, training became more and more sophisticated. In the time of Shakespeare, each licensed company would take on four to six boy apprentices, who played the female parts. Some actors were members of traditional guilds, who took their apprentices in the name of their original craft, but trained them as actors. Records show that boys began their apprenticeship between the ages of six and fourteen, and that it could last anywhere from three to twelve years. On completion, some continued as actors, others changed profession. While with the company, the apprentices were trained, fed and clothed by their teachers, who received payment for their duties by the company. In seventeenth-century France, novice actors were coached by leading colleagues while playing utility parts with a company. For the trainees/apprentices, such early stages of training included a strong element of imitation of what they saw around them. Thus, in eighteenth-century England, young actors learned by trial and error. Joining on a probationary basis, they observed and imitated experienced colleagues, from whom they also received training on occasion. Records of nineteenth-century England show that unless actors had strong family connections in the profession, which allowed them to start their work in the family business, they would begin in the provinces, sometimes unpaid, sometimes having to pay the manager. Henry Irving, later one of the leading actors of the late nineteenth century, made his debut in 1856 and had to appear in a total of 451 roles during his first three years, which meant he had to learn some 500 lines a day.[1]

Although there are some indications of a more systematic, institutionalized training in Elizabethan and Jacobean England,[2] such a system did not really begin in England or Germany until the early twentieth century (apart from a few interesting, but short-lived, endeavours in the eighteenth and nineteenth centuries). In contrast, in France the Royal Dramatic School was founded in 1786, a forerunner of today's Conservatoire, which held imitation as its main principle for many years.

Several late nineteenth- or early twentieth-century theatre artists strongly argued in favour of institutionalized actor training, and developed models for them. Harley Granville-Barker (1877–1946) was a prime example. Critical of the state of theatre in his time, Granville-Barker argued for an exemplary theatre, in which dramatic art is studied and developed, for its own sake, and disseminated 'in every demonstrable form, not only in the single one of the acted play'.[3] In the theatre he criticized, the actor has to get involved with his part to the extent of suspending 'critical faculties in regard to' the acting process altogether.[4] Because the actor's success, and with it his livelihood, depends on his acting, the actor has to exploit any play's virtues and attempt to cover its weaknesses by adding from his own resources. Against 'technique outworn and discarded', Granville-Barker sets an attempt to do without acting at all. This, however, does not yield better results either, because many actors' expression

> is fatally clogged by the outflowing of a voice they can't manage, a face
> that appears to need moving by hand, and a body they hardly dare move
> at all, unless with a violence which will mask its lack of all finer
> articulation.[5]

The newly founded drama schools did not solve the problem, Granville-

Barker argued, mainly because the problems had not been identified and formulated precisely enough. The schools' approach was considered too narrow, producing many graduates who, having acquired sufficient skills to survive, were only too aware of the vast area they would never be able to master: a devastating awareness of their own mediocrity.

The alternative Granville-Barker envisioned is complex, and I limit my summary and discussion to the issues relating directly to the actor; his ideas about most aspects of management, stage design or the choice of the repertory are thus left out. Rather than adopt one approach to all possible parts (a Shakespearean part like Romeo and a realistic role such as Torvald Helmer in Ibsen's *A Doll's House*), the actor should do each part he plays full justice within the parameters set by the play itself. Ideally, a highly qualified audience would detect weaknesses and strengths in an actor's work, and theatre critics, acting as spokesmen for the audience, would draw the actor's attention to them, serving as acceptable stimuli for the improvement of weaknesses and consolidating existing strengths.

The theatre as school provides general education as a broad basis for the theatre-specific subjects. In turn, broad education in theatre-specific subjects serves as a basis and prerequisite from which to begin the activity of acting. These subjects include voice production, elocution, dialectics, eurhythmics, playwriting, analytical criticism, theatre history, history of costume, costume design, the design, construction and painting of the set, fencing, dancing, singing and music. The rationale behind this structure of education is striking: once the foundation of general and theatre-specific education has been laid, the student is allowed to plunge into the activity of acting: 'For once he is in, he must swim unaided. His enthusiasm will survive, there's no fear, while his unexpended powers ripen.'[6] Some students will proceed to careers in theatre, some will pass on what they gained through their studies in the education system or as theatre critics, thus gradually leading to a wide-ranging reform of theatre in society.

For students of the theatre, the rehearsal process is preceded by a seminar conducting a co-operative study of the play, whose aim is to create a unity in diversity. After two or three read-throughs with varied readers, the play's meaning is discussed and agreed. Selected members of the seminar will now enact the roles, leading to further discussion as the agreed meaning derived from study is confirmed, modified or rejected in favour of a new one which could have emerged only through the acting process.

The theatre school exists side by side with a professional theatre company (the theatre as playhouse rather than as school). The theatre should provide a reliable source of income, thus doing away with the image (at times a reality) of vagabondage associated with the acting profession. With no more than four to five performances a week, and an equal amount of time spent on rehearsals as on performance, the actor must be allowed sufficient time to study in rehearsals together with fellow-actors and the director. Thus, the dangers of automatism and self-consciousness are avoided. Together with the directors and designers, actors should become generally informed and knowledgeable in all aspects of theatre, besides their obvious specializations.

Work on any production would be predominantly a process of collaboration between the actors, director, designers and, in the case of a contemporary play, the playwright. Solitary study for the actor is discouraged, as is mechanical memorizing of lines: learning them should be a result of the collaborative process. Breaks in between this ensemble rehearsal process should be left to allow ideas to incubate and develop further. The actor, Granville-Barker argues, must 'continue what the dramatist has begun by methods as nearly related to his in under-standing and intention as the circumstances allow'.[7] Granville-Barker considers the character as a

> new being that is not the actor's consistent self though partaking of it; that is not the character worn as a disguise; individual, but with no absolute existence at all, a relative being only, and now related alike to the actor as to the play.[8]

To achieve this development, debate and discussion start the rehearsal process and initially lead to certainty in the actor as to thought and feeling regarding the play and the character he has to portray. The more unconscious this process, the better. The physical action of the play should not develop, Granville-Barker maintains, before the actor has gained security in thought and feeling. Outward aspects of the character within the given situation of the play (entrances and exits, for example) must be studied and well rehearsed, and the actor has to remain in conscious control of them throughout every performance, and thus avoid slipping into automatism. There is, however, a second level to acting, involving 'demeanour, tones, gestures, and the like'.[9] To these, the actor should not oppose a 'mental bar'; only subconscious attention to them is needed. This second level is based on spontaneity, leading to freshness and vitality of acting. Both levels of acting combine to create a sophisticated performance:

> If the underlying idea is just and consistent, if the interpreter is physically trained and mentally and emotionally sensitized – if his faculties, that is to say, are sufficiently at one with his conception – then all that he does or can do will now have appropriate value and stand in right proportion to the whole.[10]

Granville-Barker published his ideas in 1922, but many of them can already be found in his work with John Vedrenne (1863–1930) at the Court Theatre, London (1904–07). In their productions, they emphasized ensemble acting. Their attention to appropriate diction was considered unique at the time, unparalleled by the approaches at the Moscow Art Theatre or Théâtre Libre in France. At the Court, speaking well meant that through training the actors appeared to be speaking naturalistically.[11] London theatres were too much under the influence of commercialism, and the theatre buildings, and with them the stage spaces, were too large to easily adopt Granville-Barker and Vedrenne's innovations. However, the repertory theatres in Manchester, Glasgow and Liverpool, and acting schools such as the Royal Academy of Dramatic Art (RADA), showed such influence in their subsequent development.[12]

As the cover of a recently published book suggests, actor 'training is arguably the most unique phenomenon of twentieth-century theatre-making'.[13] In most cases individual pioneers have developed new approaches to acting and, with that, to actor training. They include, in alphabetical order, Stella Adler, Eugenio Barba, Bertolt Brecht, Peter Brook, Joseph Chaikin, Michael Chekhov, Jacques Copeau, Jerzy Grotowski, Joan Littlewood, Sanford Meisner, Vsevolod Meyerhold, Wlodzimierz Staniewski, Konstantin Stanislavsky, Lee Strasberg and Tadashi Suzuki.

Let us review a few cases. Meyerhold placed much emphasis on the actor's physical training and discipline: he wanted an actor so 'thoroughly trained that he could respond immediately, as if by reflex action, to the needs dictated by his part or by the director'.[14] To achieve this aim, Meyerhold developed a set of simple and complex exercises which he called *biomechanics*. Theatre researchers have had difficulties in assessing this concept for two reasons: first, because 'it was a means to an end, not an end in itself'; and second, because 'it was never fully explained or codified by Meyerhold'.[15] Biomechanics incorporated many elements of acrobatics and gymnastics. Simple exercises included 'deep knee bends, with spine erect, stretching and contracting in various planes and at various tempi',[16] walking and running exercises, and various falls, backwards and forwards. The *dactyl* was a preparatory exercise carried out before more complex *études*:

> In this, the actor stands relaxed, arms down, on the balls of his feet which are placed one in front to the other as in a boxer's stance, with the toes pointing slightly inwards. Leading with the hands, which describe a wide semi-circle as they move upwards through 180°, clapping twice sharply as they go, the whole body is brought to a position stretching upwards, with the heels raised off the ground and the head thrown back. Then the hands describe a downwards semi-circle, clapping twice, ending flung backwards behind the actor; the arms again lead the movement – when they are parallel with the ground, the knees begin to bend and the head is flung backward. The knee of the rear foot is no more than an inch off the ground, the back is bowed, the head beside the forward knee. By swinging the arms forward, enough momentum is created to return the actor to the initial standing position.[17]

Especially in the *études*, the sequence of movements was based on a principle of three consecutive phases: preparation for the action, the action itself and its corresponding reaction. A marked pause separates these three elements. For example, 'Throwing the Stone': 'The actor runs, halts, crouches and leans back to pick up the imaginary stone, rises and leans forward to aim, takes the stone around in a wide arc backwards, poises, throws, leaps forward to land two-footed with a cry.'[18]

In addition to exercises for individual actors, Meyerhold developed some for pairs. Again the aim was for the actor to achieve perfect control of the body, together with an awareness, at every moment, of the body and what it looked like from outside. Once the actor had mastered biomechanics, 'he could go beyond the needs of psychological character depiction and "grip" his audience emotionally through physiological process'.

Grotowski developed various training methods to enable his actors to reach that state of mind he called *translumination*. The methods were mainly physical, aiming 'to facilitate the activation of . . . body memory: a natural reservoir of impulses to action and expression stored within the physiological make-up of an individual, an intuitive corporeal "intelligence" '.[19] In the early stages of training at the Theatre Laboratory, the actors experimented with training forms and techniques from Oriental and Asian theatre, and incorporated yoga exercises. However, Grotowski eventually abandoned such experiments, concluding that non-Western aesthetics were completely alien to him: 'I do not think that we can adopt from them any techniques, or that they could inspire us directly.'[20] Grotowski realized that Oriental or Asian theatre forms are characterized by achieving a state of sacred theatre, in which spontaneity and discipline co-exist and mutually reinforce each other. He considered such a state desirable for a Western actor, but felt that the techniques that allow, say, an Indian actor to achieve this co-existence would not work for a Western actor.

Peter Brook argues that rough theatre, holy theatre and above all total theatre need a highly trained actor. For Brook, training first implies physical training, leading to a body that is 'open, responsive, and unified in all its responses'.[21] Second is the training of the emotions, leading to the actor's 'capacity to feel, appreciate and express a range of emotions from the crudest to the most refined'.[22]

For Barba, 'training is a process of self-definition, a process of self-discipline'.[23] The emphasis on training is an emphasis on the body, which in turn is in line with the general tendency among contemporary theatre theorists and artists to stress the importance of the actor's body. Training thus appears outwardly physical, but, as Barba points out:

> it is not the exercise in itself that counts – for example, bending or somersaults – but the individual's justification for his own work, a

justification which, although perhaps banal or difficult to explain through words is physiologically perceptible, evident to the observer.[24]

What Barba appears to imply here is that the actor's physical performance as perceived by an outside observer will differ depending on the mental attitude that lies behind the actor's physical expression.

The masters' innovations were taken up, in their pure form or in further modifications, in training institutions. In the UK and the German-speaking countries (Germany, Austria, Switzerland), for example, there are numerous traditional drama schools which include one or more acting options among their portfolio of courses. In the UK there are usually three-year acting courses leading to a diploma, or, when the institution is associated with a university, or has university status itself, a BA in acting. For mature students or trained professionals seeking retraining, one-year postgraduate courses are offered. Some schools also schedule part-time or evening courses, and in some cases, training takes place within a professional theatre company, harking back to the apprentice days of past centuries. In the German-speaking countries, courses usually last for four years and are full time, eventually leading to a diploma. The majority of training institutions focus on the classical canon and related techniques. After an introduction to acting, students are subjected to textual analysis and interpretation. In university-associated UK schools there is more emphasis on theoretical subjects, which may be examined in the traditional way with essays or written examinations. In German-speaking drama schools, more emphasis is given to theoretical background than in the UK, with teaching units in theatre and drama history, theory of acting, applied dramaturgy, art history and aesthetics.

During their three- or four-year course, students of acting focus on the three areas of characterization, voice work and body training. The following headings, taken from course descriptions of US, UK and German drama schools, could be grouped under characterization: Creating a Character, The Objective, Method Acting, Acting Shakespeare, Epic Forms and Contemporary Plays. Training of the body includes movement training in general, Period Movement, work with masks, various forms of improvisation, clowning and *commedia dell'arte* exercises, as well as stage combat, including fencing, dance and mime. Classes in the Alexander Technique (mainly in the UK, occasionally in the USA), t'ai chi, aikido, Autogenes Training and Feldenkrais (mainly German-speaking countries) or Butoh (USA) are occasionally offered to enhance the actors' awareness of their bodies. The Schule für Schauspiel in Hamburg adds choreography to their body-training profile, while Tisch School of the Arts in New York offers circus games. The details of voice training are not always spelled out in the literature describing individual schools in the UK. For German-speaking countries, the Konservatorium für Musik und Theater Bern is an example: it lists proper relaxation and tension, body posture and breathing techniques to support the voice, physiology of the voice, the levels of indication, normal voice and powerful voice, the development of a wide range of vocal expression in the genres of poetry, prose and drama, and finally the enhancement of the actor's vocal abilities through singing. The graduate acting programme at the University of California at Irvine stresses that its voice work is based on the masters Kirsten Linklater and Catherine Fitzmaurice. All these aim at making actors aware of vocal processes so that they can use their voice to its fullest effect. The Hochschule für Musik und Theater 'Felix Mendels-sohn Bartholdy' in Leipzig offers phonetics courses in French and English; while the Schauspielstudio Gmelin in Munich integrates training in reading aloud and recitation.

Introductions to music theatre, storytelling and acting for TV, film and radio round off the training. Since all institutions aim to train actors for successful careers in the entertainment industry, the final year of a full-time course will usually include some information on the industry ('Professional Preparation', 'Professional Profile'), together with audi-tion practice and showcases for invited directors, casting directors and agents. Schools in the German-speaking countries also offer units of teaching in professional law.

Some mainly UK-based schools offer courses on contemporary theatre practice, covering topics such as devised theatre, environmental theatre, site-specific theatre, physical theatre, community theatre, theatre-in-education and street theatre as the main contents of a three-year course, rather than as elements of a traditional stage-acting course.

In the theatre of India, Japan and China, training originally followed patterns that are quite different from any of those we come across in the history of Western actor training. The Indian treatise on drama and theatre, the *Natyashastra*, provides a training guide for the non-enlightened actor (apprentice) to gain enlightenment himself. The elements of performance characteristic of any specific style were passed on from the teacher (*guru*) to the student (*shishya*) in an unbroken line of knowledge (*parampara*).[25] The implication here is that the *guru* does not simply teach anything he happens to know, but that he himself is firmly placed within an unbroken tradition, which he maintains by imparting it to his students. Students lived with their teacher, received room and board, and training, and were expected to follow their teacher's instructions in minute detail, respecting and honouring them almost more than a father. In return for the *guru*'s teaching, they would help in various ways: for example, cleaning the house, or providing food.

In the India of today, which has adopted much of the hectic, time-pressed Western lifestyle, such means of training no longer exist. Even earlier in the twentieth century, attending classes with the teacher for one or two hours a day, no longer in residence, was considered a luxury affordable only by well-to-do parents. To balance this loss of contact between *guru* and *shishya*, training schools were established where students spend an intensive four years of training with fellow-students and teaching staff. However, even here, institutionalization does not allow the close relationship of *guru* and *shishya*. In Indian diaspora communities, Indian cultural centres, such as the Bharatiya Vidya Bhavan, teach the major dance forms, such as bharata natyam or kathak, and the teachers are revered as *gurus* by their students, who come for one session a week. Traditionally, the *shishya* would express his gratitude to the *guru* by providing him with a gift (*guru dakshina*) on the occasion of 'graduation' (in the form of the first public performance, called *arangetram* for bharata natyam). This procedure is still maintained today, but there are plenty of anecdotes, many probably based on real events, of *gurus* exploiting this convention by asking for incredibly expensive gifts (which are due from the parents on graduation in addition to the weekly fees for training sessions).

The training of the Noh actor takes place traditionally, as in India, within the family, and begins at a very early age. The *kokata* (boy actor) may start training at the age of three. He will train as a *shite*, a *waki* or a *kyogen* actor (the comic genre which forms part of a Noh performance) with a master of the genre. The periods of training increase over the years in duration and intensity. Griffiths describes how a typical lesson he was allowed to observe, and which lasted fifteen minutes, began with 'the traditional formal, kneeling bow of greeting, the Shite and the pupil facing each other a few feet apart'.[26] He continues to describe how the *shite* and his pupil

> began their work centre stage, having arrived through the sliding door upstage left. Whilst the Shite beat out a rhythmical pattern to accompany the choral part mouthed in quiet accompaniment, the pupil established his opening posture with fan, and then, in a strident voice, gave full and rhythmical vent to his chant. When he finished, the Shite led him through a short movement pattern which circumnavigated the down stage area and led him back to his starting position, having paused and instructed at another position en route.
>
> The pupil was 'shown how' by example, in both the way he moved and arranged his body, and delivered his chant.
>
> His limbs were physically adjusted to the way of the Shite. This had to be done with exacting precision. The Shite showed, the pupil copied.[27]

At the centre of training are three fundamental elements: the position, *kamae*, strong and charged with energy, from which all movement originates, and to which it returns. *Suriashi* is the art of sliding the foot, 'ensuring that it never completely leaves the floor, even when the toes are lifted slightly at the end of a step'.[28] *Kata* denotes the movement forms. In performance, *kamae*, *suriashi* and *kata* combine, with *kata*, together with the chant (*utai*), providing the rhythmical framework for the performance.

While the boy actor today undergoes basic training in the elements described above, he will also attend state primary school; in many cases, as Griffiths points out, full commitment to 'the Noh way of life'[29] may come only after graduation from university. From the age of eleven or twelve to the age of twenty or older, the Noh student is no longer a boy actor, but has reached the second stage of training, referred to as *Uchideshi*. It is at this stage that the 'adopted' trainee will live in the family's household, and will be expected to carry out all kinds of services for the family seniors. Training is daily, fitting around secondary education. The training format is no longer only one-to-one, as during the *kokata* years, but also within a group of fellow-students, who observe and criticize each other's performances. In addition, the student now reads, studies and learns from 'the official family "*Utaibon*", a sort of vocal score which includes the markings of the rhythm of drumming, and also tiny drawings indicating the physical changes in posture at crucial moments in the dance'.[30] The student practises on his own, and presents the result to the master: the master will still demonstrate first, and the student will imitate on the basis of what he has practised on his own. The master then criticizes and improves on the student's presentation. The student has reached an important level in his development when the master asks him to present his work without any preceding demonstration.

While in the *Uchideshi* stage, the student will also assimilate backstage skills such as properly handling the Noh costumes, prop-making, costuming other actors and backstage etiquette. He also learns to use the important Noh mask, and gains proficiency in drumming and playing the flute. The student is also allowed (with the master's permission) to teach usually adult amateurs *shimai*, 'short dance sections appropriated from traditional plays', and *utai*, chant.

The next stage is the *Jun-Shokabun*, the 'pre-full professional',[31] when the student takes on more complex and challenging roles. Despite growing independence, the student still continues his lessons with the master. The master will determine if and when the student should be granted the status of *Shokabun*, full professional.

In China, actors traditionally trained within families, of which they were either natural members, or into which they had been sold. Each apprentice would learn the entire role from his teacher, who in turn had been taught by his own teacher, and so on. Thus, 'each performer embodies a whole family tradition of professionals who have gone before him'.[32] In China as well as in India and Japan, the strong relationship between master and disciple was thus at the centre of actor training. In many cases, the master was the biological father of the disciple, and if not, then he at least assumed a fatherly role to the student. The following document from 1938 is representative of the transaction between a poor student's parents and a teacher:

> Zhang Huiqing, as head of the household, gives his son Zhang Yushan, age nine, to the master Li Wanchun, to be his student. The next seven years shall be devoted to his training in the profession of *jingju*. All income he may produce during this time belongs to Li Wanchun. The student is forbidden to return home without reason, neither may he withdraw from training during this period. The sum of 500 Yuan must be provided if the student breaks off his training, or has run away and cannot be found. Sickness and suicide are the will of Heaven and neither party shall be held responsible.
>
> In gratitude to Li Wanchun. This contract was agreed by free will and not through the use of force. Signed Zhang Huiqing, Li Wanchun. Witnessed by Bai Yonggui and Jiang Tielin. Scribe: Ren Yinan. August, the twenty-seventh year of the Republic [1938].[33]

The disciple had to serve the master at table and show full obedience to him in the instruction hall. Teaching was carried out at the speed of performance, and the role was not broken into smaller units for the purposes of instruction. The student learned by imitation, and 'once the student has mastered the physical outline of the movement, the teacher withdraws his model and merely corrects the student – forms the student into the correct mould'.[34]

In the training process, each part of the body, 'hand, eye, body, finger and step',[35] is trained individually, then in combination. A student would begin with unsupervised voice exercises from 5 a.m., and continue the morning with basic physical training (stretches, leg exercises, jumps, camel spins, arm and hand positions), floor work (including tumbling, handstands, balances) and weapon training.[36] Among these, work on the legs was considered most important, because they provide the foundation of movement. In leg-stretching exercises, the 'student stretches each leg for a period of up to thirty minutes at the side of his face in a side position, and against a bar in front stretch. The foot is always flexed upwards.'[37] In the afternoon, students train individually for their roles. Role categories are decided in view of a student's physical stature, voice and temperament. The score of a role is drilled into the actor's body. In the process of training, special emphasis is placed on holding a position, which, say Chinese masters, 'provides the performer with a repertoire of "patterns" (poses) which are so drilled into the performer's body that he can execute them on stage without even having to think'.[38]

In the chapter on approaches to acting in China I discussed the concept of presence, or *qi*. To train this ability, the master will first of all insist that the student's pose positions are suitably rounded. He will 'often point to the student's abdomen and demand that the student draw up his *qi*'. And when the student needs to rest after a long session of straining exercises, the master will make sure that the student does not 'lie or sprawl exhausted on the floor, for this would dissipate the *qi*. Instead the student takes up a crouching position, with heels raised off the floor and hands resting over the thighs.'[39] This rounded position allows *qi* which has been expended through the movement of the exercises to flow to the seat of *qi* in the solar plexus.

In training, the student learns to create any role he learns on the basis of the nine-cell Luo grid, knowing precisely where each movement should be placed in relation to the grid. He will be able to adapt to any space, narrowing down or enlarging the scope of movements according to the actual size of the stage.

ℰ☯℃ℬ

9

Theatre Criticism

ഊ‍ൽ

All people involved in making theatre, including the actors, are regularly affected by theatre criticism. I have been involved in theatre criticism in various modes, which I would like to address one by one, and in relation to each other. My mother is an actress, and I remember vividly the anxious wait for the reviews in the days following an opening night (in Germany, theatre critics are not expected to write their reviews immediately, in time for the next morning's edition). I remember the elation and happiness when the reviews were good, for the production in general and for my mother in particular: those reviews were a welcome public acknowledgement of hard work. Within the institutional context of the theatre it meant popularity, which would count in the managing director's decision-making process about renewing the contract. But I also remember the disappointment following unfavourable reviews. Sometimes, the ensuing conversations at home would reveal an admission that the performance was indeed not up to the desired level, for various reasons, including personal illness on the day, or a colleague's practical joke, such as being given real red wine instead of grape juice to drink on stage, or the rehearsal method adopted by the director. In those cases, the critic's opinion was appropriate, but the way the criticism was expressed may have added to the unhappiness of the moment. At other times, however, reviews were felt not to have done justice to the production as a whole, including the performances. A respected regular critic might have been replaced by a sixth-form student interested in theatre, whose lack of experience clearly showed. All one could do then was to bemoan instances demonstrating the incompetence of the critic, which would range from incorrect names being assigned to the characters, inaccurate summaries of the plot and comments on the performers that might just as well have been made up.

My own work as a director (for productions at secondary-school level in Germany) was reviewed in the press. It was an English-language production of five one-act comedies by Ayckbourn, *Confusions*. On the opening night, the reviewer sent by the local press turned out to be a fellow-student from another school in the town, who asked for a detailed plot summary because his command of English was not very good. His subsequent review was accordingly condescending and full of factual errors, concluding that we had not really interpreted the play but merely played it (whatever that means).

When I was in London working as an assistant teacher between 1979 and 1980, I often went to the theatre, and read, in the school library, every review in all the major papers. I became acquainted with the personal styles and idiosyncrasies of the different regular critics, and before long realized that my own opinions were quite different from many of them, and closer to others. Irving Wardle came top of the list, followed, at some distance, by Michael Billington. I gave up reading the others, because I knew I would disagree anyway. During that time I read all of Wardle's *Times* reviews, and it was only in the assessment of Paul Scofield's work that I differed from his point of view (I think, contrary to Wardle at that time, that Scofield is one of the greatest actors I have come across). Apart from that, I was impressed by his ability to praise in a critical manner.

Anyone going to the theatre, critic or not, will find it much easier to enumerate all the things they did not like about a production. If a production 'does not work', you will find it easy to say, in a more or less witty form, what went wrong. Negative criticism is taking the production apart in all its aspects: the play, the director's work, set, costume, lighting, acting. This is easy; it is an intellectual activity, and as such is predominant in Western society, because the Western scientific paradigm is based on intellectual, analytic abilities, expressly seeking to exclude the subjective. Our vocabulary of negative criticism (and some may say this is a tautology) is fairly rich, and a critic can be quite funny and witty in using such vocabulary. One example that comes to mind is the review of a musical in 1979–80, about which one critic commented: 'I did not know whether to laugh, cry, or run out screaming.'

Praise, in any context, is much more difficult. Why else do educationalists have to stress the importance of praise? It is true also of theatre criticism. The problem with expressing appreciation about a production in the theatre is that the vocabulary is nowhere near as readily accessible as that appropriate for negative criticism. It takes much more effort to produce praise that is meaningful and not ultimately vapid and vague. Why is this? A production deserving of negative criticism is characterized, on the whole, by a lack of unity. This lack of unity explains why it can be easily 'taken apart' in the review. Since it never constituted a unity, its parts appeal to the intellect, which is always ready to analyse parts. A production which demands praise, however, is characterized by unity. That unity appeals not primarily to the intellect, but beyond, to the emotions, the feelings, intuition. Not to the analytic capacities of the left hemisphere of our brains, but to the synthetic capacities governed by the right hemisphere. We may intuit, feel or have a hunch that what we saw was ... what? Remarkable, great, impressive, striking, moving or stunning? All these adjectives reflect overall, holistic impressions, not instances of analyses of detail. And in the context of the predominantly analytic approach to our lives, which is able to yield high levels of precision, such holistic adjectives appear vague or poetic. It takes much effort to render such impressions in a terminology that resembles the high level of precision characteristic of negative criticism. Sometimes we may, intuitively, shy away from this translation process, because *rendering* in rational, analytically precise terms such desirable and enjoyable impressions is rather like dragging them into a medium not their own, like a fish into the air, against their, and also against our own, will and better knowledge.

Thus praise in theatre criticism suffers from several impediments. Factually, there may be more productions around that do not deserve it. As a result, critics may not often need to apply and, through application, practise it. If praise is called for, finding an appropriate idiom takes much effort, and is complicated by the tension existing between the synthetic, right hemisphere-dominated, poetic (and as such appropriate) grasp through language of a holistic experience, and the demands for analytic, left hemisphere-dominated, scientific terminology in describing and assessing our life.

Whether praise or negative criticism, it is important that critics give a balanced assessment of *all* the aspects that make up a production. How often have I come across reviews that spend two or three columns of their allocated space discussing the play, the dramatist and his or her other plays, the production and several design aspects, only to mention briefly, in some five or six lines, that there were also some actors involved in the production, too good, or too many, or too bad, to mention. This is highly disrespectful of the hard work that goes into any production, even a bad one; it is, moreover, an easy way out for the critic, possibly because of the very effort it takes to develop the terminology considered appropriate particularly for a meaningful assessment of the quality of acting.

Critics should do justice to the production reviewed. They are in a position of considerable power, and that brings with it responsibility. Their verdict can make or break a production financially, and determine whether audiences will attend or not. They have an influence on the employability of an actor, director or designer, or the playability of a dramatist. Under the tight commercial restraints governing the theatre industry, managers and artistic directors will hesitate to employ artists who have been severely slighted by the critics. As my own memories described above have shown, reviews will influence the personal lives of the artists praised or criticized. Is it worth garnering a cheap laugh at the potentially very serious expense of someone else?

This question leads us to the critics themselves. What do they get out of it? Is it just a job to earn some money? Are they professional journalists who could be writing about any subject matter, depending on the brief they get from their editors, and who just happened to get into theatre reviewing? I believe that there are still theatre critics who have a deep interest in their profession and in the theatre, and who are aware of, and acknowledge, their position of relative power, and use it to further the development of theatre. Some of them may even regard their work as an art form in itself, as, for example, was the case with Alfred Kerr (1867–1948).

For me, the ideal critic would be deeply involved in their work, inspired by high levels of knowledge of, *and* love for, the theatre. Knowledge is an intellectual aspect, while love represents the emotions, intuition and feeling. Intuition implies the vital ability, among others, to sense fruitful developments in new writing and new production work that is ahead of its own time, and points the way to the future. Both knowledge and love are needed to do full justice to any review of a production. I am reminded here of some comments I read about *New York Times* theatre critic Frank Rich, who was regarded as a highly competent writer, but without any love for the theatre, and who, in consequence, was considered incapable of doing the theatre he reviewed full justice. Knowledge can be gained through study, but love for the theatre must be a given right from the beginning. It may deepen over the course of time, and its manifestations may change, but I doubt whether it can materialize later if it was never there at the start.

Knowledge of theatre is related to the choice of an appropriate point of reference against which criticism, praise or censure is developed. Freedom of choice should be granted, in equal measure, as theatre artists should have the choice as to what kind of theatre they wish to make. Some theatres specialize in boulevard comedy or farce. Some directors work with international companies on intercultural projects. Each artistic approach, each artistic choice, that is, should be assessed on its own terms. In comparison with classical Greek tragedy, a contemporary farce may appear lightweight. However, that is hardly relevant to the critic facing the task of reviewing a contemporary farce. Rather, the criteria specific to farce, concerning the writing and production, have to be chosen as points of reference.

Knowledge of and love for the theatre, together with an appropriate frame of reference, combine with a sound awareness of the *Zeitgeist* to produce a view of what the function of theatre should be within any particular culture. Critics will make decisions as to whether a specific production as a whole, or aspects of it, meet the criteria characteristic of that overall frame. If yes, praise will result; if no, negative criticism will follow. Praise may demand more effort than negative criticism, which offers itself more easily to brilliant wit. Critics will have to decide whether it is really necessary to find an idiom for praise that is equivalent in nature to the hard terminology of analytic negative criticism, or whether they are able to create a mode of praise which is not vague and vapid despite being highly poetic and suggestive. Alfred Kerr was a master of this art, as this description of Eleonora Duse as Silvia Settala in *La Giaconda* reveals:

> Die alte, süße Magie sank herab, sie leuchtete noch einmal in überirdischer Gewalt. Sie liebkoste die Sirenetta mit den Lippen, der Hände beraubt, sich sehnsüchtig anschmiegend. Die Kleine fragt – sie vermißt etwas. Da spricht die Duse mit einer stillen, verschollenen Stimme, worin der Kummer der letzten Kreatur liegt: 'Ich habe keine Hände' – und das Merkwürdige geschieht: ihr Antlitz verfärbt sich, sie Augen füllen sich langsam mit schweren, bitteren, herabfließenden Tränen.[1]

It is difficult to translate this passage into English accurately, without losing some of its poetic value. Duse was at the end of her life when she played this part. Kerr begins by recalling her greatness: 'The old, sweet magic descended, she shone again in supernatural power.' He then focuses on one particular scene:

> She caressed Sirenetta with her lips, bereaved of her hands, yearningly nestling up to her. The little one asks – she is missing something. At that moment the Duse speaks with a quiet, lost voice, which contains the sorrow of the last creature: 'I do not have any hands' – and the remarkable happens: her countenance changes colour, the eyes slowly fill with heavy, bitter, flowing down tears.

Negative criticism will focus on bad acting, design, directing or writing, measured against the overall frame developed by the critic. If critics want to influence directly what happens in the theatre, if they want to *change* it, they might want to think which one of two diametrically opposed approaches to negative criticism will be best able to achieve this. On the one hand, sharp, biting, ironic, cynical, sarcastic and thus brilliantly witty comments; on the other hand, the much more difficult approach which does not leave issues unspoken, but manages to express them in a way such as to cause minimal, or ideally no, personal offence. There is no simple formula for the latter approach, which is governed by the critic's intuition, informed by love for the theatre; the lack of bite does not necessarily imply a lack of opportunity for demonstrating wit! Again, the work of Alfred Kerr serves as a good illustration of this. Referring to Sarah Bernhardt, no less, in *Tosca*, he describes how she should express the misery of all mankind when she hears her lover's cries while he is being tortured. Instead, Bernhardt 'macht kluge, sehr technisch-sichere Gesichtchen. Sie "macht" Qual. Sie greift keinem ans Herz'[2] – 'she makes clever, very technically secure little faces. She "makes" torment. She appeals to no one's heart.' He concludes that all her acting remains an excellently executed and thus successful act, very efficient, very clever, but without the ability to move him.

The general reader is likely to respond to the wit of negative criticism with laughter, and with *Schadenfreude* for the criticized artist. The artist at whose expense this effect has been created will simply suffer, feel humiliated, no more. The 'gentle approach' is far better able to convey the critic's serious concerns, and thus make both reader and artist *understand* the nature of the negative criticism, opening a door for the artist to change, if he so wishes. The gain for both general reader and artist is thus potentially much more substantial if the critic takes time to master the gentle approach, rather than relying on the much easier harsh approach. Let me repeat that the gentle approach does not mean evading issues: quite the contrary. Any issue of concern to the critic can be tackled much more efficiently (with a view to effecting change) by avoiding offence, even if it goes to the extreme, and hopefully rare, occasion of seriously suggesting that an artist quit the job in the interest of the theatre.

Theatre critics have an important function in the theatre, and if they take their work seriously, they *can* influence and change the art form they write about, for better or for worse. Theirs is a considerable responsibility.

∞

10

The Future of Acting

ಬಂಡಿ

Some may say that theatre can continue the way it is, that no changes are necessary. The survival of theatre as a mode of entertainment, as an art form and as an industry would support this view. In such a theatre, the acting style that has been developed up to, and during, the twentieth century would continue, with mainstream systems and methods institutionalized in state-run or private training schools, and theatres seeking to employ graduates from those schools. Within the limitations set by institutionalization, such existing and proven systems and methods may even be developed further.

However, there are tendencies among late twentieth-century approaches to acting and performance which suggest that a more exciting future of acting is possible. Readers should be able to draw their own conclusions, depending on their particular preferences. In the remainder of this chapter, I will outline my own views, which I hope, in due course, to substantiate with practice.

In my discussion of acting, postmodernism and performance, I mentioned Birringer's quest for 'acts from above and under', non-ordinary modes of perception. This quest fits in with the insight that many contemporary theatre artists share a common interest in non-Western theatre practices, mixed with religion and philosophy. What inspires their 'turn to the East' are Eastern assumptions about states of consciousness that lie beyond the intellect, beyond the emotions. I have discussed these higher states of consciousness in the context of the model of the mind proposed by Indian philosophy. Perception in such higher states of consciousness runs parallel to Birringer's 'under and above our normal ways of seeing'.[1]

The search for states of consciousness beyond the intellect, beyond the emotions, ultimately, then, the search for 'pure consciousness' together with all aspects of the waking state of consciousness is where some theatre artists, postmodern in their intercultural, intertextual activities, part company with postmodernism: Crohn-Schmitt points out that 'at the most elemental level, the description of nature necessarily becomes the description of experienced phenomena, not a representation of something more fundamental, an independent physical reality'.[2] There is, thus, no overarching universality underlying all phenomena of the world. The denial of a universal basis for creation, arrived at by the application of quantum physics to human life, is the basis for pluralism. Crohn-Schmitt's argument is thus in line with postmodernism's critique of any position that opposes in principle the pluralism characteristic of postmodernism. The emphasis of postmodern philosophers on pluralism arose as a counter-movement against metanarratives, grand narratives, such as 'dialectics of the Spirit, the hermeneutics of meaning, the emancipation of the rational and working subject or the creation of wealth'[3]: according to postmodernist philosopher Lyotard, the post-modern condition is one in which the grand narratives of modernity formulated in the eighteenth century by philosophers of the Enlightenment 'have lost all their credibility'.[4]

The theatre artists' search for desirable altered, or indeed higher, states of consciousness, as the aim of what Pavis calls ultracultural, transcultural or precultural, is nothing but a search for a new grand narrative. In this sense, theatre artists, whose endorsement of pluralism is a postmodern aspect of their work, ultimately do not share the distrust of grand narratives. However, they follow different grand narratives than Hegel or Marx. The more the artists are influenced by Western, and especially Eastern, aesthetics and psychology, the more they aim for experiences in both actors and spectators that go beyond the senses, beyond the intellect, and even beyond the emotions. The latter are mainly used to reach for the area of the mind called, with reference to Freud, Jung and other Western psychologists, the subconscious or unconscious. Through activation of the unconscious level of the mind, they hope to stimulate the experiences of *communitas*, of flow, of unification of binary opposites. They are, in other words, searching for an overarching totality, but not in the expressed fields of science, art, morality or law, as did the eighteenth-century philosophers of the Enlightenment, but in a field beyond expression, in the field of consciousness.

Thus, one area that makes the future of acting exciting is to reassess existing approaches to acting in the light of a cogent model of human consciousness. In my view, the Indian model of consciousness is a very promising candidate, because of its ability to make sense of non-ordinary experiences such as translumination, presence, the third organ of the body of theatre, or total theatre. Not only does the Indian model of consciousness make sense of such experiences, it also suggests ways of enabling the actor to systematically re-create what are considered as very helpful experiences to the acting process by those who have reported them.

Some current productions already point the way to what an intentional application of insights in consciousness studies to the theatre, and acting in particular, may look like. Usually, plays are directed in such a way that there is always only one scene on the stage. The spectator's attention is allowed to focus fully on that scene. Major characters carry the scene, while other performers occupy the background physically and emotionally so as not to upstage them. In contrast, for example, take a production by David Freeman, his *Marriage of Figaro* with Opera Factory Zurich. Freeman had assembled an international cast from Austria, Switzerland, England and Australia. The cast and production team spent the first week of a six-week rehearsal period together in a culture centre, working on improvisations to create in each singer a deep feeling for the character of his or her part. This experience, which all involved found very enriching and helpful, was enhanced further when the team later on spent five days together in a house in the country, away from twentieth-century civilization. There they not only acted, but actually lived their parts: the maids, for example, got up early to help feed the animals on the farm next door. They also had to do the cooking. Susanna and Figaro served Countess and Count Almaviva, who could sleep late because they had nothing much to do. The innovative element here is the concentration on the central importance of the house in Mozart's opera. The production is set in Count Almaviva's isolated summer castle, where all the characters of the opera live 'on top of each other, and yet everybody is separated by class and power'.[5]

In order to get the kind of hothouse atmosphere across to the audience, the life of the house is shown throughout, breaking the boundaries of ordinary opera direction. The traditional rule is that the stage should be occupied only by the characters who have to sing at that time. Not so in Freeman's *Figaro*. Life in the house goes on. The threads of the story come through the house. The focus of the scene is on the singers, but other characters go about their respective business at the same time. A few examples should illustrate this: already during the overture, Don Curzio enters, sits down at a table upstage right and starts writing. Soon he is joined by Basilio. At the same time, Antonio brings parts of a wooden bed into the small area designated as Figaro's and Susanna's chamber downstage left. After that, Antonio moves to an area centrestage right that represents the garden, indicated by flowers, and starts preparing a beautiful flowerbed. Barbarina, Susanna and two maids are busy in Figaro's and Susanna's chamber, cleaning the floor. They are joined by Cherubino, who enjoys female company. Before the end of the overture, Figaro arrives, and makes everyone except Susanna leave, so that they are now ready for their opening scene. Meanwhile, Bartolo and Marcellina have also appeared, downstage right, and during Figaro's and Susanna's scene, one of the maids brings hot water for a footbath and a camomile steambath for Marcellina's cold. Basilio moves to 'his area', indicated by a music stand, and starts composing. The maids start washing and wringing linen in the background, while Basilio eavesdrops on Susanna's and Marcellina's quarrel.

Such a liveliness of parallel action is kept up throughout the performance, breaking the boundaries of conventional productions of *Figaro*. At the same time, the perception habits of the audience are provoked. Whereas the ordinary theatre experience means focusing on one central element on the stage, in Freeman's production, a flood of visual input bombards the spectator. All elements of input are not only fascinating but make good sense, because they are logical elements of the interpretation that Freeman provides. The audience has to learn to focus on the main element, which is provided by the music: they have to focus on the singers, while at the same time allowing the other input to enrich rather than distract from the insights gained from focusing.

Simultaneity of space and time is a characteristic of both pure consciousness and the unified field discussed in quantum physics. On this level of creation, past, present and future co-exist. Pure consciousness as the source, the basis of all manifest creation, is a field of all possibilities of space and time. Therefore, if a form of drama enables an experience of simultaneity, it trains the mind in functioning more and more closely to pure consciousness.

Thus, it is not only mainstream theatre and acting that have the potential of leading to fascinating experiences in the theatre. When I asked recent final-year students about their most impressive experience while studying drama at the University of Wales, Aberystwyth, the almost unanimous response was *The Labyrinth*. This was a non-traditional, non-mainstream event, presented by a group of Columbian performers. They created a labyrinth of pathways within the theatre space, leading to individual defined spaces, such as a children's nursery, a schoolroom and a space covered with sand where a performer dressed as a gypsy would sit by a real fire and perform magic spells and manipulate the fire. Spectators went through the labyrinth on their own, groping their way along the black cloths in total darkness, sometimes guided by performers' touch or sound, encountering various 'characters' in the defined spaces, and experiencing a wide range of smells, sounds and touches without being able, in many cases, to *see* the origin of the sensory impression. In one installation, spectators had to crawl though a well-lit, comfortably padded 'umbilical cord', leading to a pitch-dark end, from where they had to slide downwards into the unknown. Some were initially too afraid to take the risk, but returning was impossible. At the bottom of the slope, they ended up in a large mass of unroasted coffee beans, where they were stroked and comforted by a performer. The reaction of individual spectators to each of the defined spaces and the installations varied, but all agreed that they were unlikely to forget the experience, and that the non-visual impressions, especially the unfamiliar but generally pleasant smells, had stayed with them for days. It was difficult to stop the students discussing the *Labyrinth* encounters on an experiential level. They found it difficult, if not impossible, to analyse their experience in traditional critical terminology. Is analysis helpful beyond being a reasonable tool for examination? You can assess if a student has grasped the meaning and implications of a specific concept, but it is much more difficult to assess a personal appreciation of a theatre impression. Are we less capable of enjoying if we are unable to analyse?

These two examples, from traditional theatre and from performance, demonstrate the potential of acting and performing for altering consciousness in transformative ways. In my own research, a project funded by the Arts and Humanities Research Board in the UK, scheduled for August 2000 (that is, after completion of the manuscript of this book), will serve as a first attempt at testing the theory presented here in practice. A ten-day workshop will be held for a group of twenty-two performers (eleven in the target group, eleven in the control group). Relevant variables (experience in meditation, suggestibility, age, gender and professional training and experience) will be measured and balanced as far as possible between the two groups. The failure of previous attempts at re-creating the desirable and beneficial experiences of non-ordinary states of consciousness through theatre was due to their eclectic non-systematic approach: theatre artists experimented with isolated elements from various unrelated performance traditions on the basis of trial and error, selecting what 'worked for them'. The hypothesis informing the research project is that desirable and beneficial transformative change of consciousness is possible through theatre, and that achievements are significantly higher if one clearly defined approach is followed. The workshop with the core group will, therefore, focus on only one source, the Indian tradition, and in particular the *Natyashastra*, taking up a selection of the instructions detailed in the text. A trained bharata natyam dancer will conduct this aspect of the workshop. Since the aim is to achieve and test higher states of consciousness, the workshop will be closely supervised by an enlightened spiritual master of India, Sri Sri Ravi Shankar. The performers in the control group will undergo theatre training which is of high quality, but differs from the approach applied to the core group by representing the non-systematic approach. A leading Western actor trainer will be invited to conduct the workshop for the control group. The professional expertise and charisma of the workshop leaders will thus be evenly distributed.

The model of the mind proposed by Indian philosophy has been subjected to numerous empirical studies. Drawing on that research, the workshop will be accompanied by empirical studies to test the hypothesis. Some tests will be administered during the workshop activities themselves, others at the beginning and end of the experiment. Measures will include heart rate, perceptual discrimination, sensory/abstract responses on the Rorschach or equivalent projective tests (rated blind by a researcher who does not know to which group each subject belonged), empathy, capacity for absorption and full attention (Tellegen Absorption Scale) and various categories on the Personal Orientation Inventory by Shostrom. Follow-up studies will be carried out six months after the workshop to test the long-term effects of the activities. Both during the workshop and for the follow-up study, some effects are expected from the control group, but if the hypothesis is adequate, then the results of the core group should be significantly higher. I expect that further research into the future of approaches to acting will develop from this pilot study.

ಏಂಅಶ

Notes

ᘒᘖ

Chapter 1: Worldwide Origins of Acting

1. Oscar G. Brockett, *History of the Theatre*. London: Allyn and Bacon, 1987, 5th edition, p. 5.
2. *Ibid.*
3. Benito Ortolani, 'Das japanische Theater', in Heinz Kindermann (ed.), *Einführung in das ostasiatische Theater*. Wien: Hermann Böhlhaus, 1985, p. 321.
4. *Ibid.*, p. 322.
5. Benito Ortolani, *The Japanese Theatre: From Shamanistic Ritual to Contemporary Pluralism*. Leiden: E. J. Brill, 1990.

Chapter 2: Greece and Rome

1. Brockett, *History of the Theatre*, p. 18.
2. *Ibid.*, p. 23.
3. Peter D. Arnott, *Public and Performance in the Greek Theatre*. London: Routledge, 1991, p. 51.
4. *Ibid.*, p. 61.
5. *Ibid.*, p. 64.
6. *Ibid.*
7. *Ibid.*, p. 63.
8. Rush Rehm, *Greek Tragic Theatre*. London and New York: Routledge, 1992, p.39.
9. *Ibid.*, p.41.
10. *Ibid.*
11. David Wiles, *The Masks of Menander: Sign and Meaning in Greek and Roman Performance*. Cambridge: Cambridge University Press, 1991, p. 129.
12. *Ibid.*, p. 130.

Chapter 3: The Middle Ages and the Renaissance

1. Brockett, *History of the Theatre*, p. 106.
2. William Tydeman, *The Theatre in the Middle Ages: Western European Stage Conditions, c. 800–1576*. Cambridge: Cambridge University Press, 1978, p. 190.
3. *Ibid.*, p. 193.
4. John R. Elliott, Jr, 'Medieval acting', in Marianne G. Briscoe and John C. Coldewey (eds), *Contexts for Early English Drama*. Bloomington: Indiana University Press, 1989, p. 245.
5. Tydeman, *The Theatre in the Middle Ages*, p. 203.
6. John Wesley Harris, *Medieval Theatre in Context: An Introduction*. London and New York: Routledge, 1992, p. 170.
7. Alfred S. Golding, 'Nature as symbolic behavior: Crésol's *Autumn Vacations* and early Baroque acting technique', *Renaissance and Reformation*, 10:1 (1986), p. 148.
8. *Ibid.*, p. 151.
9. *Ibid.*, p. 152.
10. *Ibid.*, p. 154.

Chapter 4: From 1550 to 1900

1. A. J. von Schack, *Geschichte der Literatur und dramatischen Kunst in Spanien*. Berlin: Duncker and Humblot, 1845/6, p. 258ff.
2. Michael Patterson, *The First German Theatre: Schiller, Goethe, Kleist and Büchner in Performance*. London and New York: Routledge, 1990, p. 2.
3. George W. Brandt and Wiebe Hogendoorn, *German and Dutch Theatre, 1600–1848*. Cambridge: Cambridge University Press, 1993, p. 123.
4. Ann Marie Koller, *The Theatre Duke: Georg II of Saxe-Meiningen and the German Stage*. Stanford: Stanford University Press, 1984, p. 136.
5. *Ibid.*, p. 129.
6. *Ibid.*, p. 120.
7. George Taylor, 'The just delineation of the passions: theories of acting in the age of Garrick', in Kenneth Richards and Peter Thomson (eds), *The Eighteenth-Century English Stage: The Proceedings of a Symposium Sponsored by the Manchester University Department of Drama*. London: Methuen, 1972, p. 51.
8. John Russell Brown, 'On the acting of Shakespeare's plays', *Quarterly Journal of Speech*, 34 (1953), pp. 477–84.
9. Schack, *Geschichte der Literatur und dramatischen Kunst in Spanien*, pp. 358, A 109.
10. Kenneth Richards and Laura Richards, *The Commedia dell'Arte: A Documentary History*. Oxford: Basil Blackwell, 1990, p. 113.

11. Taylor, 'The just delineation of the passions . . .', p. 62.
12. *Ibid.*, p. 60.
13. *Ibid.*, p. 55.
14. *Ibid.*, p. 60.
15. Marvin Carlson, *Theories of the Theatre: A Historical and Critical Survey, from the Greeks to the Present.* Ithaca and London: Cornell University Press, 1984, pp. 59–61.
16. *Ibid.*, pp. 65–6.
17. *Ibid.*, p. 159.
18. Denis Diderot, *The Paradox of Acting*. New York: Hill and Wang, 1955, p. 15.
19. Lionel Gossman and Elizabeth MacArthur, 'Diderot's displaced paradox', in Jack Undank and Herbert Josephs (eds), *Diderot Digression and Dispersion: A Bicentennial Tribute.* Lexington, KE: French Forum Publishers, 1984, pp.113–14.
20. Diderot, *The Paradox of Acting*, p. 14.
21. *Ibid.*, p. 19.
22. *Ibid.*, pp. 32–3.
23. Allison Grear, 'A background to Diderot's *Paradoxe sur le Comédien*: the role of imagination in spoken expression of emotion', *Forum for Modern Language Studies*, 21:3 (1985), p. 225.
24. *Ibid.*
25. *Ibid.*, p. 226.
26. *Ibid.*, pp. 226–7.
27. *Ibid.*, p. 229.
28. *Ibid.*, p. 233.
29. Joseph R. Roach, Jr, 'Diderot and the actor's machine', *Theatre Survey*, 22:1 (1981), p. 52.
30. *Ibid.*
31. John R. Battista, 'The science of consciousness', in Kenneth S. Pope and Jerome L. Singer (eds), *The Stream of Consciousness: Scientific Investigation into the Flow of Human Consciousness.* Chichester, New York, Brisbane and Toronto: John Wiley and Sons, 1978, p. 70.
32. *Ibid.*
33. *Ibid.*
34. D. W. Hamlyn, *The Penguin History of Western Philosophy.* London: Penguin, 1990, p. 211.
35. Roach, 'Diderot and the actor's machine', p. 58.
36. *Ibid.*, p. 54.
37. *Ibid.*
38. *Ibid.*, p. 56.
39. *Ibid.*, p. 57.
40. Diderot, *The Paradox of Acting*, p. 61.
41. *Ibid.*, p. 62.

42. *Ibid.*
43. *Ibid.*, p. 53.
44. Gerard de Lairesse, *Groot Schilderboek*. Amsterdam: Hendrick Desbordes, 1712.
45. Brandt and Hogendoorn, *German and Dutch Theatre*, p. 482.
46. Patterson, *The First German Theatre*, p. 36.
47. John Prudhoe, *The Theatre of Goethe and Schiller*. Oxford: Basil Blackwell, 1973, p. 21.
48. Brandt and Hogendoorn, *German and Dutch Theatre*, p. 161.
49. Eduard Devrient, *Geschichte der deutschen Schauspielkunst*, Vol. 2. Berlin: Otto Elsner, 1905, p. 162.
50. Heinz Kindermann, *Theatergeschichte Europas*, Vol. IV. Salzburg: Otto Müller, 1961, p. 386.
51. Brandt and Hogendoorn, *German and Dutch Theatre*, p. 148.
52. Devrient, *Geschichte der Deutschen Schauspielkunst*, p. 76.
53. Patterson, *The First German Theatre*, p. 119.
54. Kindermann, *Theatergeschichte Europas*, Vol. IV, p. 202.
55. Michael R. Booth, *Theatre in the Victorian Age*. Cambridge: Cambridge University Press, 1991, p. 134.
56. *Ibid.*
57. *Ibid.*, p. 125.
58. *Ibid.*, p. 130.
59. Brockett, *History of the Theatre*, p. 470.
60. Booth, *Theatre in the Victorian Age*, p. 134.
61. *Ibid.*, p. 137.
62. Stephen C. Schultz, 'Toward an Irvingesque theory of Shakespearean acting', *Quarterly Journal of Speech*, 61 (1975), pp. 437–8.
63. Heinz Kindermann, *Theatergeschichte Europas*, Vol. VII. Salzburg: Otto Müller, 1965, p. 61.
64. Brockett, *History of the Theatre*, p. 536.
65. J. L. Styan, *Max Reinhardt* (Directors in Perspective). Cambridge: Cambridge University Press, 1982, p. 17.
66. Oscar G. Brockett and Robert R. Findlay, *Century of Innovation: A History of European and American Theatre and Drama since the Late 19th Century*. Boston and London: Allyn and Bacon, 1991, p. 68.
67. *Ibid.*, p. 73.

Chapter 5: The Twentieth Century

1. Constantin Stanislavsky, *An Actor Prepares*. Translated by Elizabeth Reynolds Hapgood. London: Methuen, 1986, p. 15.
2. *Ibid.*, p. 14.
3. *Ibid.*

4. *Ibid.*, p. 13.
5. Diderot, *The Paradox of Acting* p. 17.
6. Stanislavsky, *An Actor Prepares*, p. 13.
7. *Ibid.*, p. 114.
8. *Ibid.*, p. 116.
9. *Ibid.*, p. 15.
10. *Ibid.*, p. 118.
11. *Ibid.*, p. 119.
12. *Ibid.*, p. 175.
13. *Ibid.*
14. *Ibid.*, p. 176.
15. *Ibid.*, p. 177.
16. *Ibid.*, p. 168.
17. *Ibid.*, p. 190.
18. Constantin Stanislavsky, *Building a Character*. Translated by Elizabeth Reynolds Hapgood. New York: Theatre Arts Books, 1949, p. 266.
19. *Ibid.*, p. 181.
20. *Ibid.*, p. 192.
21. *Ibid.*
22. *Ibid.*, p. 193.
23. *Ibid.*, p. 185.
24. Stanislavsky, *An Actor Prepares*, p. 249.
25. *Ibid.*
26. *Ibid.*, p. 250.
27. *Ibid.*, p. 247.
28. *Ibid.*, pp. 250–1.
29. *Ibid.*, p. 274.
30. Stanislavsky, *Building a Character*, p. 108.
31. *Ibid.*
32. Constantin Stanislavsky, *Creating a Role*. Translated by Elizabeth Reynolds Hapgood and edited by Hermine I. Popper. New York: Theatre Arts Books, 1961, p. 52.
33. *Ibid.*
34. *Ibid.*
35. *Ibid.*
36. Stanislavsky, *An Actor Prepares*, p. 267.
37. Diderot, *The Paradox of Acting*, p. 14.
38. Marianne Kesting, 'Stanislavsky–Meyerhold–Brecht', *Forum Modernes Theater*, 4:2 (1989), p. 123.
39. Richard M. Ryckman, *Theories of Personality*. Monterey: Brooks/Cole Publishers, 3rd edition, 1985, p. 46.
40. Kesting, 'Stanislavsky–Meyerhold–Brecht', p. 123.
41. Ryckman, *Theories of Personality*, p. 33.

42. Benvenuto Bice, and Roger Kennedy, *The Work of Jaques Lacan*. London: Free Association Books, 1986, p. 48.
43. Joseph R. Roach, *The Player's Passion: Studies in the Science of Acting*. Newark: University of Delaware Press, 1985, p. 205.
44. Lee Strasberg, 'Working with live material', in Erika Munk (ed.), *Stanislavsky and America: The 'Method' and Its Influence on the American Actor*. New York: Hill and Wang, 1966, p. 198.
45. Roach, *The Player's Passion*, p. 205.
46. Strasberg, 'Working with live material', p. 111.
47. Roach, *The Player's Passion*, pp. 204–5.
48. Vasily Osipovich Toporkov, *Stanislavsky in Rehearsal: The Final Years*. New York: Routledge, 1998, p. 154.
49. *Ibid.*, p. 159.
50. *Ibid.*
51. *Ibid.*, p. 162.
52. *Ibid.*, p. 169.
53. *Ibid.*, p. 195.
54. *Ibid.*
55. Phillip Zarrilli, ' "On the edge of a breath, looking": disciplining the actor's bodymind through the martial arts in the Asian/ Experimental Theatre Program', in Phillip Zarrilli (ed.), *Acting (Re)Considered: Theories and Practices*. London and New York: Routledge, 1995, pp. 177–96.
56. Lee Strasberg, *A Dream of Passion: The Development of the Method*. Edited by Evangeline Morphos. London: Bloomsbury, 1988, p. 85.
57. *Ibid.*
58. *Ibid.*
59. *Ibid.*, p. 60.
60. David Krasner, 'Strasberg, Adler and Meisner: method acting', in Alison Hodge (ed.), *Twentieth Century Actor Training*. London and New York: Routledge, 2000, p. 141.
61. Uta Hagen, *A Challenge for the Actor*. New York: Scribner, 1991, p. 42.
62. *Ibid.*, p. 57.
63. *Ibid.*, p. 63.
64. *Ibid.*, p. 66.
65. *Ibid.*, p. 89.
66. Nick Worrall, *Modernism to Realism on the Soviet Stage: Tairov–Vakhtangov–Okhlopkov*. Cambridge: Cambridge University Press, 1989, p. 106.
67. *Ibid.*
68. *Ibid.*, p. 15.
69. *Ibid.*, p. 35.
70. James Roose-Evans, *Experimental Theatre: From Stanislavsky to Peter Brook*. London: Routledge, 1989, p. 29.

71. Samuel Leiter, *From Stanislavsky to Barrault: Representative Directors of the European Stage* (Contributions to Drama and Theatre Studies No. 34). London: Greenwood Press, 1991, p. 56.

72. Robert Leach, *Vsevolod Meyerhold*. Cambridge: Cambridge University Press, 1989, p. 52.

73. *Ibid.*, p. 61.

74. *Ibid.*

75. *Ibid.*, pp. 64–5.

76. Leiter, *From Stanislavsky to Barrault*, p. 56.

77. *Ibid.*, p. 57.

78. *Ibid.*, p. 56.

79. Johannes Hirschberger, *Geschichte der Philosophie: Neuzeit und Gegenwart*. Freiburg, Basel and Wien: Herder, 1981, p. 468.

80. *Ibid.*, p. 482.

81. Leiter, *From Stanislavsky to Barrault*, p. 56.

82. *Ibid.*

83. Cheshire Calhoun and Robert C. Solomon, *What Is an Emotion? Classical Readings in Philosophical Psychology*. New York and Oxford: Oxford University Press, 1984, p. 126.

84. *Ibid.*

85. *Ibid.*

86. Nico H. Frijda, *The Emotions*. Cambridge: Cambridge University Press, 1986, p. 125.

87. Robert Levenson, Paul Ekman and Wallace V. Friesen, 'Voluntary facial action generates emotion-specific autonomous nervous system activity', *Psychophysiology*, 27:4 (1990), p. 363.

88. Oliver M. Sayler (ed.), *Max Reinhardt and His Theatre*. New York: Benjamin Blom, 1968 (first published 1924), p. 65.

89. Styan, *Max Reinhardt*, p. 23.

90. Michael Patterson, *The Revolution in German Theatre, 1900–1933*. Boston and London: Routledge and Kegan Paul, 1981, p. 35.

91. *Ibid.*, p. 42.

92. *Ibid.*

93. Brockett, *History of the Theatre*, p. 598.

94. *Ibid.*, p. 17.

95. *Ibid.*, p. 18.

96. *Ibid.*, p. 50.

97. *Ibid.*, p. 51.

98. *Ibid.*, p. 52.

99. *Ibid.*, p. 51.

100. *Ibid.*, p. 57.

101. *Ibid.*

102. *Ibid.*, p. 74.

103. *Ibid.*, p. 77.

104. *Ibid.*

105. *Ibid.*, p. 80.
106. *Ibid.*, p. 82.
107. Walter Gropius (ed.), *The Theater of the Bauhaus*. London: Eyre Methuen, 1961, p. 8.
108. Oskar Schlemmer, 'Man and art figure', in Gropius (ed.), *The Theater of the Bauhaus*, pp. 22–3.
109. *Ibid.*, p. 17.
110. Oskar Schlemmer, 'Theater (Bühne)', in Gropius (ed.), *The Theater of the Bauhaus*, p. 95.
111. *Ibid.*, p. 97.
112. *Ibid.*
113. T. Lux Feininger, quoted in Gropius (ed.), *The Theater of the Bauhaus*, pp. 8–9.
114. Brockett and Findlay, *Century of Innovation*, p. 163.
115. Annabelle Henkin Melzer, *Dada and Surrealist Performance*. Baltimore and London: The Johns Hopkins University Press, 1994, p. 43.
116. *Ibid.*, pp. 62–3.
117. *Ibid.*, p. 53.
118. *Ibid.*
119. *Ibid.*, p. 57.
120. *Ibid.*, p. 60.
121. *Ibid.*, p. 61.
122. Patterson, *The Revolution in German Theatre*, p. 116.
123. *Ibid.*, pp. 127–8.
124. John Willett (ed. and trans.), *Brecht on Theatre: The Development of an Aesthetic*. New York: Hill and Wang, 1978, p. 14.
125. Jan Knopf, *Brecht-Handbuch. Theater: Eine Ästhetik der Widersprüche*. Stuttgart: J. B. Metzlersche Verlagsbuchhandlung, 1980, p. 383.
126. Willett, *Brecht on Theatre*, p. 137.
127. *Ibid.*
128. *Ibid.*, p. 139.
129. *Ibid.*
130. Christopher Innes, *Holy Theatre: Ritual and the Avant-Garde*. Cambridge: Cambridge University Press, 1981, p. 11.
131. Leiter, *From Stanislavsky to Barrault*, p. 170.
132. Innes, *Holy Theatre*, pp. 11–12.
133. Susan L. Stern, 'Drama in second language learning from a psycholinguistic perspective', *Language Learning*, 3:1 (1980), p. 81.
134. Willett, *Brecht on Theatre*, p. 145.
135. *Ibid.*, p. 193.
136. *Ibid.*
137. Aage H. Hansen-Löve, *Der Russische Formalismus: Methodologische Rekonstruktion seiner Entwicklung aus dem Prinzip der Verfremdung*. Austrian Academy of Sciences, Philosophical-historical Class.

Minutes, Vol. 336. Publication of the Commission for Literary Studies, No. 5. Vienna: Publishing House of the Austrian Academy of Sciences, 1978, p. 19.

138. *Ibid.*, pp. 361–2.

139. Knopf, *Brecht-Handbuch*, p. 379.

140. Julian Hilton, *Performance* (New Directions in Theatre). London: Macmillan, 1987, p. 61.

141. Knopf, *Brecht-Handbuch*, 379.

142. Edward Braun, *Meyerhold on Theatre*. London: Methuen, 1969, p. 168.

143. Daphna Ben Chaim, *Distance in the Theatre: The Aesthetics of Audience Response* (Theatre and Dramatic Studies No. 17). Ann Arbor and London: UMI Research Press, 1984, p. 32.

144. *Ibid.*

145. Antonin Artaud, *The Theatre and Its Double*. Collected Works, Vol. 4. Translated by Victor Corti. London: Calder and Boyars, 1974, p. 4.

146. *Ibid.* Innes considers Artaud's position in twentieth-century theatre history as that of a 'theatrical litmus, sensitive to the cultural physiology of the twentieth century' (Innes, *Holy Theatre*, p. 109).

147. Artaud, *The Theatre and Its Double*, p. 4.

148. Innes, *Holy Theatre*, p. 110.

149. Artaud, *The Theatre and Its Double*, p. 77.

150. *Ibid.*, p. 78.

151. *Ibid.*

152. *Ibid.*, p. 25.

153. *Ibid.*

154. *Ibid.*, p. 26.

155. *Ibid.*, p. 100.

156. *Ibid.*, p. 101.

157. *Ibid.*, p. 102.

158. *Ibid.*, p. 75.

159. Innes, *Holy Theatre*, p. 60.

160. Artaud, *The Theatre and Its Double*, p. 62.

161. *Ibid.*, p. 63.

162. Jacqueline Martin, *Voice in Modern Theatre*. London and New York: Routledge, 1991, p. 58.

163. Philip Auslander, '*Holy Theatre* and catharsis', *Theatre Research International*, 9:1 (1984), p. 23.

164. Innes, *Holy Theatre*, p. 58.

165. Auslander, '*Holy Theatre* and catharsis', p. 23.

166. Claude Schumacher, *Artaud on Theatre*. London: Methuen Drama, 1989, p. 92.

167. *Ibid.*, p. 38.

168. *Ibid.*

169. Ronald Hayman, *Artaud and After*. Oxford: Oxford University Press, 1977, p. 77.
170. *Ibid.*
171. *Ibid.*, p. 39.
172. *Ibid.*, p. 40.
173. *Ibid.*, p. 44.
174. *Ibid.*, p. 46.
175. Artaud, *The Theatre and Its Double*, p. 43.
176. James R. Brandon (ed.), *The Cambridge Guide to Asian Theatre*. Cambridge: Cambridge University Press, 1997, p. 119.
177. Artaud, *The Theatre and Its Double*, p. 38.
178. Jerzy Grotowski, *Towards a Poor Theatre*. Edited by Eugenio Barba with a preface by Peter Brook. London: Methuen, 1969, p. 89.
179. Harold G. Coward, *The Sphota Theory of Language: A Philosophical Analysis*. Delhi, Varanasi and Patna: Motilal Banarsidass, 1980, p. 3.
180. *Ibid.*
181. *Ibid.*, p. 128.
182. *Ibid.*, p. 129.
183. *Ibid.*, p. 131.
184. *Ibid.*
185. *Ibid.*, p. 73.
186. *Ibid.*
187. *Ibid.*, p. 12.
188. *Ibid.*
189. *Ibid.*
190. William Haney II, 'Unity in Vedic aesthetics: the self-interacting dynamics of the knower, the known, and the process of knowing', *Analecta Husserliana*, 233 (1991), p. 316.
191. Coward, *The Sphota Theory of Language*, 76.
192. Artaud, *The Theatre and Its Double*, p. 45.
193. Grotowski, *Towards a Poor Theatre*, p. 15.
194. David Bradby and David Williams, *Directors' Theatre* (Macmillan Modern Dramatists). London: Macmillan, 1988, p. 124.
195. Grotowski, *Towards a Poor Theatre*, p. 18.
196. Bradby and Williams, *Directors' Theatre*, p. 124.
197. Grotowski, *Towards a Poor Theatre*, p. 16.
198. *Ibid.*, p. 7.
199. *Ibid.*
200. Bradby and Williams, *Directors' Theatre*, p. 123.
201. *Ibid.*
202. Jennifer Kumiega, *The Theatre of Grotowski*. London and New York: Methuen, 1987, pp. 128–9.
203. *Ibid.*, p. 139.
204. Grotowski, *Towards a Poor Theare*, p. 16.
205. *Ibid.*, p. 39.

206. Chaim, *Distance in the Theatre*, p. 40.
207. Grotowski, *Towards a Poor Theare*, p. 43.
208. Jan Kott, 'Grotowski or the limit', *New Theatre Quarterly*, 6:23 (1990), pp. 203–4.
209. Brian Bates, *The Way of the Actor: A New Path to Personal Knowledge and Power*. London: Century, 1986, p. 39.
210. Grotowski, *Towards a Poor Theatre*, pp. 22–3.
211. *Ibid.*, p. 23.
212. *Ibid.*
213. Roose-Evans, *Experimental Theatre*, p. 147.
214. Ryckman, *Theories of Personality*, p. 65.
215. *Ibid.*
216. *Ibid.*
217. Richard Gilman, 'Jerzy Grotowski', *New American Review*, 9 (April 1970), pp. 206, 216.
218. Daniel Davy, 'Grotowski's Laboratory: a speculative look back at the Poor Theatre', *Essays in Theatre*, 7:2 (1989), p. 136.
219. Grotowski, *Towards a Poor Theatre*, p. 40.
220. Chaim, *Distance in the Theatre*, p. 41.
221. Kumiega, *The Theatre of Grotowski*, p. 148.
222. *Ibid.*, p. 147.
223. Innes, *Holy Theatre*, p. 163.
224. Grotowski, *Towards a Poor Theatre*, pp. 16, 125, 162.
225. David S. Werman, 'The oceanic experience and states of consciousness', *Journal of Psychoanalytic Anthropology*, 9:3 (1986), p. 340.
226. Sigmund Freud, *Civilisation and Its Discontents*. The standard edition of the complete psychological works of Freud, translated from the German under the general editorship of James Strachey in collaboration with Anna Freud assisted by Alex Strachey and Alan Tyson, Vol. 21, 1927–31. London: Hogarth Press and the Institute of Psychoanalysis, 1961, p. 64.
227. *Ibid.*, p. 65.
228. *Ibid.*, p. 68.
229. *Ibid.*
230. *Ibid.*
231. Werman, 'The oceanic experience and states of consciousness', p. 348.
232. Ryckman, *Theories of Personality*, p. 64.
233. *Ibid.*, p. 65.
234. Grotowski, *Towards a Poor Theatre*, p. 89.
235. Kumiega, *The Theatre of Grotowski*, p. 121.
236. Kott, 'Grotowski or the limit', p. 204.
237. Innes, *Holy Theatre*, p. 175.
238. Kumiega, *The Theatre of Grotowski*, p. 6.

239. *Ibid.*, p. 29.
240. *Ibid.*, p. 32.
241. *Ibid.*, p. 115.
242. *Ibid.*
243. *Ibid.*, p. 116.
244. Daniel Meyer-Dinkgräfe, *Consciousness and the Actor: A Reassessment of Western and Indian Approaches to the Actor's Emotional Involvement from the Perspective of Vedic Psychology*. Frankfurt am Main: Peter Lang, 1996.
245. Rhoda Orme-Johnson, 'A unified field theory of literature', *Modern Science and Vedic Science*, 1:3 (1987), p. 336.
246. Hagen, *A Challenge for the Actor*, p. 27.
247. Simon Callow, *Being an Actor*. Harmondsworth: Penguin, 1995.
248. Francis Hodge, *Play Directing: Analysis, Communication and Style*. London: Allyn and Bacon, 1994.
249. Yvette Daoust, *Roger Planchon: Director and Playwright* (Directors in Perspective). Cambridge: Cambridge University Press, 1981, p. 21.
250. Lise-Lone Marker and Frederick J. Marker, *Ingmar Bergman: Four Decades in the Theater* (Directors in Perspective). Cambridge: Cambridge University Press, 1982, p. 8.
251. *Ibid.*, p. 217.
252. Daoust, *Roger Planchon*, p. 20.
253. Maria M. Delgado and Paul Heritage (eds), *In Contact with the Gods? Directors Talk Theatre*. Manchester and New York: Manchester University Press, 1996, pp. 86–7.
254. *Ibid.*, p. 74.
255. *Ibid.*
256. William Ball, *A Sense of Direction: Some Observations on the Art of Directing*. New York: Drama Book Publishers, 1984, p. 5.
257. *Ibid.*
258. *Ibid.*, p. 7.
259. Delgado and Heritage, *In Contact with the Gods?*, p. 271.
260. Ball, *A Sense of Direction*, p. 55.
261. Daoust, *Roger Planchon*, p. 19.
262. Ball, *A Sense of Direction*, p. 61.
263. Delgado and Heritage, *In Contact with the Gods?*, p. 169.
264. *Ibid.*, p. 254.
265. *Ibid.*, p. 359.
266. Philip Auslander, *From Acting to Performance: Essays in Modernism and Postmodernism*. London and New York: Routledge, 1997, p. 28.
267. *Ibid.*, p. 30.
268. *Ibid.*
269. *Ibid.*
270. *Ibid.*, p. 36.
271. *Ibid.*, p. 92.

272. Wolfgang Welsch, 'Postmoderne: Genealogie und Bedeutung eines umstrittenen Begriffs', in Peter Kemper (ed.), *Postmoderne, oder: Der Kampf um die Zukunft. Die Kontroverse in Wissenschaft, Kunst und Gesellschaft.* Frankfurt am Main: Fischer, 1988, p. 9.

273. *Ibid.*

274. *Ibid.*, p.10.

275. *Ibid.*

276. *Ibid.*

277. *Ibid.*, p. 15.

278. Johannes Birringer, *Theatre, Theory, Postmodernism.* Bloomington and Indianapolis: Indiana University Press, 1991, p. xi.

279. *Ibid.*

280. Ulrich Broich and Manfred Pfister (eds), *Intertextualität: Formen, Funktionen, anglistische Fallbeispiele.* Tübingen: Narr, 1985, p. 15.

281. *Ibid.*

282. *Ibid.*, p. 25.

283. *Ibid.*

284. David George, 'On ambiguity: towards a post-modern performance theory', *Theatre Research International*, 14:1 (1989), p. 71.

285. *Ibid.*

286. *Ibid.*, p. 75.

287. *Ibid.*

288. *Ibid.*

289. *Ibid.*, p. 83.

290. Anika Lemaire, *Jacques Lacan.* Translated by David Macey. London, Henley and Boston: Routledge and Kegan Paul, 1977, p. 67.

291. *Ibid.*

292. *Ibid.*, p. 48.

293. George, 'On ambiguity', p. 74.

294. Natalie Crohn-Schmitt, *Actors and Onlookers: Theatre and Twentieth-Century Scientific Views of Nature.* Evanston: Northwestern University Press, 1990, p. 1.

295. *Ibid.*, p. 2.

296. *Ibid.*, p. 9.

297. *Ibid.*, p. 14.

298. *Ibid.*, p. 28.

299. *Ibid.*, p. 130.

300. Birringer, *Theatre, Theory, Postmodernism*, p. 79.

301. *Ibid.*, p. 31.

302. *Ibid.*, p. 100.

303. Auslander, *From Acting to Performance*, p. 93.

304. Mike Pearson, lecture 1 from the module *Principles of Performance I*, part of the newly launched undergraduate degree scheme in Performance Studies at the University of Wales, Aberystwyth. URL: http://www.aber.ac.uk/~psswww/pf20110/lecture1.htm

305. *Ibid.*, Glossary. URL: http://www.aber.ac.uk/~psswww/general/glossary.htm
306. *Ibid.*
307. *Ibid.*, Lecture 2, URL http://www.aber.ac.uk/~psswww/pf20110/lecture2.htm
308. *Ibid.*
309. *Ibid.*
310. *Ibid.*
311. *Ibid.*, Glossary.
312. Josette Féral, 'What is left of performance art? Autopsy of a function. Birth of a genre', *Discourse*, 14:2 (1992), p. 148.
313. RoseLee Goldberg, *Performance Art: From Futurism to the Present*. London: Thames and Hudson, 1988, p. 29.
314. *Ibid.*, p. 31.
315. Herschel B. Chipp, *Theories of Modern Art: A Source Book by Artists and Critics*. Berkeley, Los Angeles and London: University of California Press, 1968, p. 366.
316. *Ibid.*
317. Goldberg, *Performance Art*, p. 89.
318. *Ibid.*, p. 96.
319. Xerxes Mehta, 'Performance art: problems of description and evaluation', *Journal of Dramatic Theory and Criticism*, 5:1 (1990), 189.
320. *Ibid.*
321. *Ibid.*, p. 190.
322. *Ibid.*, p. 192.
323. *Ibid.*, p. 194.
324. *Ibid.*, p. 195.
325. Féral, 'What is left of performance art?', p. 157.
326. *Ibid.*, p. 146.
327. *Ibid.*, p. 147.
328. *Ibid.*, p. 149.
329. *Ibid.*, p. 158.

Chapter 6: Non-Western Approaches

1. William F. Sands, 'Maharishi's program of reading the Vedic literature: unfolding the total potential of natural law', *Modern Science and Vedic Science*, 7:1 (1997), p. 94.
2. Coward, *The Sphota Theory of Language*, p. 3.
3. *Ibid.*, p. 7.
4. Adapted from Tony Nader, *Human Physiology: Expression of Veda and Vedic Literature*. Vlodrop: Maharishi Vedic University Press, 1995, p. 34.

5. Maharishi Mahesh Yogi, *Perfection in Education*. Jabalpur: Maharishi Vedic University Press, 1997, p. 168.
6. Maharishi Mahesh Yogi, *On the Bhagavad-Gita: A New Translation and Commentary, Chapters 1–6*. Harmondsworth: Penguin, 1969, p. 128.
7. *Ibid.*, p. 482.
8. *Ibid.*, pp. 482–3.
9. Gabriel Hartmann, *Maharishi-Gandharva-Ved. Die klassische Musik der Vedischen Hochkultur: Eine Einführung in die musiktheoretischen Grundlagen*. Vlodrop: Maharishi Vedic University Press, 1992, p. 62.
10. *Ibid.*
11. Srinivasa Ayya Srinivasan, *On the Composition of the Natyasastra* (Studien zur Indologie und Iranistik Monographie 1). Reinbek: Dr Inge Wezler Verlag für Orientalische Fachpublikationen, 1980, p. 1.
12. Pramod Kale, *The Theatrical Universe: A Study of the Natyasastra*. Bombay: Popular Prakashan, 1974, p. 5.
13. Maharishi Mahesh Yogi, *On the Bhagavad-Gita*, p. 252.
14. *Ibid.*, pp. 253–4.
15. Manomohan Ghosh (ed. and trans.), *The Natyasastra: A Treatise on Hindu Dramaturgy and Histrionics*. Calcutta: The Royal Asiatic Society of Bengal, 1950, pp. 2–3. Future references to this text will be indicated by *NS*.
16. *NS*, p. 3.
17. *NS*, pp. 3–4.
18. *NS*, p. 4.
19. Kale, *The Theatrical Universe*, p. 1.
20. Hari Ram Mishra, *The Theory of Rasa in Sanskrit Drama: With a Comparative Study of General Dramatic Literature*. Bhopal, Sayar and Chhatapur: Vindhyachal Prakashan, 1964.
21. Kapila Chandra Pandey, *Comparative Aesthetics*, Vol. 1: *Indian Aesthetics*. Banaras: The Chpwkhamba Sanskrit Series Office, 1950, p. 10.
22. Mishra, *The Theory of Rasa in Sanskrit Drama*, p. 198.
23. V. Rhagavan, *The Concept of the Beautiful in Sanskrit Literature*. Madras: The Kuppuswami Sastri Research Institute, 1988.
24. *NS*, p. 102.
25. *NS*, p. 109.
26. *NS*, pp. 108–9.
27. *NS*, p. 109.
28. *NS*, p. 102.
29. *NS*, p. 109.
30. *NS*, p. 102.
31. *NS*, pp. 102–3.
32. *NS*, p. 105.
33. E. W. Marasinghe, *The Sanskrit Theatre and Stagecraft* (Sri Garib

Dass Oriental Series No. 78). Delhi: Sri Satguru Publications, 1989, p. 198.

34. *NS*, Chapter 14.
35. *NS*, p. 143.
36. R. R. Ambardekar, *Rasa Structure of the Meghaduta*. Bombay: Prakashan, 1979, p. 26.
37. *NS*, p. 143.
38. *NS*, p. 143.
39. Suresh Dhayagude, *Western and Indian Poetics: A Comparative Study* (Bhandarkar Oriental Research Series No. 18). Poona: Bhandarkar Oriental Research Institute, 1981, p. 14.
40. *Ibid.*, p. 172.
41. *Ibid.*, p. 15.
42. G. K. Bhat, *Rasa Theory and Allied Problems*. Baroda: The MS University of Baroda, 1984, p. 48.
43. *Ibid.*
44. Rekha Jhanji, *The Sensuous in Art: Reflections on Indian Aesthetics* (Indian Institute of Advanced Studies). Delhi: Shimla in association with Motilal Barnasidass, 1989, p. 35.
45. *Ibid.*
46. Shveni Pandya, *A Study of the Technique of Abhinaya in Relation to Sanskrit Drama*. Bombay and New Delhi: Somaiya Publications, 1988, p. 256.
47. *Ibid.*
48. Minakshi Dalal, *Conflict in Sanskrit Drama*. Bombay and New Delhi: Somaiya Publications, 1973, p. 36.
49. *Ibid.*
50. G. K. Bhat, *Sanskrit Dramatic Theory* (Bhandarkar Oriental Institute Postgraduate and Research Series No. 13). Poona: Bhandarkar Oriental Research Institute, 1981, p. 51.
51. Marasinghe, *The Sanskrit Theatre and Stagecraft*, p. 188.
52. Richard Schechner, *Between Theatre and Anthropology*. Philadelphia: University of Pennsylvania Press, 1985, p. 136.
53. *Ibid.*, p. 140.
54. Ian Watson, *Towards a Third Theatre: Eugenio Barba and the Odin Teatret*. London and New York: Routledge, 1993, p. 14.
55. *Ibid.*
56. *Ibid.*, p. 15.
57. *NS*, pp. 245–6.
58. Kumiega, *The Theatre of Grotowski*, p. 116.
59. Peter Brook, lecture at Temenos Academy, London, 1 November 1993.
60. Richard E. Kramer, 'The *Natyasastra* and Stanislavsky: points of contact', *Theatre Studies*, vol. 36 (1991), p. 56.
61. *Ibid.*

62. *Ibid.*
63. John Miletich, *States of Awareness: An Annotated Bibliography*. New York, Westport and London: Greenwood, 1988, p. ix.
64. Arnold M. Ludwig, 'Altered states of consciousness', in Charles T. Tart (ed.), *Altered States of Consciousness: A Book of Readings*. New York, London, Sydney and Toronto: John Wiley and Sons, 1969, pp. 13–16.
65. *Ibid.*, pp. 10–12.
66. *Ibid.*, pp. 18–20.
67. Charles Tart, 'Some assumptions of orthodox, Western psychology', in Charles Tart (ed.), *Transpersonal Psychologies*. London: Routledge and Kegan Paul, 1975, p. 81.
68. Miletich, *States of Awareness*, p. 68.
69. John H. Clark, *A Map of Mental States*. London, Boston, Melbourne and Henley: Routledge and Kegan Paul, 1983, pp. 13–14.
70. *Ibid.*, p. 16.
71. *Ibid.*, p. 20.
72. *Ibid.*
73. *Ibid.*, pp. 22–4.
74. *Ibid.*, p. 25.
75. W. T. Stace, *Mysticism and Philosophy*. London: Macmillan, 1960.
76. Robert K. C. Forman, 'Introduction: mysticism, constructivism, and forgetting', in Robert K. C. Forman (ed.), *The Problem of Pure Consciousness: Mysticism and Philosophy*. New York and Oxford: Oxford University Press, 1990, p. 7.
77. *Ibid.*, p. 8.
78. *Ibid.*, p. 3.
79. *Ibid.*, p. 28.
80. Charles N. Alexander, Ken Chandler and Robert W. Boyer, 'Experience and understanding of pure consciousness in Vedic Science of Maharishi Mahesh Yogi', unpublished paper, 5–6, quoted in Robert K. C. Forman, *The Problem of Pure Consciousness: Mysticism and Philosophy*. New York and Oxford: Oxford University Press, 1990, pp. 27–8.
81. Forman, *The Problem of Pure Consciousness*, p. 27.
82. Alexander *et al.*, in Forman, *The Problem of Pure Consciousness*, pp. 27–8.
83. Paul Gelderloos and Zaid H. A. D. Beto, 'The TM and TM-Sidhi Program and reported experiences of transcendental consciousness', *Psychologia*, 32:2 (1989), pp. 91–103.
84. Charles N. Alexander, J. L. Davies, C. A. Dixon, M. C. Dillbeck, S. M. Druker, R. M. Oet, J. M. Muehlman and D. W. Orme-Johnson, 'Growth of higher stages of consciousness: Maharishi's Vedic Psychology of human development', in Charles N. Alexander

and Ellen J. Langer (eds), *Higher Stages of Human Development: Perspectives on Human Growth.* Oxford: Oxford University Press, 1990, p. 290.

85. Charles N. Alexander, Robert W. Cranson, Robert W. Boyer and David W. Orme-Johnson, 'Transcendental consciousness: a fourth state of consciousness beyond sleep, dream, and waking', in Jayne Gackenbach (ed.), *Sleep and Dream: A Sourcebook.* New York and London: Garland Publishing, 1986, p. 291.

86. Charles N. Alexander, Steven M. Druker and Ellen J. Langer, 'Introduction: major issues in the exploration of adult growth', in Charles N. Alexander and Ellen J. Langer (eds), *Higher Stages of Human Development. Perspectives on Human Growth.* Oxford: Oxford University Press, 1990, p. 3.

87. *Ibid.*

88. *Ibid.*, p. 5.

89. *Ibid.*

90. *Ibid.*, p. 3.

91. *Ibid.*, pp. 9–10.

92. Charles N. Alexander and Robert W. Boyer, 'Seven states of consciousness: unfolding the full potential of the cosmic psyche in individual life through Maharishi's Vedic Psychology', *Modern Science and Vedic Science*, 2:4 (1989), p. 342.

93. H. D. Thoreau, *Walden.* New York, New American Library, 1960 (first published 1854), pp. 94–5.

94. B. J. King and K. Chapin, *Billie Jean.* New York: Harper & Row, 1974, p. 199.

95. Alexander and Boyer, 'Seven states of consciousness', p. 355.

96. Kathleen Raine, *The Land Unknown.* New York: George Braziller, 1975, p. 119.

97. Alexander and Boyer, 'Seven states of consciousness', pp. 359–60.

98. Orme-Johnson, 'A unified field theory of literature', p. 339.

99. *NS*, p. 102.

100. *NS*, p. 102.

101. *NS*, p. 109.

102. Yogashiromani Shri Shri Ravi Shankar, interview with Daniel Meyer-Dinkgräfe, 5 August 1992.

103. *Ibid.*

104. *Ibid.*

105. *Ibid.*

106. Padma Subrahmanyam, renowned bharata natyam exponent in Madras, who produced a thirteen-part TV series about the *Natyashastra* at the request of Indian Television.

107. James Brandon (ed.), *The Cambridge Guide to Asian Theatre*, p. 143.

108. Ortolani, *The Japanese Theatre*, chapter on Noh, on which the rest of this chapter is based.

109. Josephine Hung-Hung, 'Das chinesische Theater', in Heinz Kinder-
     mann (ed.), *Einführung in das ostasiatische Theater*. Wien: Hermann
     Böhlhaus, 1985, pp. 116–17. My own translation into English.
110. Jo Riley, *Chinese Theatre and the Actor in Performance*. Cambridge:
     Cambridge University Press, 1997, p. 13.
111. *Ibid.*, p. 22.
112. *Ibid.*, p. 30.
113. *Ibid.*, p. 206.
114. *Ibid.*
115. *Ibid.*, p. 237.
116. *Ibid.*
117. *Ibid.*, p. 70.
118. *Ibid.*, p. 249.
119. Don Rubin (ed.), *The World Encyclopedia of Contemporary Theatre*,
     Vol. IV: *The Arab World*. London and New York: Routledge, 1999,
     p. 90.
120. *Ibid.*

Chapter 7: The Intercultural Paradigm

1. Chris Jenks, *Culture*. London and New York: Routledge, 1995, p. 6.
2. *Ibid.*, p. 9.
3. F. R. Leavis, *Mass Civilization and Minority Culture*. Cambridge: The
   Minority Press, 1930, p. 19.
4. H. J. Gans, *Popular Culture and High Culture*. New York: Basic Books,
   1974, pp. 3–5.
5. Patrice Pavis, *Theatre at the Crossroads of Culture*. London and New
   York: Routledge, 1992, p. 9.
6. Camille Camelleri, 'Culture et sociétés: caractères et fonctions',
   Les Amis de Sèvre, 4 (1982), p. 16.
7. *Ibid.*
8. Pavis, *Theatre at the Crossroads of Culture*, p. 2.
9. *Ibid.*, p. 4.
10. *Ibid.*, p. 186.
11. *Ibid.*
12. *Ibid.*, p. 20.
13. *Ibid.*
14. *Ibid.*
15. *Ibid.*
16. Erika Fischer-Lichte, 'Das Theater auf der Suche nach einer
    Universalsprache', *Forum Modernes Theater*, 4:2 (1989), pp. 115–
    21.
17. Pavis, *Theatre at the Crossroads of Culture*, p. 20.
18. *Ibid.*, pp. 20–1.

19. *Ibid.*, p. 21.
20. Jatinder Verma, article on 'Binglish' on the Internet, 1996. URL: http://www.tara-arts.com
21. Innes, *Holy Theatre*, p. 11.
22. Watson, *Towards a Third Theatre*, p. 101.
23. *Ibid.*, pp. 3–4.
24. *Ibid.*, p. 149.
25. *Ibid.*
26. *Ibid.*
27. Eugenio Barba and Nicola Savarese, *The Secret Art of the Performer: A Dictionary of Theatre Anthropology*. London and New York: Routledge, 1991, p. 8.
28. *Ibid.*
29. *Ibid.*, p. 8.
30. Eugenio Barba, 'Interview with Gautam Dasgupta', *Performing Arts Journal*, January 1985, p. 12.
31. Watson, *Towards a Third Theatre*, p. 32.
32. *Ibid.*
33. *Ibid.*
34. Barba and Savarese, *The Secret Art of the Performer*, p. 188.
35. Watson, *Towards a Third Theatre*, p. 33.
36. *Ibid.*
37. *Ibid.*, p. 34.
38. *Ibid.*, p. 35
39. Eugenio Barba, 'The fiction of duality', *New Theatre Quarterly*, 5:20 (1989), p. 312.
40. Watson, *Towards a Third Theatre*, p. 39.
41. *Ibid.*
42. *Ibid.*
43. Eugenio Barba, *The Floating Islands: Reflections with Odin Teatret*. Edited by Ferdinando Taviani. Gråsten: Drama, 1979, p. 134.
44. Watson, *Towards a Third Theatre*, p. 40.
45. *Ibid.*
46. Barba, *The Floating Islands*, p. 35.
47. *Ibid.*, p. 73.
48. *Ibid.*
49. Eugenio Barba, 'The way of refusal: the theatre's body-in-life', *New Theatre Quarterly*, 4:16 (1988), p. 291.
50. *Ibid.*
51. *Ibid.*
52. *Ibid.*
53. David Williams, *Peter Brook: A Theatrical Casebook*. London: Methuen, 1991, p. 1.
54. *Ibid.*, p. 74.
55. Martin, *Voice in Modern Theatre*.

56. Peter Brook, *The Shifting Point: Forty Years of Theatrical Exploration 1946–1987*. London: Methuen, 1987, p. 31.
57. Kott, 'Grotowski or the limit', p. 203.
58. Bradby and Williams, *Directors' Theatre*, p. 31.
59. Brook, *The Shifting Point*, p. 30.
60. Williams, *Peter Brook*, p. 332.
61. Peter Brook, *The Empty Space*. Harmondsworth: Penguin, 1972, p. 151.
62. *Ibid.*
63. Brook, *The Shifting Point*, p. 41.
64. *Ibid.*
65. Brook, *The Empty Space*, pp. 79–80.
66. *Ibid.*, p. 47.
67. Eugenio Barba, 'Eugenio Barba to Phillip Zarrilli: about the visible and the invisible in the theater, and about ISTA in particular', *The Drama Review*, 32:3 (1988), p. 12.
68. Brook, *The Empty Space*, p. 63.
69. *Ibid.*
70. Brook, *The Shifting Point*, p. 233.
71. *Ibid.*
72. Bradby and Williams, *Directors' Theatre*, p. 147.
73. Brook, *The Shifting Point*, p. 128.
74. Leonard Pronko, 'L.A. Festival: Peter Brook's *The Mahabharata*', *Asian Theatre Journal*, 5: 2 (1988), p. 110.
75. Innes, *Holy Theatre*, p. 139.
76. *Ibid.*, p. 142.
77. David Williams, 'Theatre of innocence and of experience: Peter Brook's International Centre. An introduction', in David Williams (ed.), *Peter Brook and the Mahabharata: Critical Perspectives*. London and New York: Routledge, 1991, pp. 3–28.
78. Rustom Bharucha, *Theatre and the World: Essays on Performance and Politics of Culture*. London and New York: Routledge, 1993.
79. Patrice Pavis, 'Theory and practice in the Theatre Studies at the University', *Proceedings of Disorientations Conference*. Monash University, 1998.
80. Rustom Bharucha, 'A view from India', in Williams (ed.), *Peter Brook and the Mahabharata*, p. 233.
81. *Ibid.*, p. 237.
82. *Ibid.*, p. 245.
83. Mallika Sarabhai, in 'Energy and the ensemble: actors' perspectives', in Williams (ed.), *Peter Brook and the Mahabharata*, pp. 99–100.
84. Vijay Mishra, 'The great Indian epic and Peter Brook', in Williams (ed.), *Peter Brook and the Mahabharata*, p. 200.
85. Williams, 'Theatre of innocence and experience', p. 19.

86. Bharucha, 'A view from India', pp. 230–1.
87. Bharucha, *Theatre and the World*, p. 4.
88. Bharucha, 'A view from India', p. 229.
89. Maria Shevtsova, 'Interaction–interpretation: *The Mahabharata* from a socio-cultural perspective', in Williams (ed.), *Peter Brook and the Mahabharata*, p. 226
90. David Williams, 'Transculturalism and myth in the theatre of Peter Brook', in Patrice Pavis (ed.), *The Intercultural Performance Reader*. London and New York: Routledge, 1996, p. 70.
91. Bharucha, 'A view from India', p. 236.
92. *Ibid.*, p. 231.
93. Jean-Claude Carrière, 'What is not in *The Mahabharata* is nowhere', in Williams (ed.), *Peter Brook and the Mahabharata*, p. 64.
94. Bharucha, 'A view from India', p. 242.
95. *Ibid.*
96. Marvin Carlson, 'Brook and Mnouchkine: passages to India?', in Patrice Pavis (ed.), *The Intercultural Performance Reader*. London and New York: Routledge, 1996, p. 88.
97. *Ibid.*
98. Peter Brook, 'Theatre, popular and special, and the perils of cultural piracy', in Williams (ed.), *Peter Brook and the Mahabharata*, p. 52.
99. Carlson, 'Brook and Mnouchkine', p. 91.
100. Gautam Dasgupta, 'Peter Brook's *Orientalism*', in Williams (ed.), *Peter Brook and the Mahabharata*, p. 263.
101. Pavis, 'Theory and Practice in the Theatre Studies at the University', p. 226.

Chapter 8: Training Past and Present

1. Booth, *Theatre in the Victorian Age*, p. 103.
2. Gerald Eades Bentley, *The Profession of the Player in Shakespeare's Time 1590–1642*. Princeton: Princeton University Press, 1984, pp. 143–4.
3. Harley Granville-Barker, *The Exemplary Theatre*. New York and London: Benjamin Blom, 1969 (first published 1922), p. 77.
4. *Ibid.*
5. *Ibid.*, p. 88.
6. *Ibid.*, p. 111.
7. *Ibid.*, p. 228.
8. *Ibid.*, p. 232.
9. *Ibid.*, p. 245.
10. *Ibid.*
11. Jan McDonald, 'The promised land of the London stage: acting

style at the Court Theatre London, 1904–1907', in Milan Lukes (ed.), *The Role of the Actor in the Theatrical Reform of the Late 19th and Early 20th Centuries*. Seventh International Congress on Theatre Research, 3–8 September 1973. University of Prague, 1976, p. 84.

12. *Ibid.*
13. Alison Hodge (ed.), *Twentieth Century Actor Training*. London and New York: Routledge, 2000.
14. Leiter, *From Stanislavsky to Barrault*, p. 56.
15. Leach, *Vsevolod Meyerhold*, p. 52.
16. *Ibid.*, p. 61.
17. *Ibid.*
18. *Ibid.*, pp. 64–5.
19. Bradby and Williams, *Directors' Theatre*, p. 123.
20. *Ibid.*, p. 116.
21. Brook, *The Shifting Point*, p. 233.
22. *Ibid.*
23. *Ibid.*, p. 73.
24. *Ibid.*
25. Barba and Savarese, *The Secret Art of the Performer*, p. 30.
26. David Griffiths, *The Training of Noh Actors and The Dove. Mask. A Release of Acting Resources*, Vol. 2. Amsterdam: Harwood Academic, 1998, p. 33.
27. *Ibid.*, pp. 33–4.
28. *Ibid.*, p. 38.
29. *Ibid.*, p. 39.
30. *Ibid.*, p. 41.
31. *Ibid.*, p. 44.
32. Riley, *Chinese Theatre*, p. 22.
33. *Ibid.*, p. 37.
34. *Ibid.*, p. 22.
35. *Ibid.*, p. 88.
36. *Ibid.*, p. 90.
37. *Ibid.*
38. *Ibid.*, p. 177.
39. *Ibid.*, p. 208.

Chapter 9: Theatre Criticism

1. Alfred Kerr, *Die Welt im Drama*. Edited by Gerhard F. Hering. Köln and Berlin: Kiepenheuer & Witsch, 1964 (first published 1954), p. 466.
2. *Ibid.*, p. 470.

Chapter 10: The Future of Acting

1. Kerr, *Die Welt im Drama*, p. 470.
2. Crohn-Schmitt, *Actors and Onlookers*, p. 8.
3. Madan Sarup, *An Introductory Guide to Post-Structuralism and Postmodernism*. New York, London, Toronto, Sydney and Tokyo: Harvester Wheatsheaf, 1988, p. 131.
4. *Ibid.*, p. 132.

∞

Bibliography

ૹ൫ൟ

Alexander, Charles N., Robert W. Cranson, Robert W. Boyer and David W. Orme-Johnson, 'Transcendental consciousness: a fourth state of consciousness beyond sleep, dream, and waking', in Jayne Gackenbach (ed.), *Sleep and Dream: A Sourcebook*. New York and London: Garland Publishing, 1986, pp. 282–315.

Alexander, Charles N. and Robert W. Boyer, 'Seven states of consciousness: unfolding the full potential of the cosmic psyche in individual life through Maharishi's Vedic Psychology', *Modern Science and Vedic Science*, 2:4 (1989), pp. 324–71.

Alexander, Charles N., J. L. Davies, C. A. Dixon, M. C. Dillbeck, S. M. Draker, R. M. Oet, J. M. Muehlman and D. W. Orme-Johnson, 'Growth of higher stages of consciousness: Maharishi's Vedic Psychology of human development', in Charles N. Alexander and Ellen J. Langer (eds), *Higher Stages of Human Development: Perspectives on Human Growth*. Oxford: Oxford University Press, 1990, pp. 286–341.

Alexander, Charles N., Steven M. Druker and Ellen J. Langer, 'Introduction: major issues in the exploration of adult growth', in Charles N. Alexander and Ellen J. Langer (eds), *Higher Stages of Human Development: Perspectives on Human Growth*. Oxford: Oxford University Press, 1990, pp. 3–32.

Alexander, Charles N., Ken Chandler and Robert W. Boyer, 'Experience and understanding of pure consciousness in Vedic Science of Maharishi Mahesh Yogi', unpublished paper, 5–6, quoted in Robert K. C. Forman, *The Problem of Pure Consciousness: Mysticism and Philosophy*. New York and Oxford: Oxford University Press, 1990, pp. 27–8.

Ambardekar, R. R., *Rasa Structure of the Meghaduta*. Bombay: Prakashan, 1979.

Arnott, Peter D. *Public and Performance in the Greek Theatre*. London: Routledge, 1991.

Artaud, Antonin, *The Theatre and Its Double*. Collected Works, Vol. 4. Translated by Victor Corti. London: Calder and Boyars, 1974.

Auslander, Philip, '*Holy Theatre* and catharsis', *Theatre Research International*, 9:1 (1984), pp. 16–29.

Auslander, Philip, *From Acting to Performance: Essays in Modernism and Postmodernism*. London and New York: Routledge, 1997.

Ball, William, *A Sense of Direction: Some Observations on the Art of Directing*. New York: Drama Book Publishers, 1984.

Barba, Eugenio, *The Floating Islands: Reflections with Odin Teatret*. Edited by Ferdinando Taviani. Holstebro, 1979.

Barba, Eugenio, 'Interview with Gautam Dasgupta', *Performing Arts Journal*, January (1985), pp. 3–10.

Barba, Eugenio, 'The way of refusal: the theatre's body-in-life', *New Theatre Quarterly*, 4:16 (1988), pp. 291–9.

Barba, Eugenio, 'Eugenio Barba to Phillip Zarrilli: about the visible and the invisible in the theater, and about ISTA in particular', *The Drama Review*, 32:3 (1988), pp. 7–14.

Barba, Eugenio, 'The fiction of duality', *New Theatre Quarterly*, 5:20 (1989), 311–14.

Barba, Eugenio and Nicola Savarese, *The Secret Art of the Performer: A Dictionary of Theatre Anthropology*. London and New York: Routledge, 1991.

Bates, Brian, *The Way of the Actor: A New Path to Personal Knowledge and Power*. London: Century, 1986.

Battista, John R., 'The science of consciousness', in Kenneth S. Pope and Jerome L. Singer (eds), *The Stream of Consciousness: Scientific Investigation into the Flow of Human Consciousness*. Chichester, New York, Brisbane and Toronto: John Wiley and Sons, 1978, pp. 55–87.

Battock, Gregory and Robert Nickas, *The Art of Performance: A Critical Anthology*. New York: Dutton, 1984.

Bentley, Gerald Eades, *The Profession of the Player in Shakespeare's Time 1590–1642*. Princeton: Princeton University Press, 1984.

Bharucha, Rustom, 'A view from India', in David Williams (ed.), *Peter Brook and the Mahabharata: Critical Perspectives*. London and New York: Routledge, 1991, pp. 228–52.

Bharucha, Rustom, *Theatre and the World: Essays on Performance and Politics of Culture*. London and New York: Routledge, 1993.

Bhat, G. K., *Sanskrit Dramatic Theory* (Bhandarkar Oriental Institute Post-graduate and Research Series No. 13). Poona: Bhandarkar Oriental Research Institute, 1981.

Bhat, G. K., *Rasa Theory and Allied Problems*. Baroda: The MS University of Baroda, 1984.

Bice, Benvenuto and Roger Kennedy, *The Work of Jaques Lacan*. London: Free Association Books, 1986.

Birringer, Johannes, *Theatre, Theory, Postmodernism*. Bloomington and Indianapolis: Indiana University Press, 1991.

Booth, Michael R., *Theatre in the Victorian Age*. Cambridge: Cambridge University Press, 1991.

Bradby, David and David Williams, *Directors' Theatre* (Macmillan Modern Dramatists). London: Macmillan, 1988.

Brandon, James R. (ed.), *The Cambridge Guide to Asian Theatre*. Cambridge: Cambridge University Press, 1997.

Brandt, George W. and Wiebe Hogendoorn, *German and Dutch Theatre, 1600–1848*. Cambridge: Cambridge University Press, 1993.

Braun, Edward, *Meyerhold on Theatre*. London: Methuen, 1969.

Brockett, Oscar G., *History of the Theatre*, 5th edition. London: Allyn and Bacon, 1987.

Brockett, Oscar G. and Robert R. Findlay, *Century of Innovation: A History of European and American Theatre and Drama since the Late 19th Century*. Boston and London: Allyn and Bacon, 1991.

Broich, Ulrich and Manfred Pfister (eds), *Intertextualität: Formen, Funktionen, anglistische Fallbeispiele*. Tübingen: Narr, 1985.

Brook, Peter, *The Empty Space*. Harmondsworth: Penguin, 1972.

Brook, Peter, *The Shifting Point: Forty Years of Theatrical Exploration 1946–1987*. London: Methuen, 1987.

Brook, Peter, 'The presence of India: an introduction', in David Williams (ed.), *Peter Brook and the Mahabharata: Critical Perspectives*. London and New York: Routledge, 1991, pp. 41–4.

Brook, Peter, 'Theatre, popular and special, and the perils of cultural piracy', in David Williams (ed.), *Peter Brook and the Mahabharata: Critical Perspectives*. London and New York: Routledge, 1991, pp. 52–8.

Brook, Peter, lecture at Temenos Academy, London, 1 November 1993.

Brown, John Russell, 'On the acting of Shakespeare's plays', *Quarterly Journal of Speech*, 34 (1953), pp. 477–84.

Calhoun, Cheshire and Robert C. Solomon, *What Is an Emotion? Classical Readings in Philosophical Psychology*. New York and Oxford: Oxford University Press, 1984.

Callow, Simon, *Being an Actor*. Harmondsworth: Penguin, 1995.

Camilleri, Camille, 'Culture et sociétés: caractères et fonctions', *Les Amis de Sèvre*, 4 (1982).

Carlson, Marvin, *Theories of the Theatre: A Historical and Critical Survey, from the Greeks to the Present*. Ithaca and London: Cornell University Press, 1984.

Carlson, Marvin, 'Brook and Mnouchkine: passages to India?', in Patrice Pavis (ed.), *The Intercultural Performance Reader*. London and New York: Routledge, 1996, pp. 79–92.

Carrière, Jean-Claude, 'What is not in *The Mahabharata* is nowhere', in David Williams (ed.), *Peter Brook and the Mahabharata: Critical Perspectives*. London and New York: Routledge, 1991, pp. 59–64.

Carter, Huntley, *The Theatre of Max Reinhardt*. New York: Benjamin Blom, 1964 (first published 1914).

Chaim, Daphna Ben, *Distance in the Theatre: The Aesthetics of Audience*

Response (Theatre and Dramatic Studies No. 17). Ann Arbor and London: UMI Research Press, 1984.

Chekhov, Mikhail, 'About Vakhtangov', in Lyubov Vendrovskaya and Galena Kaptereva (compilers), *Evgeny Vakhtangov*. Moscow: Progress, 1982, pp. 208–10.

Chipp, Herschel B., *Theories of Modern Art: A Source Book by Artists and Critics*. Berkeley, Los Angeles and London: University of California Press, 1968.

Clark, John H., *A Map of Mental States*. London, Boston, Melbourne and Henley: Routledge and Kegan Paul, 1983.

Coward, Harold G., *The Sphota Theory of Language: A Philosophical Analysis*. Delhi, Varanasi and Patna: Motilal Banarsidass, 1980.

Crohn-Schmitt, Natalie, *Actors and Onlookers: Theatre and Twentieth-Century Scientific Views of Nature*. Evanston: Northwestern University Press, 1990.

Dalal, Minakshi, *Conflict in Sanskrit Drama*. Bombay and New Delhi: Somaiya Publications, 1973.

Daoust, Yvette, *Roger Planchon: Director and Playwright* (Directors in Perspective). Cambridge: Cambridge University Press, 1981.

Dasgupta, Gautam, 'Peter Brook's *Orientalism*', in David Williams (ed.), *Peter Brook and the Mahabharata: Critical Perspectives*. London and New York: Routledge, 1991, pp. 262–7,

Davy, Daniel, 'Grotowski's Laboratory: a speculative look back at the Poor Theatre', *Essays in Theatre*, 7:2 (1989), pp. 127–38.

Delgado, Maria M. and Paul Heritage (eds), *In Contact with the Gods? Directors Talk Theatre*. Manchester and New York: Manchester University Press, 1996.

Devrient, Eduard, *Geschichte der deutschen Schauspielkunst*, Vol. 2. Berlin: Otto Elsner, 1905.

Dhayagude, Suresh, *Western and Indian Poetics: A Comparative Study* (Bhandarkar Oriental Research Series No. 18). Poona: Bhandarkar Oriental Research Institute, 1981.

Diderot, Denis, *The Paradox of Acting*. New York: Hill and Wang, 1955.

Elliott, John R. Jr, 'Medieval acting', in Marianne G. Briscoe and John C. Coldewey (eds), *Contexts for Early English Drama*. Bloomington: Indiana University Press, 1989, pp. 238–51.

Féral, Josette, 'What is left of performance art? Autopsy of a function. Birth of a genre', *Discourse*, 14:2 (1992), pp. 142–62.

Fischer-Lichte, Erika, 'Das Theater auf der Suche nach einer Universalsprache', *Forum Modernes Theater*, 4:2 (1989), pp. 115–21.

Forman, Robert K. C., 'Introduction: mysticism, constructivism, and forgetting', in Robert K. C. Forman (ed.), *The Problem of Pure Consciousness: Mysticism and Philosophy*. New York and Oxford: Oxford University Press, 1990.

Freud, Sigmund, *Civilisation and Its Discontents*, The standard edition of the complete psychological works of Freud, translated from the German under the general editorship of James Strachey in collaboration with Anna Freud assisted by Alex Strachey and Alan Tyson, Vol. 21, 1927–31. London: Hogarth Press and the Institute of Psychoanalysis, 1961.

Frijda, Nico H., *The Emotions*. Cambridge: Cambridge University Press, 1986.

Gans, H. J., *Popular Culture and High Culture*. New York: Basic Books, 1974.

Gelderloos, Paul and Zaid H. A. D. Beto, 'The TM and TM-Sidhi Program and reported experiences of transcendental consciousness', *Psychologia*, 32:2 (1989), pp. 91–103.

George, David, 'On ambiguity: towards a post-modern performance theory', *Theatre Research International*, 14:1 (1989), pp. 71–85.

Ghosh, Manomohan (ed. and trans.), *The Natyasastra: A Treatise on Hindu Dramaturgy and Histrionics*. Calcutta: The Royal Asiatic Society of Bengal, 1950.

Gilman, Richard, 'Jerzy Grotowski', *New American Review*, 9 (April 1970), pp. 206, 216.

Goldberg, RoseLee, *Performance Art: From Futurism to the Present*. London: Thames and Hudson, 1988.

Golding, Alfred S., 'Nature as symbolic behavior: Crésol's *Autumn Vacations* and early Baroque acting technique', *Renaissance and Reformation*, 10:1 (1986), pp. 147–57.

Gossman, Lionel and Elizabeth MacArthur, 'Diderot's displaced paradox', in Jack Undank and Herbert Josephs (eds), *Diderot Digression and Dispersion: A Bicentennial Tribute*. Lexington, Kentucky: French Forum Publishers, 1984, pp. 106–19.

Granville-Barker, Harley, *The Exemplary Theatre*. New York and London: Benjamin Blom, 1969 (first published 1922).

Grear, Allison, 'A background to Diderot's *Paradoxe sur le Comédien*: the role of imagination in spoken expression of emotion', *Forum for Modern Language Studies*, 21:3 (1985), pp. 225–38.

Griffiths, David, *The Training of Noh Actors and The Dove. Mask. A Release of Acting Resources*, Vol. 2. Amsterdam: Harwood Academic, 1998.

Gropius, Walter (ed.), *The Theater of the Bauhaus*. London: Eyre Methuen, 1961.

Grotowski, Jerzy, *Towards a Poor Theatre*. Edited by Eugenio Barba with a preface by Peter Brook. London: Methuen, 1969.

Hagen, Uta, *A Challenge for the Actor*. New York: Scribner, 1991.

Hamlyn, D. W., *The Penguin History of Western Philosophy*. London: Penguin, 1990.

Haney, William II, 'Unity in Vedic aesthetics: the self-interacting dynamics of the knower, the known, and the process of knowing', *Analecta Husserliana*, 233 (1991), pp. 295–319.

Hansen-Löve, Aage H., *Der russische Formalismus: Methodologische Rekonstruktion seiner Entwicklung aus dem Prinzip der Verfremdung.* Austrian Academy of Sciences, Philosophical-historical Class. Minutes, Vol. 336. Publication of the Commission for Literary Studies, No. 5. Vienna: Publishing house of the Austrian Academy of Sciences, 1978.

Harris, John Wesley, *Medieval Theatre in Context: An Introduction.* London and New York: Routledge, 1992.

Hartmann, Gabriel, *Maharishi-Gandharva-Ved. Die klassische Musik der Vedischen Hochkultur: Eine Einführung in die musiktheoretischen Grundlagen.* Vlodrop: Maharishi Vedic University Press, 1992.

Hayman, Ronald, *Artaud and After.* Oxford: Oxford University Press, 1977.

Hilton, Julian, *Performance* (New Directions in Theatre). London: Macmillan, 1987.

Hirschberger, Johannes, *Geschichte der Philosophie: Neuzeit und Gegenwart.* Freiburg, Basel and Wien: Herder, 1981.

Hodge, Alison (ed.), *Twentieth Century Actor Training.* London and New York: Routledge, 2000.

Hodge, Francis, *Play Directing: Analysis, Communication and Style.* London: Allyn and Bacon, 1994.

Hung-Hung, Josephine, 'Das chinesische Theater', in Heinz Kindermann (ed.), *Einführung in das ostasiatische Theater.* Wien: Hermann Böhlhaus, 1985.

Innes, Christopher, *Holy Theatre: Ritual and the Avant-Garde.* Cambridge: Cambridge University Press, 1981.

Jenks, Chris, *Culture.* London and New York: Routledge, 1995.

Jhanji, Rekha, *Aesthetic Communication: The Indian Perspective.* Delhi: Munshiram Mancharlal Publishers, 1985.

Jhanji, Rekha, *The Sensuous in Art: Reflections on Indian Aesthetics* (Indian Institute of Advanced Studies). Delhi: Shimla in association with Motilal Barnasidass, 1989.

Johnson, Claudia D., *American Actress: Perspective on the 19th Century.* Chicago: Nelson Hall, 1984.

Kale, Pramod, *The Theatrical Universe: A Study of the Natyasastra.* Bombay: Popular Prakashan, 1974.

Kerr, Alfred, *Die Welt im Drama.* Edited by Gerhard F. Hering. Köln and Berlin: Kiepenheuer & Witsch, 1964 (first published 1954).

Kesting, Marianne, 'Stanislavsky–Meyerhold–Brecht', *Forum Modernes Theater*, 4:2 (1989), pp. 122–38.

Kindermann, Heinz, *Theatergeschichte Europas.*
  Vol. I: *Das Theater der Antike und des Mittelalters.* Salzburg: Otto Müller, 1957.
  Vol. II: *Das Theater der Renaissance.* Salzburg: Otto Müller, 1957
  Vol. III: *Das Theater der Barockzeit.* Salzburg: Otto Müller, 1959.

Vol. IV: *Von der Aufklärung zur Romantik (Part 1)*. Salzburg: Otto Müller, 1961.

Vol. VII. *Realismus*. Salzburg: Otto Müller, 1965.

King, B. J. and K. Chapin, *Billie Jean*. New York: Harper & Row, 1974.

Knopf, Jan, *Brecht-Handbuch. Theater. Eine Ästhetik der Widersprüche*. Stuttgart: J. B. Metzlersche Verlagsbuchhandlung, 1980.

Koller, Ann Marie, *The Theatre Duke: Georg II of Saxe-Meiningen and the German Stage*. Stanford: Stanford University Press, 1984.

Kott, Jan, 'Grotowski or the limit', *New Theatre Quarterly*, 6:23 (1990), pp. 203–6.

Kramer, Richard E., 'The *Natyasastra* and Stanislavsky: points of contact', *Theatre Studies*, vol. 36 (1991), pp. 46–62.

Krasner, David, 'Strasberg, Adler and Meisner: method acting', in Alison Hodge (ed.), *Twentieth Century Actor Training*. London and New York: Routledge, 2000, pp. 129–50.

Krivitsky, Kim, 'Vakhtangov and the modern theatre', in Lyubov Vendrovskaya and Galena Kaptereva (compilers), *Evgeny Vakhtangov*. Moscow: Progress, 1982, pp. 255–68.

Kumiega, Jennifer, *The Theatre of Grotowski*. London and New York: Methuen, 1987.

Lairesse, Gerard de, *Groot Schilderboek*. Amsterdam: Hendrick Desbordes, 1712.

Leach, Robert, *Vsevolod Meyerhold*. Cambridge: Cambridge University Press, 1989.

Leavis, F. R., *Mass Civilization and Minority Culture*. Cambridge: The Minority Press, 1930.

Leiter, Samuel, *From Stanislavsky to Barrault: Representative Directors of the European Stage* (Contributions to Drama and Theatre Studies No. 34). London: Greenwood Press, 1991.

Lemaire, Anika, *Jacques Lacan*. Translated by David Macey. London, Henley and Boston: Routledge and Kegan Paul, 1977.

Levenson, Robert, Paul Ekman and Wallace V. Friesen, 'Voluntary facial action generates emotion-specific autonomous nervous system activity', *Psychophysiology*, 27:4 (1990), pp. 363–84.

Ludwig, Arnold M., 'Altered states of consciousness', in Charles T. Tart (ed.), *Altered States of Consciousness: A Book of Readings*. New York, London, Sydney and Toronto: John Wiley and Sons, 1969, pp. 9–22.

McDonald, Jan, 'The promised land of the London stage: acting style at the Court Theatre London, 1904–1907', in Milan Lukes (ed.), *The Role of the Actor in the Theatrical Reform of the Late 19th and Early 20th Centuries*. Seventh International Congress on Theatre Research, 3–8 September 1973. University of Prague, 1976 pp. 75–89.

Maharishi Mahesh Yogi, *On the Bhagavad-Gita: A New Translation and Commentary, Chapters 1–6*. Harmondsworth: Penguin, 1969.

Maharishi Mahesh Yogi, *Perfection in Education*. Jabalpur: Maharishi Vedic University Press, 1997.

Marasinghe, E. W., *The Sanskrit Theatre and Stagecraft* (Sri Garib Dass Oriental Series No. 78). Delhi: Sri Satguru Publications, 1989.

Marker, Lise-Lone and Frederick J. Marker, *Ingmar Bergman: Four Decades in the Theater* (Directors in Perspective). Cambridge: Cambridge University Press, 1982.

Martin, Jacqueline, *Voice in Modern Theatre*. London and New York: Routledge, 1991.

Mehta, Xerxes, 'Performance art: problems of description and evaluation', *Journal of Dramatic Theory and Criticism*, 5:1 (1990), pp. 187–99.

Melzer, Annabelle Henkin, *Dada and Surrealist Performance*. Baltimore and London: The Johns Hopkins University Press, 1994.

Meyer-Dinkgräfe, Daniel, *Consciousness and the Actor: A Reassessment of Western and Indian Approaches to the Actor's Emotional Involvement from the Perspective of Vedic Psychology*. Frankfurt am Main: Peter Lang, 1996.

Miletich, John, *States of Awareness: An Annotated Bibliography*. New York, Westport and London: Greenwood, 1988.

Mishra, Hari Ram, *The Theory of Rasa in Sanskrit Drama: With a Comparative Study of General Dramatic Literature*. Bhopal, Sayar and Chhatapur: Vindhyachal Prakashan, 1964.

Mishra, Vijay, 'The great Indian epic and Peter Brook', in David Williams (ed.), *Peter Brook and the Mahabharata: Critical Perspectives*. London and New York: Routledge, 1991, pp. 195–205.

Mitter, Shomit, *Systems of Rehearsal: Stanislavsky, Brecht, Grotowski and Brook*. London and New York: Routledge, 1992.

Nader, Tony, *Human Physiology: Expression of Veda and Vedic Literature*. Vlodrop: Maharishi Vedic University Press, 1995.

Napier, A. David, *Foreign Bodies: Essays in Performance, Art and Symbolic Anthropology*. Berkeley: University of California Press, 1990.

Orme-Johnson, Rhoda, 'A unified field theory of literature', *Modern Science and Vedic Science*, 1:3 (1987), pp. 323–73.

Ortolani, Benito, 'Das japanische Theater', in Heinz Kindermann (ed.), *Einführung in das ostasiatische Theater*. Wien: Hermann Böhlhaus, 1985.

Ortolani, Benito, *The Japanese Theatre: From Shamanistic Ritual to Contemporary Pluralism*. Leiden: E.J. Brill, 1990.

Pandey, Kapila Chandra, *Comparative Aesthetics*, Vol. 1: *Indian Aesthetics*. Banaras: The Chpwkhamba Sanskrit Series Office, 1950.

Pandya, Shveni, *A Study of the Technique of Abhinaya in Relation to Sanskrit Drama*. Bombay and New Delhi: Somaiya Publications, 1988.

Patterson, Michael, *The Revolution in German Theatre, 1900–1933*. Boston and London: Routledge and Kegan Paul, 1981.

Patterson, Michael, *The First German Theatre: Schiller, Goethe, Kleist and Büchner in Performance*. London and New York: Routledge, 1990.

Pavis, Patrice, *Theatre at the Crossroads of Culture*. London and New York: Routledge, 1992.

Pavis, Patrice, 'Theory and practice in the Theatre Studies at the University', *Proceedings of Disorientations Conference*. Monash University, 1998.

Pearson, Mike, lecture 1 from the module *Principles of Performance I*, part of the newly launched undergraduate degree scheme in Performance Studies at the University of Wales, Aberystwyth.
URL: http://www.aber.ac.uk/~psswww/pf20110/lecture1.htm

Pearson, Mike, lecture 2, from the module *Principles of Performance I*, part of the newly launched undergraduate degree scheme in Performance Studies at the University of Wales, Aberystwyth.
URL: http://www.aber.ac.uk/~psswww/pf20110/lecture2.htm

Pearson, Mike, glossary of the Internet material for the newly launched undergraduate degree scheme in Performance Studies at the University of Wales, Aberystwyth.
URL http://www.aber.ac.uk/~psswww/general/glossary.htm

Pronko, Leonard C., 'LA Festival: Peter Brook's *The Mahabharata*', *Asian Theatre Journal*, 5:2 (1988), pp. 220–4.

Prudhoe, John, *The Theatre of Goethe and Schiller*. Oxford: Basil Blackwell, 1973.

Raine, Kathleen, *The Land Unknown*. New York: George Braziller, 1975.

Rehm, Rush, *Greek Tragic Theatre*. London and New York: Routledge, 1992.

Rennert, H. A., *The Spanish Stage in the Times of Lope de Vega*. New York, 1909.

Rhagavan, V., *The Concept of the Beautiful in Sanskrit Literature*. Madras: The Kuppuswami Sastri Research Institute, 1988.

Richards, Kenneth and Laura Richards, *The Commedia dell'Arte: A Documentary History*. Oxford: Basil Blackwell, 1990.

Riley, Jo, *Chinese Theatre and the Actor in Performance*. Cambridge: Cambridge University Press, 1997.

Roach, Joseph R. Jr, 'Diderot and the actor's machine', *Theatre Survey*, 22:1 (1981), pp. 51–68.

Roach, Joseph R., *The Player's Passion: Studies in the Science of Acting*. Newark: University of Delaware Press, 1985.

Roose-Evans, James, *Experimental Theatre: From Stanislavsky to Peter Brook*. London: Routledge, 1989.

Rubin, Don (ed.), *The World Encyclopedia of Contemporary Theatre*, Vol. 4: *The Arab World*. London and New York: Routledge, 1999.

Ryckman, Richard M., *Theories of Personality*, 3rd edition. Monterey: Brooks/Cole Publishers, 1985.

Sands, William F., 'Maharishi's program of reading the Vedic literature: unfolding the total potential of natural law', *Modern Science and Vedic Science*, 7:1 (1997), pp. 93–108.

Sarabhai, Mallika, 'Energy and the ensemble: actors' perspectives', in David Williams (ed.), *Peter Brook and the Mahabharata: Critical Perspectives*. London and New York: Routledge, 1991, pp. 99–103.

Sarup, Madan, *An Introductory Guide to Post-Structuralism and Postmodernism*. New York, London, Toronto, Sydney and Tokyo: Harvester Wheatsheaf, 1988.

Sayler, Oliver M. (ed.), *Max Reinhardt and His Theatre*. New York: Benjamin Blom, 1968 (first published 1924).

Schack, A. J. von, *Geschichte der Literatur und dramatischen Kunst in Spanien*. Berlin: Duncker and Humblot, 1845/6.

Schechner, Richard, *Between Theatre and Anthropology*. Philadelphia: University of Pennsylvania Press, 1985.

Schlemmer, Oskar, 'Man and art figure', in Walter Gropius (ed.), *The Theater of the Bauhaus*. London: Eyre Methuen, 1961, pp. 17–48.

Schlemmer, Oskar, 'Theater (Bühne)', in Walter Gropius (ed.), *The Theater of the Bauhaus*. London: Eyre Methuen, 1961, pp. 81–104.

Schultz, Stephen C., 'Toward an Irvingesque theory of Shakespearean acting', *Quarterly Journal of Speech*, 61 (1975), pp. 428–38.

Schumacher, Claude, *Artaud on Theatre*. London: Methuen Drama, 1989.

Shankar, Yogashiromani Shri Shri Ravi, interview with Daniel Meyer-Dinkgräfe, 5 August 1992.

Shevtsova, Maria, 'Interaction–interpretation: *The Mahabharata* from a socio-cultural perspective', in David Williams (ed.), *Peter Brook and the Mahabharata: Critical Perspectives*. London and New York: Routledge, 1991, pp. 206–27.

Sprinkle, Annie, *Hardcore from the Heart: The Pleasures, Profits and Politics of Sex in Performance. Annie Sprinkle: SOLO*. London: Continuum, 2001.

Srinivasan, Srinivasa Ayya, *On the Composition of the Natyasastra* (Studien zur Indologie und Iranistik Monographie 1). Reinbek: Dr Inge Wezler Verlag für Orientalische Fachpublikationen, 1980.

Stace, W. T., *Mysticism and Philosophy*. London: Macmillan, 1960.

Stanislavsky, Constantin, *Building a Character*. Translated by Elizabeth Reynolds Hapgood. New York: Theatre Arts Books, 1949.

Stanislavsky, Constantin, *Creating a Role*. Translated by Elizabeth Reynolds Hapgood and edited by Hermine I. Popper. New York: Theatre Arts Books, 1961.

Stanislavsky, Constantin, *An Actor Prepares*. Translated by Elizabeth Reynold Hapgood. London: Methuen, 1986.

Stein, Jack, *Richard Wagner and the Synthesis of the Arts*. Westport, CT.: Greenwood, 1973.

Stern, Susan L., 'Drama in second language learning from a psycholinguistic perspective', *Language Learning*, 3:1 (1980), pp. 77–100.

Strasberg, Lee, 'Working with live material', in Erika Munk (ed.), *Stanislavsky and America: An Anthology from the Tulane Drama Review*. New York: Hill and Wang, 1966.

Strasberg, Lee, *A Dream of Passion: The Development of the Method.* Edited by Evangeline Morphos. London: Bloomsbury, 1988.

Styan, J. L., *Max Reinhardt* (Director in Perspective). Cambridge: Cambridge University Press, 1982.

Subrahmanyam, Padma, renowned bharata natyam exponent in Madras, who produced a thirteen-part TV series about the *Natyashastra* at the request of Indian Television.

Tart, Charles, 'Some assumptions of orthodox, Western psychology', in Charles Tart (ed.), *Transpersonal Psychologies.* London: Routledge and Kegan Paul, 1975, pp. 59–111.

Taylor, George, 'The just delineation of the passions: theories of acting in the age of Garrick', in Kenneth Richards and Peter Thomson (eds), *The Eighteenth-Century English Stage: The Proceedings of a Symposium Sponsored by the Manchester University Department of Drama.* London: Methuen, 1972, pp. 51–72.

Thomas, David (ed.), *Restoration and Georgian England, 1666–1788.* Theatre in Europe: a documentary history. Cambridge: Cambridge University Press, 1989.

Thoreau, H. D., *Walden.* New York: New American Library, 1960 (first published 1854).

Toporkov, Vasily Osipovich, *Stanislavsky in Rehearsal: The Final Years.* New York: Routledge, 1998.

Tydeman, William, *The Theatre in the Middle Ages: Western European Stage Conditions, c. 800–1576.* Cambridge: Cambridge University Press, 1978.

Vendrovskaya, Lyubov and Galena Kaptereva (compilers), *Evgeny Vakhtangov.* Moscow: Progress, 1982.

Verma, Jatinder, Article on 'Binglish' on the Internet, 1996. URL: http://www.tara-arts.com

Walton, J. Michael, *Greek Theatre Practice.* Westport, CT, and London: Greenwood Press, 1980.

Watson, Ian, *Towards a Third Theatre: Eugenio Barba and the Odin Teatret.* London and New York: Routledge, 1993.

Welsch, Wolfgang, 'Postmoderne: Genealogie und Bedeutung eines umstrittenen Begriffs', in Peter Kemper (ed.), *Postmoderne, oder: Der Kampf um die Zukunft. Die Kontroverse in Wissenschaft, Kunst und Gesellschaft.* Frankfurt am Main: Fischer, 1988, pp. 9–36.

Werman, David S., 'The oceanic experience and states of consciousness', *Journal of Psychoanalytic Anthropology,* 9:3 (1986), pp. 339–57.

Wiles, David, *The Masks of Menander: Sign and Meaning in Greek and Roman Performance.* Cambridge: Cambridge University Press, 1991.

Willett, John (ed. and trans.), *Brecht on Theatre: The Development of an Aesthetic.* New York: Hill and Wang, 1978.

Williams, David, *Peter Brook: A Theatrical Casebook.* London: Methuen, 1991.

Williams, David, 'Theatre of innocence and of experience: Peter Brook's International Centre. An introduction', in David Williams (ed.), *Peter Brook and the Mahabharata: Critical Perspectives*. London and New York: Routledge, 1991, pp. 3–28.

Williams, David, 'Transculturalism and myth in the theatre of Peter Brook', in Patrice Pavis (ed.), *The Intercultural Performance Reader*. London and New York: Routledge, 1996, pp. 67–78.

Witham, Barry B. (ed.), *Theatre in the US: A Documentary History*, Vol. 1: *1750–1915: Theatre in the Colonies and US*. Cambridge: Cambridge University Press, 1996.

Worrall, Nick, *Modernism to Realism on the Soviet Stage: Tairov–Vakhtangov–Okhlopkov*. Cambridge: Cambridge University Press, 1989.

Worrall, Nick, *The Moscow Art Theatre*. London and New York: Routledge, 1996.

Zarrilli, Phillip. ' "On the edge of a breath, looking": disciplining the actor's bodymind through the martial arts in the Asian/Experimental Theatre Program', in Phillip Zarrilli (ed.), *Acting (Re)Considered: Theories and Practices*. London and New York: Routledge, 1995, pp. 177–96.

ଓଔ

Index

𝇁ꙮ𝇁